The War on Drugs

the War on Drugs

A Failed Experiment

PAULA MALLEA

DUNDURN
TORONTO

Project Editor: Diane Young
Editor: Allison Hirst
Design: Courtney Horner
Printer: Webcom
Cover design by Courtney Horner
Cover images © plainpicture/Maskot

Library and Archives Canada Cataloguing in Publication

Mallea, Paula, 1949-, author
    The war on drugs : a failed experiment / Paula Mallea.

Includes bibliographical references and index.
Issued in print and electronic formats.
ISBN 978-1-4597-2289-7

    1. Drug control--History. 2. Drug abuse--History. 3. Drug traffic--History. I. Title.

HV5801.M34 2014   363.45   C2014-901038-9
                                          C2014-901039-7

1 2 3 4 5   18 17 16 15 14

 Conseil des Arts du Canada   Canada Council for the Arts   Canada    ONTARIO ARTS COUNCIL CONSEIL DES ARTS DE L'ONTARIO

We acknowledge the support of the **Canada Council for the Arts** and the **Ontario Arts Council** for our publishing program. We also acknowledge the financial support of the **Government of Canada** through the **Canada Book Fund** and **Livres Canada Books**, and the **Government of Ontario** through the **Ontario Book Publishing Tax Credit** and the **Ontario Media Development Corporation**.

Care has been taken to trace the ownership of copyright material used in this book. The author and the publisher welcome any information enabling them to rectify any references or credits in subsequent editions.

                                          J. Kirk Howard, President

The publisher is not responsible for websites or their content unless they are owned by the publisher.

Printed and bound in Canada.

Visit us at
Dundurn.com
@dundurnpress
Facebook.com/dundurnpress
Pinterest.com/dundurnpress

Dundurn	Gazelle Book Services Limited	Dundurn
3 Church Street, Suite 500	White Cross Mills	2250 Military Road
Toronto, Ontario, Canada	High Town, Lancaster, England	Tonawanda, NY
M5E 1M2	LA1 4XS	U.S.A. 14150

For the many casualties of the War on Drugs

Contents

Acknowledgements

I would like to acknowledge the assistance of everyone at Dundurn, including editorial director Diane Young, senior editor Allison Hirst, and the production and publicity staff. Thank you also to the Ontario Arts Council, which supported the preparation of this book. Many people and sources were responsible for helping me understand the "war on drugs" and its far-reaching consequences, and I am grateful for their wisdom.

I would especially like to thank John for his tolerance of my writing schedule, and for his continued support of me and of this project, even while working on his own. Thank you so much, John.

Introduction

The War on Drugs was never about the drugs. If it were, there would be consistency and logic about which drugs are prohibited. Science and evidence would determine what gets banned. Instead, drugs have been selected for prohibition arbitrarily, and not according to which ones cause harm, or whether they cause harm at all. Decisions to ban drugs have been based upon political expediency, prejudice, and ignorance. Those affected by this unfair "war" are disproportionately the marginalized of our society. Prison sentences are the sanction of choice, even though most drug offences are victimless and non-violent.

The champions of this war have sent the users of certain substances to prison while they have simultaneously allowed organized crime bosses to reap the profits and thumb their noses at the justice system. They have allowed people to get sick and die from drug use because gangsters don't care about the quality of their product, or the age or health of their buyers.

It is by now indisputable that the War on Drugs has failed in all of its objectives. It has not reduced the drug trade, eliminated production, or decreased the number of users. Governments have thrown billions of dollars and thousands of police and military resources at the issue, and they have also opened and expanded many prisons to deal with it, but the illegal drug trade persists and grows. More drugs than ever are available today; they are cheaper, and they are being moved around the world by means of the Internet and paid for with virtual currencies. More violence than ever is attributed to gangster turf wars over this very lucrative industry.

The War on Drugs was an invention of American politicians. It has spawned a system of criminalization that has incarcerated millions of citizens who choose to use recreational drugs other than tobacco or alcohol. In the 1960s and 1970s, drug abuse was not high on the list of concerns for Americans. They were more preoccupied with the war in Vietnam, with civil rights, and with the assassinations of Bobby Kennedy and Martin Luther King Jr. In an effort to distract voters from these serious and difficult issues, politicians chose an easy target — the demonization of drug users.

In the late 1960s, the Republican Party was desperately searching for an issue that would distinguish it from the Democrats and would appeal to the public, thus returning the Grand Old Party to the White House. Taking careful aim at the social programs and progressive philosophy of Lyndon Baines Johnson's "Great Society," the GOP objected to the idea that fighting crime included fighting poverty, inadequate housing, and unemployment.[1] As aspiring president Richard Nixon wrote in 1967, "The country should stop looking for the 'root causes' of crime and put its money instead into increasing the number of police. America's approach to crime must be 'swift and sure' retribution." That fight against crime swiftly focused on the young, rebellious Americans who used marijuana and other illegal drugs. The mantra of "sex, drugs and rock 'n' roll" was despised by those in power, who quickly used drugs as an excuse to lock up troublemakers and position the GOP as tough on crime.

Nixon thus ranks high among politicians who have adopted the reliable tactic of replacing evidence-based policy with hide-bound ideology. Having avoided talking about the real issues of the day, he won the presidency and promptly declared drug abuse "public enemy number one," calling it a national emergency. He placed a considerable amount of funding and other resources into waging "total war" on the "slave traders of our time"; hence, the War on Drugs. Ironically, his own *National Commission on Marijuana and Drug Abuse* in 1972 recommended legalizing marijuana, but his government steadfastly pursued the War on Drugs anyway.

After Nixon resigned in disgrace, presidents Gerald Ford and Jimmy Carter both made moves to climb down from the War on Drugs. The Democrat Carter even supported eliminating federal penalties for possession of up to one ounce of marijuana. By 1979–1980, though, he was fighting for re-election. At the time, Americans were being held hostage in Tehran, the domestic economy was ailing, and Ronald Reagan was waiting in the wings. Political expediency ruled the day, and Carter's administration announced a new "war on marijuana."

This about-face was not enough to win the election for the Democrats. Within two years, Republican president Reagan announced a re-energized War on Drugs, singling out marijuana for special attention. "We're taking down the surrender flag that has flown over so many drug efforts," he said. "We're running up a battle flag."[2] The president's wife, Nancy Reagan, urged schoolchildren to "Just Say No" to drugs, and called casual drug users "accomplice[s] to murder." From the early 1980s onward, both Democratic and Republican governments ratcheted up the war, with an extraordinary amount of violence and countless citizens incarcerated.

Today, former president Jimmy Carter is among many who argue that this war cannot be won. In an op-ed for the *New York Times*, he appealed to the government to call off the global drug war.[3] He urged the government to adopt the recommendations of a new Global Commission on Drug Policy to stop incarcerating drug users who do no harm to others, and to concentrate instead on fighting violent criminal organizations. He argued convincingly that "penalties against possession of a drug should not be more damaging to an individual than the use of the drug itself."

Former president Bill Clinton has also admitted the failure of the War on Drugs. In a documentary film produced by Sam Branson, *Breaking the Taboo*, Clinton said, "Well, obviously if the expected result was that we would eliminate serious drug use in America and eliminate the narcotrafficking networks, it hasn't worked." President Obama has allowed that marijuana is not as harmful as alcohol, and his Attorney General has taken the first steps to releasing thousands of prisoners incarcerated for drug offences. They also appear ready to allow Washington and Colorado to proceed with legal regimes for marijuana.

Admitting that the War on Drugs has failed, though, is only a first step. Recognizing the inappropriateness of lengthy incarceration for non-violent, victimless offences is not adequate to address the issue of drug prohibition. We need to consider new ways of thinking about illegal drugs: how they first became illegal and why; what health and other consequences they have for users and communities; what the impact of criminalization has been; what other solutions are being sought around the world. A War on Drugs premised upon prejudice, fear, and moralism needs to be replaced with policies that are based upon public health concerns, scientific evidence, and, not least, compassion.

This book begins with an overview of how we have arrived at this place, and then reviews the health consequences of using drugs, together with the myths surrounding their use and their potential therapeutic uses. It examines the economic costs of the War on Drugs, and the potential economic benefits of alternatives to drug prohibition. It highlights the difference between the harm caused by drugs and the harm caused by their prohibition. I will explore what other countries around the world are thinking and doing to deal with the issue of drug use and the worldwide shift that began in the dawn of the twenty-first century. Proposals for decriminalizing and legalizing drugs in a number of jurisdictions, including the United States, Europe, and Latin America, are leading the way to a new approach to the problem.

The final chapters of this book examine the disconnect between Canada and virtually every other nation. I advocate for a reasoned and sensible solution to the problem of drug prohibition. At the risk of "committing sociology" — to use our prime minister's disparaging terminology — I conclude that we must consider the root causes of drug abuse and then direct resources to those. We must also stop dealing with drug abuse through the criminal justice system and treat it as a public health problem. Prevention, treatment, and harm reduction should be priorities, and saving individual lives and helping families and communities should be paramount. Perhaps we could instead describe this as "committing decency."

This is a book for a lay audience, so I have taken some liberties in order to make it more accessible. Instead of referring to "cannabis," I talk about "marijuana" in all cases, even though hash and hash oil may be included in the discussion. I also refer to "addictions" and "drug addicts," even though today the politically correct terms would be "substance dependence" and "substance abusers."

I have also concentrated the discussion around three illegal drugs — heroin, cocaine, and marijuana. Arguments about how to end the War on Drugs and find new solutions to the problems of addiction, illness, crime, and violence can be made based upon our knowledge of and experience with these three drugs. I could have gone on to examine methamphetamines, new psychoactive drugs, and prescription drug abuse, but this would only make for a longer book, not for a more comprehensive argument.

Many advocates of change appeal to our experience with the legalization of alcohol as a justification for legalizing other drugs. Opponents, on the other hand, argue that the harms caused by legal alcohol provide the best reason for never legalizing other drugs. I have not offered a detailed comparison of illegal drugs and alcohol because many others have already done so. It is enough for our purposes to assert that the two main legal drugs — alcohol and tobacco — cost society much more in dollars and suffering than all of the illegal drugs combined.[4]

One final thought. Before I began to work on this research, I had my own ideas about what might be an acceptable alternative to the War on Drugs. There are two general possibilities — decriminalization or legalization.

Decriminalization is also described by some as "prohibition lite" because it leaves prohibition intact. It generally allows adults to possess, grow, or even share a small quantity of drugs. These activities, though, remain prohibited and may attract criminal sanctions in the event of non-compliance with any imposed fines or drug treatment programs. Trafficking and production continue to be strictly banned, leaving criminal organizations in control of the drug trade, with the attendant concerns about violence and quality control.

Legalization eliminates prohibition altogether. Some advocates recommend a wide open, free market model in which there are no regulations. Most, though, envisage a government-controlled regime with regulations tailored to the particular drug. Regulations appropriate for heroin, for example, might not be sensible for marijuana, and vice versa. Legalization would generally allow adults to possess, sell, or produce drugs, but within strictly controlled and regulated regimes. This has the advantage of removing control of the drug trade from criminal organizations altogether, ensuring the drugs are not adulterated with dangerous substances or sold to children, and eliminating the violence associated with organized crime.

My own ideas about an acceptable alternative to the War on Drugs were modest. They ran along the lines of decriminalizing, not legalizing, marijuana and then working on a solution for other drugs. The evidence, though, pulled me along inexorably and I was drawn to an unexpected conclusion.

What follows is based upon the best work of the best minds in the field. The science and research are as solid as they can be when dealing with a regime that is illegal and necessarily conducted underground. If nothing else comes from this book, I hope that readers will begin to think differently about the drugs that we have chosen to label "illegal." The future of our children may depend upon it.

Chapter One

How We Got into This Predicament

SHIFTING GROUND

The ground is shifting under the War on Drugs. After more than forty years of tough-on-drugs rhetoric, countries around the world are withdrawing from the law enforcement model espoused by Richard Nixon and Ronald Reagan as well as by the international community and its many nation states. One by one, starting in Europe and Latin America, they are beginning to question the wisdom of using the criminal justice system to deal with a problem that they now feel requires a public health model. In turn they are beginning to remove criminal sanctions from some or all drug infractions. Astonishingly, even the United States is rethinking its approach, with two states voting to legalize marijuana and the Attorney General announcing a less harsh approach to some non-violent drug offenders.

Many of those who used to be dedicated drug warriors are renouncing the War on Drugs in order to work for the liberalization of drug laws. A good example revolves around the story of a Canadian advocate for marijuana legalization who is currently serving five years in an American prison. Marc Emery, Canada's "Prince of Pot," sold marijuana seeds to American buyers and was convicted in Washington State in 2010 for that offence. The man who put him in prison, District Attorney John McKay, took to a podium in Vancouver two years later and argued for the outright legalization of that very drug.[1] "Criminal prohibition of marijuana is a complete failure," he said, adding that it allowed gangs and cartels to generate billions in profits and cause mayhem while doing so. At time of writing, Marc Emery is still serving his sentence in the United States. The Harper government has refused, so far, to permit his transfer to a Canadian prison.

John McKay is by no means the only one who has moved from one side of this debate to the other. Prosecutors, police, medical doctors, mayors, Attorneys General, former and current heads of state, and many others now urge the legalization, regulation, and taxation of marijuana. Many also argue that the prohibition of other illegal drugs should be lifted and replaced with a legal regime appropriate to each. How has this sea change occurred, and will it result in the wholesale adoption by nations of a new approach to illegal drugs?

Where is Canada in this developing scenario? Ten years ago we were toying with the idea of decriminalizing marijuana — a very modest proposal. Today, we are outliers, denying the science and research that show the criminal justice model to be counterproductive to public safety, to our fiscal health, and to the health of our communities. We are cracking down on illegal drugs, increasing prison sentences, and reducing funding to the many treatment and prevention programs that we know work. How did we get here and why are we virtually alone in ramping up the demonization of certain drugs?

Canada's position from the beginning has been fraught with contradiction. We were the first in North America to ban marijuana, but also the first to allow for its use as a medication (spurred on, it must be admitted, by the Supreme Court of Canada). Parliamentary reports as early as 1972 and as recently as 2002 have recommended that the prohibition of marijuana be lifted and that a regime of decriminalization or outright legalization be instituted. In 2004, a Liberal government even tabled legislation that purported to effect some minor changes.

However, in 2006, a Conservative minority was elected that solidly backed the War on Drugs. It swiftly hardened its position on punishment of all drug infractions, including harsh mandatory minimum sentences.

As of November 2012, judges no longer have any discretion in sentencing most drug offences. If, for example, an offender grows six marijuana plants, he will face a mandatory prison sentence of six months. If the offender is growing his six plants in a rented unit (a house he shares while attending university, for example), the mandatory minimum is nine months.

Conservative legislators have ensured maximum coverage by designing additional "health and safety factors" and "aggravating factors." These factors are vague, mandating the application of higher sentences to drug offenders. For example, if an offender is in possession of more than three kilograms of marijuana or resin for the purpose of trafficking, he will receive at least a two-year sentence if he did so "for the abuse of authority or position" or if he did so "in or near a school, in or near an area normally frequented by youth, or in the presence of youth." Both factors are so vague and/or all-encompassing (for example, where in the average city can you go and not be near an area frequented by youth?) as to virtually guarantee the mandatory minimum will be applied. Prisons are already bursting with the influx of inmates sentenced under this new regime.

Only recently have Canadian politicians opposed to the Conservatives begun to revise their positions on illegal drugs. The New Democratic Party (NDP) now recommends decriminalization of marijuana possession, while the Greens support marijuana's outright legalization. The Liberal Party of Canada has recently adopted a policy to legalize marijuana, and has designed proposed regulations to this end. None has suggested changes concerning the treatment of other illegal drugs.

Among nations around the world, Canada is now one of the toughest when it comes to waging the War on Drugs. This can only partly be explained by our historic close relationship with the United States. It is true that we are the main trading partner of the United States and share a four-thousand-mile border. Or, as famed author and wit Margaret Atwood put it, we share the longest undefended one-way mirror in the world.[2] If illegal drugs were to be decriminalized or legalized in Canada, it has always been thought that this would negatively affect our relationship with the United States in ways that could only be imagined.

But now the ground is shifting south of the border, sowing confusion among Canadian hardliners who have always been able to rely upon American drug czars and their colossal budgets to support an all-out war.

American voters have been retreating from the drug war, electing to legalize pot — in Washington and Colorado in 2013 — and expand the number of states allowing for the use of medical marijuana. Currently, twenty states and Washington, DC, allow the prescribing of medical marijuana,[3] while seven more states are considering this policy change.[4] Recent developments also show that President Obama is becoming less inclined to vigorously prosecute marijuana laws.

There have been many high-profile Americans calling for a new approach to this issue. One of the most influential was broadcaster Walter Cronkite. He said America needed to admit it was wrong about the War on Drugs in the same way that Robert McNamara had later admitted not only that the Vietnam War was "wrong, terribly wrong," but that he had thought so at the very time he was helping wage it.[5] Cronkite urged then-president Bill Clinton to appoint a bipartisan commission to review the evidence and produce a comprehensive drug policy for the future:

> It's surely time for this nation to stop flying blind, stop accepting the assurances of politicians and other officials that if only we keep doing what we're doing, add a little more cash, break down a few more doors, lock up a few more [people], then we would see the light at the end of the tunnel. Victory would be ours.... We cannot go into tomorrow with the same formulas that are failing today. We must not blindly add to the body count and the terrible cost of the war on drugs only to learn from another Robert McNamara thirty years from now that what we've been doing is wrong, terribly wrong.

Cronkite made these remarks in 1995. Almost twenty years later, his plea continues to be ignored.

One American who changed his mind in a hurry was California state assemblyman Pat Nolan. Mr. Nolan had been all in favour of longer sentences for drug offences until he himself served two years in prison on corruption charges. In a reference to the United States's moralistic approach to drugs, and to its indiscriminate use of prison sentences, he said, "We should reserve our prison space for people we are afraid of, instead of people we are mad at."[6]

Among those around the world who now advocate for a repeal of drug prohibition are high-ranking scientists who have over time changed their minds about illegal drugs. Dr. David Nutt first assumed his responsibilities as Chair of the Advisory Council on the Misuse of Drugs (ACMD) in Britain thinking that the country was on the right track in its determined prosecution of illegal drugs.[7] However, he soon decided that the criminal justice approach was doing more harm than good, producing perverse consequences. He also came to deplore a world view shared by drug warriors that "taking certain drugs in certain kinds of ways is not just harmful but *immoral.*"

Dr. Nutt's Waterloo moment arrived when Britain's Home Secretary rejected the ACMD's advice as to the proper categorization of marijuana. The ACMD had recommended that it should continue to be listed in the less-harmful category, but the government instead reclassified it to a category indicating a higher level of harmfulness. Dr. Nutt argued that this ran against the scientific evidence and maintained that, while marijuana was not harmless, it was much less harmful than, say, alcohol. He was determined to provide a consistent public-health message, and maintained that this was an impossible task if the government refused to talk about the harmfulness of certain legal drugs. As he put it, "The more hysterical and exaggerated any Home Secretary was about the harms of cannabis, the less credibility they would have in the eyes of the teenagers binge-drinking themselves into comas every day."

As a result of the inevitable confrontation, Dr. Nutt was fired and a number of ACMD's scientific experts resigned. They have since gone on to form the Independent Scientific Committee on Drugs (ISCD), which urges people and governments to consider drug policy in the light of objective evidence. Dr. Nutt says, "Being willing to change our minds in the light of new evidence is essential to rational policy-making." British police officers, medical professionals, politicians, and many others have also changed their minds and are lobbying hard for change.

In Latin America, heads of state and former heads of state are seeking a different approach to illegal drugs. Writing in *The Wall Street Journal*, Fernando Henrique Cardoso (former president of Brazil), César Gaviria (former president of Colombia), and Ernesto Zedillo (former president of Mexico) were unequivocal: "The War on Drugs has failed.... Prohibitionist policies based on eradication, interdiction, and criminalization of consumption simply haven't worked. Violence and the organized crime associated with the narcotics trade remain critical problems in our countries."[8] They claimed that "U.S.–inspired drug policies" had led to the corruption of their judicial and political systems. They tentatively suggested the decriminalization of marijuana, and recommended focusing on a health and education approach to drug use, rather than repression.

Another former president of Mexico, Vicente Fox, has been vocal about the drug war. "The War on Drugs convoked by President Nixon 40 years ago has been a total failure," he says.[9] He recommends legalizing all drugs, stating that "freedom of choice exercised in an educated, responsible manner" should be the objective.[10] He speaks eloquently of the thousands of young Mexicans who have died because of the drug war: "These people were not born criminals; they did not possess criminality in their genes. And yet because of a flawed public policy, because of lack of education and disinformation, because of lack of better economic incentives and opportunities, they became victims of an insane war against an enemy we can never defeat with the current prohibitions in place." He says the prerequisite to legalization will be the repeal of prohibition by the United States.

Felipe Calderón (whose repressive regime is widely credited with the deaths of tens of thousands of Mexicans), speaking before he stepped down as Mexico's president, mused that it was "impossible" to stop the drug trade, and called for "market alternatives." Most observers have interpreted "market alternatives" to mean a legalized, controlled market in drugs.

Other current Latin American leaders calling for change include Guatemalan president Otto Pérez Molina, a former military strongman. At the 2012 Summit of the Americas, he called the War on Drugs "a global deceit," saying drugs cannot be eradicated.[11] He urged leaders to stop being ideologues and start thinking about drug use as a public health issue. He would prefer to see all drugs legalized, with limits and conditions.

Juan Manuel Santos, current president of Colombia, has emerged as a leading voice on the international political stage calling for major changes.[12] He is concerned that the consuming countries appear not to be interested in change. He would be inclined to legalize marijuana and perhaps cocaine, but only "if there is a world consensus." He says that "a new approach should try [to] take away the violent profit that comes with drug trafficking…. If that means legalising, and the world thinks that's the solution, I will welcome it." He, too, deplores the corruption that comes with the drug trade.

Two Latin American leaders have already moved away from the prohibition model. President Evo Morales of Bolivia has managed to make the growing of coca leaves in his country legal, and their use permitted by the United Nations.[13] And President José Mujica of Uruguay has just succeeded in legalizing marijuana.[14] No wild-haired radical, Mujica is a seventy-eight-year-old former guerrilla who spent fourteen years in prison. He says, "Nowhere in the world has repression yielded results [in the War on Drugs]." President Mujica has just been nominated for the Nobel Peace Prize for his leadership on drug policy.

It will not be lost on the reader that the national leaders who are calling for change are all heads of drug-producing states. These are countries whose citizens are dying in the tens of thousands. The War on Drugs is wrecking their economies, their environments are being destroyed, and corruption and violence are endemic, threatening the very foundations of their states. In the words of President Santos, they are losing their best politicians, best journalists, best police, and best judges to the drug war.[15]

The consuming countries, on the other hand — Canada, the United States, European nations — continue to be mostly resistant to policy change. Although small incursions against the all-out drug war are being made in the United States and in some European nations, by and large the consuming countries are content to let producing nations take the fall for consumers' habits. As one Uruguayan legislator said, "The U.S. provides the arms and we provide the dead."[16]

When thinking about how best to push for change, it's helpful to understand the history. How is it that certain drugs became the subject of prohibition while others did not? What lies behind the distinctions that were made over the past century? Do these distinctions make any sense? Are they distinctions that today should not be acceptable because they smack of discrimination and moralism? Why did incarceration become the default mode for what is essentially a public health problem? How do we strip away this history and deal with problems of drug abuse in ways that accord with the science and evidence?

THE EARLY HISTORY OF CRIMINALIZATION

Today's illegal drugs were regularly used — by respectable society no less — as legal drugs until quite recently in our history. Any number of patented medicines once contained cocaine or morphine.[17] Coca-Cola contained cocaine until 1900, and Bayer Pharmaceutical Products sold heroin over the counter in 1898. Even Queen Victoria was known to take and enjoy both marijuana and cocaine.[18] During the late 1800s, there were cough medicines for children that contained extracts of marijuana, heroin, and cocaine. British department store Harrods sold both cocaine and heroin over the counter until 1916, and prepared gift packs for First World War soldiers that contained morphine and cocaine.[19] Heroin has always been available on prescription in the United Kingdom with certain restrictions (with the exception of a short time in the mid-1950s when pressure from the United States convinced the government to ban it). Marijuana, cocaine, and heroin were, in fact, almost mainstream drugs until the beginning of the twentieth century.

Some American states passed laws in the late 1800s that limited the commerce in cocaine, marijuana, and opium. As will be seen, these were largely racist laws targeting mainly black, Mexican, and Chinese men. They were intended to protect white women from predation by these minorities and to sideline populations that were seen to be taking jobs away from white people.[20] But how did this all come to pass?

In 1906, the federal *Pure Food and Drug Act* was passed in the United States, and this resulted in the demise of the patent medicine industry.[21] This was followed by the 1914 *Harrison Narcotic Act*, which imposed so many regulations that it was virtually impossible to conduct legal commerce in opium and cocaine. Finally, in 1919, the Supreme Court, in *Webb v. United States*, cruelly decided that it was illegal for doctors to prescribe drugs to alleviate symptoms of withdrawal. This ushered in the black market that still flourishes today. It drove the industry underground while ensuring that the quality of available drugs became unreliable and therefore dangerous to users.

In 1937, the United States passed its *Marijuana Tax Act*, which prohibited the non-medicinal and unlicensed possession or sale of marijuana. The hysteria around the use of marijuana by this time had reached its peak.

In 1936, *Reefer Madness* (propaganda thinly disguised as a melodramatic feature film) warned against the dangers of marijuana. In 1937, Harry J. Anslinger, commissioner of the U.S. Federal Bureau of Narcotics (now the Drug Enforcement Agency or DEA), wildly claimed, "Marijuana is the most violence-causing drug in the history of mankind. Most marijuana smokers are Negroes, Hispanics, Filipinos, and entertainers. Their satanic music, jazz and swing, result from marijuana usage. This marijuana causes white women to seek sexual relations with Negroes."[22]

Thus Mr. Anslinger neatly encapsulated the moral outrage, racial prejudice, and unfocused fear that informed the prohibition of marijuana. It should be noted that the American Medical Association (AMA) spoke out against the criminalization of the drug in 1937.

The 1937 law, coupled with considerable red tape and an exorbitant tax, succeeded in removing marijuana from the commercial market and driving it, too, underground. Even hemp, a harmless substance much-prized for its commercial uses as rope, paper, and textiles (it is the stalk of the marijuana plant, with no active THC content) was outlawed after the Second World War.[23]

In Canada, early legislation followed almost in lockstep with the United States. In 1908, the *Opium Act* made it illegal to import, manufacture, or sell opium for non-medicinal purposes.[24] However, in imitation of the racist approach of the United States, Canadian law enforcement ensured that only the Chinese manufacturers of opium for smoking were put out of business. At the same time, the patent-medicine industry was allowed to continue dispensing opiated liquids to its primarily white customers. In 1922, changes to *The Opium and Narcotic Control Act* resulted in high conviction rates and harsh sentences against the Chinese population in British Columbia, including deportation back to China.[25]

Cocaine was banned for use in medicines in 1908, and was later included in the 1911 *Opium and Drugs Act*, which provided for harsher sentences for drug convictions.

Canada was ahead of the United States in banning marijuana. Feminist Emily Murphy is widely credited with helping convince the government to do so. She demonized the drug, describing drug users as "dope fiends," and received an extraordinary amount of publicity by writing a book and a series of articles for *Maclean's* magazine on the subject. The government obliged by the simple expedient of adding cannabis to the schedule of prohibited drugs in 1923. This was announced quietly, succinctly, and somewhat ominously: "There is a new drug in the schedule."

Eighty years later, a Senate committee excoriated Canada's 1923 law. It said that the law had provided a solution where there was no problem.[26] It had amounted to a pre-emptive strike. The committee concluded that the 1923 marijuana prohibition was based upon "moral panic, racist sentiment and a notorious absence of debate."[27]

The rationale for criminalizing drugs in North America relied upon neither science nor public health concerns. Moral indignation, racial prejudice, classism, and cultural differences were responsible for the wholesale outlawing of drugs that had been seen as largely beneficial when used sensibly. It is not going too far to suggest that drug prohibition has been employed as a means of social control.

The ban on marijuana provides a good example of the effect of racism upon drug policy. At the time of its prohibition in the United States, marijuana was considered to be the drug of choice of African-Americans, who used it in speakeasies where jazz — an "immoral" new type of music — was prominent. Raw sex was widely thought to be central to the atmosphere of these clubs, and combined with a widespread fear of black men as predators on white women, these factors were enough for legislators to outlaw the drug associated with them.

An additional factor associated with marijuana prohibition was that Mexican men were immigrating to the United States in significant numbers and were bringing a penchant for the drug with them. The Mexicans were regarded as a threat to jobs for white men at the time, and so criminalizing the drug was one way of ridding the employment market of these interlopers.

The racism implicit in these developments continues today, and African-Americans are incarcerated in the United States at a much higher rate for drug use, even where they use drugs less than Caucasians. In every major county of California, African-Americans are two to four times more likely to be arrested than Caucasians for marijuana offences, even though they are less likely to smoke marijuana.[28] In more general terms, although black and non-black use of marijuana is "similar" across the board, 74 percent of those in American prisons for using marijuana are black. A recent report by the American Civil Liberties Union (ACLU) confirms this, saying that Caucasians and African-Americans use marijuana about equally, but the latter are 3.73 times more likely to be arrested for marijuana possession.[29]

A recent *New York Times* editorial described the "war on marijuana" as a tool of racial oppression.[30] It noted that in some U.S. states, African-Americans are eight times more likely to be arrested for marijuana offences and in some counties up to thirty times more likely. Police are targeting these communities, largely in response to numerical arrest goals, which encourage petty arrests and illegal stops. Officers are evaluated on the numbers of arrests they make.

Two recent books set out, in stark and damning detail, the history of continuing oppression of the African-American community through drug laws. Dr. Carl Hart is a neuropsychopharmacologist who demolishes many of the myths surrounding illegal drugs and the generally accepted ideas about who is using them.[31] And civil rights lawyer Michelle Alexander has written a flaming indictment of how the prosecution of illegal drugs has marginalized and disenfranchised millions of African-Americans.[32] She maintains in her book *The New Jim Crow* that mass incarceration is the new tool of social control, replacing slavery, and that the most effective part of that tool is the War on Drugs.

Political philosopher Noam Chomsky has placed his considerable weight behind this argument, speaking of the reinstitution of criminalization of the African-American population in the late 1970s.[33] He calls it a race war, and says, "It's not based on crime. The device that was used to recriminalize the black population was drugs. The drug wars are fraud — a total fraud. They have nothing to do with drugs; the price of drugs doesn't change. What the drug war has succeeded in doing is to criminalize the poor. And the poor in the United States happen to be overwhelmingly black and Latino."

Then he explains how this selective criminalization was accomplished: "Almost entirely, from the first moment, the orders given to the police as to how to deal with drugs were, 'You don't go into the suburbs and arrest the white stockbroker sniffing coke in the evening, but you do go into the ghettos, and if a kid has a joint in his pocket, you put him in jail.'"

Western countries have recently banned another substance that is used traditionally by a specific ethnic community, even though no science exists to justify the prohibition. Qat, a traditional herb chewed in parts of Africa and in some Arab countries for its mild stimulus, was outlawed by the United States in 1993 and by Canada in 1998. Twenty years went by before the United Kingdom followed the U.S. example. Its decision to ban qat in 2013, despite the recommendation of the ACMD, was highly controversial.[34] David Nutt said the decision "shows contempt for reason and evidence, disregard for the sincere efforts of the ACMD, and most of all, indifference to the welfare and rights of the communities in which qat is used." He claimed that the U.K. had bowed to persistent pressure from the United States.

The ACMD had found that there was insufficient evidence that chewing qat caused health or other problems. It also found no evidence that qat was linked to organized crime, or used to fund the Somalia-based Al-Shabaab Islamist group, as was alleged by some. On the other hand, the ban risks criminalizing as many as ninety thousand members of the Somali, Yemeni, and Ethiopian communities in Britain who chew qat as part of their social lives. The racism implicit in the decision to ban qat is clear.

Qat is still legal in many east African countries, and can be imported under licence in Australia. Only fourteen European countries have banned the substance. The World Health Organization (WHO) in 2006 blocked the scheduling of qat under United Nations international controls — so under WHO rules, it is still legal.[35] However, the International Narcotics Control Board (INCB), which was set up by the 1961 United Nations *Single Convention on Narcotic Drugs*, persists in trying to overturn this decision.

In addition to the racist element, there has always been a prejudice along socio-economic lines affecting the prosecution of the War on Drugs. For example, among organized crime hierarchies, it is most often street-level dealers and consumers of drugs who are caught by law enforcement and punished.[36] High-end dealers and financiers largely remain untouched and continue in the trade.

A quick survey of the socio-economic status of prison inmates in Canada today shows that it is still mainly the poor and marginalized, particularly Native people, who are successfully prosecuted and incarcerated. This is as true for drug offences as for violent, anti-social behaviour.[37] It is rare for a well-to-do cocaine or heroin user to spend time in prison.

Case in point: Keith Richards, famed guitarist with the Rolling Stones, was arrested in Toronto in 1977 and charged with possession for the purpose of trafficking of twenty-two grams of high-grade heroin.[38] The maximum sentence for this offence at the time was life in prison. Two things then happened. The prosecutor reduced the charge to simple possession and asked for a sentence of six months to one year. And the judge sentenced Richards to probation, on the condition that his band would give a free concert performance in aid of the blind within six months. In view of the fact that Richards had a record of five drug charges over the previous ten years, this was a result that left others convicted of heroin offences speechless. One law for the rich; one for the poor. One for the famous; one for the rest.

Over time, a trend has been established of banning substances used by ethnic minorities, marginalized people, and immigrants, and then of treating preferentially those in the prosperous mainstream who choose to indulge. Substances like alcohol and tobacco that have long been accepted by the dominant community continue to be legal.

Despite the fact that most illegal drugs were outlawed some time ago, the orgy of prosecution and imprisonment that we are familiar with today did not really begin until the 1960s. Both the international community and individual nations became part of an historic effort to eliminate the use of particular drugs. They chose to tackle the problem, not through education and treatment, but by punishing drug offenders with prison sentences, even where offences were victimless and non-violent. A dependency on drugs was not treated as a public health issue. Instead, it was prosecuted as evidence of an individual's moral failure.

The Role of International Institutions

The international community stepped into the game in 1961. In that year, under pressure from the United States, the United Nations passed the *Single Convention on Narcotic Drugs*, which enshrined the prohibition of selected drugs in domestic law across the globe. This and subsequent conventions signed in 1971 (and its 1972 Protocol) and 1988 had the effect of ensuring a regime of outright prohibition of certain drugs virtually everywhere in the world.

A close reading of the conventions shows that they did allow for a more flexible approach with respect to some minor drug infractions. However, over the years they became a hammer, enforcing a strict criminal justice model and preventing individual nations from adopting public health approaches (or any other alternative approaches).[39] The International Narcotics Control Board (INCB), set up by the 1961 convention, has always taken a particularly hard line, endorsing repressive drug policies. The Global Commission on Drug Policy says that "the U.N. drug control system continues to act largely as a straitjacket.... For most of the last century, it has been the U.S. government that has led calls for the development and maintenance of repressive drug policies."[40] The commission goes on to say that there is "strong institutional resistance" to new ideas within the United Nations.

Only very recently has the international community, represented by the United Nations, started to soften its tone. This is partly because it has begun to admit that the science does not support its punitive approach. For years its representatives tried to massage the message to support its law-and-order stance. For example, in 2002, a scandal erupted at the United Nations Office of Drug Control and Crime Prevention (ODCCP). The executive director had edited the *World Drug Report 2000* to make it appear as if the ODCCP's policy of suppression by law enforcement was successfully driving illegal drug use down. Research showed that this was not the case. The Global Commission on Drug Policy has said that public leaders need to admit what they know privately: "That the evidence overwhelmingly demonstrates that repressive strategies will not solve the drug problem, and that the war on drugs has not, and cannot, be won."[41]

Yet in 2012, the United Nations report on drugs and crime (*World Drug Report 2012*) was still making a mighty effort to reconcile its preferred conclusions with the facts on the ground.[42] It repeatedly asserted, against the evidence, that increased enforcement was driving drug production and use down, that illegal drugs were more dangerous than alcohol and tobacco, and that most people supported the drug war. It referred to drug "epidemics." These assertions were offered as justification for continued interdiction and more stringent law enforcement. Unfortunately, they too did not accord with the science and statistics.

The U.N. did admit that traffickers are quick to adapt to increased law enforcement by changing the routes and methods they use to bring drugs north. Western Africa is a new route to Europe, while organized crime is beginning to use containers and airplanes in response to the crackdown on Caribbean and Central American sea and land routes. European markets have also shifted from Colombia to Bolivia and Peru for their supply of cocaine.

Other organizations and nations dedicated to the War on Drugs also do not address the fact that drug lords are always one step ahead of law enforcement, and always will be. There is simply so much money to be made from the illicit market that organized crime can afford equipment and technology that are out of the reach of the average enforcement budget. And traffickers are agile in moving to places where the law has not yet reached, or where it can be readily corrupted.

The U.N. report went on to say that drug use has stabilized worldwide over the past decade, including in Canada, and that marijuana use in the United States has dropped 50 percent from its peak in 1979. After lengthy discussions of marijuana, cocaine, and the opioids, the report admitted that, except for marijuana, the most prevalent type of illegal drug use is none of these. It is, in fact, the non-medical use of (legal) pharmaceuticals.

The report discussed the "direct" costs of illegal drug use (losses in productivity, costs of health care, crime committed by users to obtain the price of their drugs, costs of drug treatment). However, it paid scant attention to the costs of organized crime violence, adulterated and dangerous products, the spread of disease, and other costs that are directly attributable to criminalization and the black market that it creates.

The report predicted the success of the drug war in the future. At the same time, in a baffling display of inconsistency and incoherence, it estimated that the total number of drug users could increase by 25 percent by 2050 (an implicit admission that the enforcement model will not succeed in driving the percentages down). Then it agreed that few people who use an illicit drug one time ever progress to frequent or regular (monthly) use.

If this seems like a collection of self-contradictory statements, it is. Having created confusion around the issue of worldwide drug use, the report then made passing reference to what it called the "unintended effects" of drug control: black markets, organized crime, replacement or displacement of the markets to other regions, and so on. But these kinds of "unintended consequences" are wholly predictable. They are the results, not of the use of drugs, but of the criminalization of those drugs. They are also, by all accounts, responsible for the most extensive harms that are created. The report, however, did not deal seriously with these consequences of prohibition.

There are notable international efforts to shift the discussion away from the law enforcement model and toward a variety of alternatives. For example, there are teams of scientists working on HIV/AIDS who are encouraging a public health approach. In 2010, the XVIII International AIDS Conference (chaired by Canadian Dr. Julio Montaner) adopted the Vienna Declaration.[43] It sought "to improve community health and safety by calling for the incorporation of scientific evidence into illicit drug policies." It recommended redirecting enforcement budgets to programs of "evidence-based prevention, regulatory, treatment and harm reduction interventions." The declaration was signed by former presidents of Brazil, Mexico, and Colombia. Canada has refused to sign the Vienna Declaration.

In another significant recent development, the Global Commission on Drug Policy declared in its 2011 report that the War on Drugs had failed, and recommended a new approach.[44] The Global Commission states as its purpose: "to bring to the international level an informed, science-based discussion about humane and effective ways to reduce the harm caused by drugs to people and societies."

The commission is a significant organization because its membership comprises a number of luminaries whose opinions are sought after and respected around the world. Among these are former heads of state César Gaviria (Colombia), Ernesto Zedillo (Mexico), Fernando Henrique Cardoso (Brazil), George Papandreou (Greece),[45] and Ruth Dreifuss (Switzerland). Louise Arbour, former U.N. High Commissioner for Human Rights and former justice of the Supreme Court of Canada, is also a commissioner. So are George P. Shultz, former secretary of state for the United States, and Paul Volcker, former chair of the United States Federal Reserve. Kofi Annan, former secretary general of the United Nations, was a founding commissioner, as was entrepreneur Richard Branson.

The recommendations of the Global Commission's 2011 report (and subsequent reports dealing with the effects of the drug war on epidemics of HIV/AIDS and Hepatitis C) are thoughtful and based upon the best evidence available. They do not rule out any option, including full legalization. Encouraging experimentation by governments with different models of legal regulation of drugs, the commission says, "It is unhelpful to ignore those who argue for a taxed and regulated market for currently illicit drugs. This is a policy option that should be explored with the same rigor as any other."[46]

In a remarkable turnaround, the Executive Summary of the *World Drug Report 2013* has also admitted that "the international drug control system is floundering."[47] This report is the closest that the United Nations has come to admitting that the law enforcement system is inadequate to the task. Since the driving force behind much of the international prohibition effort has been the United States, it is helpful to identify the origins of the War on Drugs and its development there, as well as to trace its influence upon other western and Latin American countries.

Chapter Two

A Declaration of War Leads to a Shambles

THE UNITED STATES, ORIGINATOR OF THE WAR ON DRUGS

In the 1960s, young people began to use marijuana openly while simultaneously and noisily indulging in free love, flower power, and opposition to the Vietnam War. "Sex, drugs, and rock 'n' roll" was the mantra. In a moralistic fervour, the United States government launched an all-out offensive upon marijuana users, sending thousands to prison. In 1972, President Richard Nixon first declared a War on Drugs. Legislation produced harsher penalties and expanded the number of offences that could be prosecuted. Although President Carter later campaigned for the decriminalization of marijuana, this idea soon disappeared.

In 1986, under Ronald Reagan, the United States re-dedicated itself to the War on Drugs and passed the *Anti-Drug Abuse Act*. The provenance of this law is especially interesting. On June 19, 1986, Len Bias, a young basketball star and acknowledged successor to Michael Jordan, died of what was described as a cocaine overdose. (It was, in fact, a combination of cocaine and alcohol.) The country was so shaken at this loss of a promising young athlete that politicians went to work to draft a new criminal law. The *Anti-Drug Abuse Act* introduced mandatory minimum sentences that were draconian, especially for the new drug on the market, crack cocaine.

Eric Sterling, who was legal counsel to the U.S. House Committee at the time, helped create the law. He now admits that the bill was completed in haste in a couple of months and was "terribly drafted."[1] The terms were "purely arbitrary," there was no science involved, and the law produced a sudden and shocking increase in the federal prison population from thirty-six thousand in 1986 to 219,000 today. About half of these people are imprisoned for drug offences.

Mr. Sterling now says this was the worst thing he had ever been involved in as a lawyer. If Len Bias had not died, everything would have been "profoundly different." Thus, a law that destroyed the lives of millions of Americans was written "on the back of a napkin." It is only today that politicians are beginning to correct some of those errors made more than twenty-five years ago.

The same *Anti-Drug Abuse Act* required the U.S. president to evaluate the performance of drug-producing and drug-transit countries every year and certify those that were co-operating with the United States. Decertification meant that the United States could withdraw foreign aid, impose trade sanctions, and oppose international loans. Latin American drug-producing countries (like Colombia) or transit countries (like Mexico) are consequently obliged to demonstrate their zeal in prosecuting the drug war. This has increased the violence and number of deaths in both countries.

In an ever-escalating determination to prosecute illegal drugs, President H.W. Bush in 1990 increased the budget for the War on Drugs by 50 percent. The extraordinary expenditures continued through the presidency of Bill Clinton, who nevertheless was the first (but not the last) American president to admit that he had tried marijuana.

Some American politicians did question the efficacy of the War on Drugs through those years. A 1995 Sentencing Commission noted the disparity in sentencing between powder cocaine (used mainly by middle-class people) and crack cocaine (used mainly by people with lower incomes). Crack cocaine offences were, by law, punished by one hundred times as much prison time as powder cocaine.[2] The Sentencing Commission made recommendations to rectify this state of affairs and related issues, but its recommendations were rejected by the United States

Congress. The Obama administration later reduced the disparity of 100:1 to 18:1 with the *Fair Sentencing Act* of 2010. Clearly, to be equitable, the ratio should be 1:1, a change which now is also being supported by the Obama administration.[3]

Currently, both medical marijuana and legal marijuana regimes are being successfully organized in some American states. Twenty-one states have already legalized the use of marijuana for medical purposes, while two states have legalized the recreational use of marijuana as well. The federal Attorney General has recently issued instructions not to prosecute every single case of marijuana possession. This is an important departure for an office that has always insisted upon its right to prosecute drug offences over state preferences.

Further, the Obama administration is implementing other changes, including releasing some prisoners from their long sentences.[4] The administration is asking defence lawyers to help identify people who are serving long sentences for crack offences so that Obama can use his executive authority (avoiding Congress) to have them released. Prison officials are also spreading the word. At the end of 2011, about thirty thousand inmates were serving sentences for crack offences (15 percent of all inmates). The president kick-started this process by pardoning eight inmates in December 2013. Unfortunately, as of February 2014, there were 3,500 petitions on the administration's desk and no adequate system for processing them. Since Obama is the "stingiest" president in history when it comes to granting pardons, inmates still serving sentences under the old regime do not hold out much hope for an early reprieve.[5]

CANADA: A RELIABLE ALLY

Canada, too, laid down long sentences and harsh punishment for drug users beginning in the 1960s. A seven-year minimum sentence for importing drugs was not removed until it was struck down by the Supreme Court of Canada in the 1980s. Many young people went to prison for simple possession of soft drugs or for trafficking, which includes sharing (that is, passing a joint from one person to the next). A single marijuana seed in a shirt pocket could result in an arrest.

Rosie Rowbotham famously spent decades in the Canadian penitentiary system for his participation in the drug trade.[6] In the 1970s, as a young man, he set up shop selling marijuana in Rochdale College in Toronto, where the lineup of buyers stretched down the corridor. Later, he imported tons of hashish, receiving sentences amounting to decades of prison time. He served the longest sentence in Canadian history for marijuana offences, and grew old in prison.

Yet as early as 1972 — at the same time the United States was declaring its War on Drugs — Canada's Le Dain Commission was recommending lifting the prohibition on marijuana possession. Gerald Le Dain of Osgoode Hall Law School chaired the *Commission of Inquiry into the Non-Medical Use of Drugs*, which also recommended lowering sentences for importing/exporting and trafficking and removing the prohibition on producing marijuana unless it was for the purpose of trafficking. The Le Dain report languished for years and no action was taken upon its recommendations. On the contrary, Canada continued to prosecute the War on Drugs with increased vigour.

In 1988, the Canadian Centre on Substance Abuse (CCSA) was created by Parliament as the national non-governmental organization (NGO) on addictions.[7] In 1990, the Health and Welfare secretariat was created to coordinate activities around illegal drugs within the federal government and abroad. In 1992, the government established Canada's Drug Strategy. It called for a balanced approach to illegal drugs, including control and enforcement, prevention, treatment, and rehabilitation and harm reduction. These changes were made by the Progressive Conservative government of the day. (The current ruling Conservative Party of Canada takes a different approach, emphasizing control, enforcement, and incarceration.)

Then in 1997, amid much controversy, the *Controlled Drugs and Substances Act* — a very severe law — was passed by a Liberal government. Witnesses who gave testimony at parliamentary committees were highly critical of this punishment-oriented law. They said it perpetuated 1920s-style prohibition without placing any emphasis upon harm reduction or prevention. The Liberal government at the time nonetheless ignored expert advice and ramped up its policy of incarceration. By 1998, Canada's Drug Strategy (the one with the balanced approach, led by Health Canada) was receiving no funding at all.

The 1997 tough-on-crime legislation proved to be an abject failure, however. Despite the fact that many more people were in prison, almost twice as many people were using marijuana in 2001 as in 1991.[8] By 2012, Canada's consumption rate was one of the highest in the world.[9] About three million Canadians today use marijuana, including 17 percent of those between the ages of fifteen and sixty-four. Although one poll from 2012 showed that 66 percent of Canadians support reforming the marijuana laws to reflect this reality, prohibition and severe penalties continue to be government policy. Costs are soaring and prisons are double-bunking in record numbers.

Back in 2001, Canada had become the first country in the world to permit medical marijuana use. This was a singular accomplishment, but it only happened because the courts compelled it.[10] The resulting Marihuana Medical Access Regulations (MMAR) have been less than adequate, entailing much red tape, poor-quality marijuana, reluctant doctors, and a continuing risk of prosecution. Today, the Conservative government is revising the system in ways that will make it even more difficult and more expensive for patients to acquire their medical marijuana.

In 2002, the *Senate Special Committee Report on Cannabis* surprisingly recommended outright legalization of marijuana for those over sixteen years of age, including an amnesty for all those who had been convicted of possession of small amounts of marijuana and elimination of their criminal records. Having considered the pros and cons of decriminalization as opposed to legalization, the committee decided that decriminalization represented the "worst case scenario." Why? Because it did not allow for governments to control and regulate the drug, thus leaving organized crime in the driver's seat.

The Senate Committee noted Canada's high rate of marijuana use, despite extraordinary and expensive efforts to eradicate the industry. Enforcement had become particularly severe since the attack on the World Trade Center in 2001. While agreeing that "at-risk" behaviour is possible with marijuana use, the committee questioned the strategy of resorting to criminal sanctions as the best way of controlling its use. "Even if cannabis were to have serious harmful effects, one would have to question the relevance of using the criminal law to limit these effects," it said. As far as the committee was concerned, the main social costs incurred by marijuana use were those incurred as a result of its criminalization, not as a result of its consumption.

Faced with the international implications of what it was recommending, the Senate Committee was careful to note a North-South geopolitical disconnect in drug laws. They pointed out that organic substances mainly originating in the South, where they were often part of the local tradition and culture, were strictly prohibited in the North. These included coca, poppy, and marijuana. Substances mainly originating and produced in the North, however, were merely regulated as legal substances. These included alcohol, tobacco, and pharmaceuticals. Yet all of the latter demonstrably represent a serious threat to the health and well-being of users and others.

Neil Boyd, a Canadian expert on illegal drugs from Simon Fraser University, is even more pointed in his analysis. He notes that the United Nations power brokers who signed the 1961 *Single Convention on Narcotic Drugs* did not themselves have territorial control of the production and distribution of some of these drugs, including the opiates. He thinks it was for this reason that these drugs were prohibited. The power brokers did, however, control alcohol, tobacco, and pharmaceuticals. These were thus deemed to be properly the subject of regulation rather than prohibition.[11] The implications of this analysis are clear. The world body appears to have been complicit in legitimizing the use of those drugs that are more likely to provide profits to the North, while prohibiting those that do not.

According to the Senate committee, the United Nations international drug control conventions codified arbitrary classifications of illegal drugs that were not supported by science. These conventions made no mention at all of alcohol or tobacco, even though the international community claimed to be curtailing the use of dangerous drugs. Especially with respect to marijuana, the committee said that international conventions represented "an utterly irrational restraint that has nothing to do with scientific or public health considerations."

Canada's political response to illegal drugs has been reliably tough on crime for fifty years, with one short-lived legislative attempt to liberalize. Prime Minister Paul Martin's minority government tabled a timid law in 2004 decriminalizing small amounts of marijuana. Less than fifty grams could attract a fine of up to four hundred dollars, but there would be no criminal record. On the other hand, the law provided for a doubling of sentences for growers. Advocates of more liberal marijuana laws were appalled, saying the new law would be worse than before. Martin's government fell before Bill C-17 could be passed, but his party in 2012 voted to support a policy of outright legalization.

Since the election of the Conservative government in 2006, though, and up until the time of writing, Prime Minister Harper has taken an extremely hard line on drugs, establishing long mandatory minimum sentences for all illicit drugs, including marijuana, and prosecuting drug laws with renewed vigour. Approaches that stress public health or harm reduction are fought tooth and nail in the face of Supreme Court decisions allowing for the application of these models.

On the one hand, the government has opposed harm-reduction projects like InSite, the safe injection site in Vancouver. On the other hand, having lost its bid to shut InSite down, in 2011 the government endorsed a heroin research project called SALOME (The Study to Assess Longer-term Opioid Medication Effectiveness) in which addicts will be provided with treatment in the form of either heroin or hydromorphone (both are opiates, but the latter is legal).[12]

An earlier project, NAOMI (North American Opiate Management Initiative), had found that methadone (a synthetic opiate) was not as successful as heroin in helping addicts get into treatment, stop taking street drugs, and stop committing crimes to support their habit. For some addicts, therefore, prescribed heroin is the only effective option. However, the Conservative government has a visceral antipathy to providing heroin to heroin addicts under any circumstances for any reason. Hydromorphone is the more palatable alternative for this government, if it can be proved to work, because hydromorphone is, unaccountably, legal.

Researchers say that abstinence from opioids is not a realistic objective when dealing with addicts.[13] The addiction must be recognized as a chronic condition and treated by long-term, maintenance-oriented substitution methods. Methadone, for example, must be provided on a long-term basis. But using methadone to detoxify a user to get him to abstain carries a "really high risk of death." Abstinence is simply not an option for some users.

Prescribed heroin is commonplace in Europe as a treatment for heroin addiction. The European Monitoring Centre for Drugs and Drug Addiction (EMCDDA) said in its 2007 annual report that virtually all nations in the EU provided opioid substitution treatment and needle exchange programs. These programs had increased in number tenfold over ten years.[14]

The evidence accepted by these nations — that prescribed heroin is a proven successful therapy — has so far not been accepted by the Canadian government. The myopia engendered by a tough-on-crime approach to drugs thus has the direct result of endangering the lives of addicts and their friends and families. This is just one illustration of the intransigence of the current government in the face of overwhelming evidence.

HIGH TECHNOLOGY, DESIGNER DRUGS, AND OLD-FASHIONED PRESCRIPTIONS

If we needed further proof that the War on Drugs cannot be won, it lies in the ingenious and continual invention of new synthetic drugs, and in new methods of distribution that better enable dealers to circumvent law enforcement.

One of the most innovative distribution networks to emerge depends upon neither a geographical location nor a physical currency. It is known as the Silk Road, and first came to light in 2011.[15] The Silk Road is an online marketplace (somewhat like eBay) that sells many products, but largely drugs. Law enforcement officials know where to find it online, but until recently they were unable to shut down the drug sales. The Silk Road uses a popular Internet anonymizer tool called "Tor," which makes it virtually impossible to locate the computers. And it uses the new anonymous, stateless, encrypted online currency called "Bitcoin."

It took the FBI more than two years to arrest the purveyor of the Silk Road in October 2013.[16] But within one month of Ross Ulbricht's arrest, a new Silk Road drug bazaar was up and running. The new operator continues to use Tor (which is still safe — Edward Snowden used it when he released information from the National Security Agency in 2013), and has improved the technology so as to keep buyers' identities secret. Traffickers have thus proved themselves remarkably capable of adapting swiftly to the pressure of law enforcement, as they have in other areas of the drug trade.

Key players in creating the Silk Road say that selling drugs over the Internet is a way of bypassing criminal gangs as it allows people to buy their drugs straight from the producer. Users who buy from the Silk Road say that "the quality is more consistent, the sale is safer, and the experience better than trying to find a street dealer." Some even claim that the site helps combat addiction by requiring buyers to confirm their intentions and make decisions carefully.

Canadians are among the top buyers and sellers on the Silk Road. Canada places fifth on a list of the twelve most frequent shipping and originating destinations.[17] When asked what law enforcement is doing about the Internet trade, though, the Royal Canadian Mounted Police (RCMP) say simply that they do not monitor anonymous websites.

Drugs are delivered over the Silk Road by the mundane means of private shipping companies or by registered mail, and often arrive in vacuum-sealed bags to avoid drug-sniffer dogs. Elaborate measures are taken by the site to protect its clients, but even so, a handful of users have been arrested in the United States and one was convicted in Australia in 2013. The amount of money changing hands is not yet significant (about $2.21 million in today's Canadian dollars per month, according to researchers at Carnegie Mellon University),[18] but drug warriors regard it as important to nip this new development in the bud. As cyber security professor Dr. Nicolas Christin says, though, "It's not a matter of the police locking a few guys up to end this. It is very distributed: we are looking at more than 600 sellers each month."[19]

One large problem law enforcement faces in trying to put a stop to the Internet drug trade is the human rights issue. It is expected that officials will try to tackle the industry through the vulnerabilities of Bitcoin. However, if Bitcoin were to be banned, bloggers in places like Saudi Arabia and Vietnam — who use Bitcoin to host services on alternative, dissident websites — would be vulnerable. And Tor is a "staple of activists avoiding Internet censorship or government crackdowns the world over, including China, Iran and Syria." Thus, officials who try to interfere with these technologies in search of drug dealers will also be likely to expose the identities of dissidents, placing their lives in grave danger. In a supreme irony, a large proportion of Tor's funding comes (indirectly) from the U.S. State Department's Internet freedom budget.[20]

Another recent trend compels law enforcement to work hard to keep up. This is the determined and perpetual development of a host of new drugs that allow dealers to stay one step ahead of the law. While the latest *World Drug Report 2013* says that the world has achieved stability in the use of traditional drugs (meaning mainly heroin, cocaine, and marijuana), it also says there has been an alarming increase in new psychoactive substances (NPS).[21] The number of NPS has increased more than 50 percent in less than three years, from 166 to 251. This means there are more NPS now than there are banned drugs. These new "legal highs" or "designer drugs" are being created in order to foil prohibition. As the report says, "Given the almost infinite scope to alter the chemical structure of NPS, new formulations are outpacing efforts to impose international control." As fast as one drug is declared illegal, a new one is developed. One commentator has observed that this means the drug war has not been so much "lost" as it has become "obsolete."[22]

The *World Drug Report 2013* admits that "the international drug control system is floundering … under the speed and creativity of the phenomenon [of new designer drugs]." In a statement that comes close to conceding defeat, this report says that banning the new drugs is possible, but a "very challenging undertaking" due to "the sheer rapidity of emerging NPS." In Canada alone, fifty-nine NPS were created over the first two quarters of 2012. Users were also experimenting with salvia, jimson weed, datura, and ketamine.

Whereas the U.N. report insists that public health is "pivotal to [the United Nations'] overall strategy," in fact, the United Nations is and has always been mainly preoccupied with how to control the new trade in designer drugs by law enforcement. One observer, noting the new attitude to legalizing marijuana in Latin American countries, says, "The distinct sounds of circling wagons characterized the rhetoric at the launch of the 2013 *World Drug Report*."[23] And at the same time that NPS are proliferating, the United Nations reports that cocaine use decreased by 40 percent in the United States between 2006 and 2011, while heroin use was stable or falling around the world.

Most of the new designer drugs are stand-ins for MDMA (ecstasy), marijuana, LSD, and magic mushrooms.[24] Ecstasy is the only one of these drugs that is known to cause overdoses in users, and this only happens if the drug is not taken properly. All of them, though, are illegal. NPS, on the other hand (which are emerging at the rate of one per week) are created in labs and are legal until banned.[25] There is no way for a user to know how dangerous they are. There are seven hundred websites in the European Union alone that are selling them. "Moves to ban new drugs simply inspire chemical innovation that sidesteps the law," so this is yet another way that the law enforcement model is failing to prevail.

A final recent area of concern is the abuse of prescription drugs. A new report from the Canadian Council on Substance Abuse (CCSA) describes the problem, which is generally agreed to be serious.[26] Double-doctoring and the diversion of pharmaceuticals are practices that feed addictions to painkillers and other drugs. The rash of deaths attributed to abuse of oxycodone, for example, is well documented. No mention is made by the CCSA of the fact that drug companies aggressively market their drugs, or that they sometimes fail to reveal side effects identified in clinical trials. The report does not talk about possible treatment options for those already addicted.[27] Much, though, is made of the need for more resources for law enforcement.

A prime example of prescription drug abuse is illustrated by the recent removal of oxycodone from pharmacy shelves in the United States. Twenty years ago, this drug was marketed by its manufacturer, Purdue Pharma, as the new miracle painkiller.[28] By 2012, the addiction numbers were so high that the company replaced the drug with an equivalent formulation that was harder for people to abuse (because it could not be dissolved and injected). In 2007, Purdue and three of its top executives pleaded guilty to misleading doctors, regulators, and patients about the risk of addiction, and paid millions of dollars in fines. In the meantime, though, many addicts had turned to heroin as a cheaper alternative. They also turned to alternatives such as morphine and codeine. These alternatives have the same or a higher risk of over-dose. They also present a scenario where needle-sharing is likely, leading to the spread of disease. Meanwhile, the withdrawal of the original formula for oxycodone led to an increase in street prices for it, resulting in increased market volatility and related crime. The fact that Canada still permits oxycodone to be prescribed in its original form is causing friction with the United States, since users are smuggling the Canadian product — known as hillbilly heroin — across the border.[29]

Withdrawal from oxycodone is excruciating and long-lasting. Once it was banned in its injectable form, addicts turned to alternatives. One of those was fentanyl, a synthetic opioid. Fentanyl is legal and prescribed as a patch so that the active ingredient can be released gradually. Addicts learned that they could scrape the substance off a patch and smoke it to obtain relief.[30] Or they could ingest the whole patch, or cut it up and apply it to their gums. Fentanyl is one hundred times stronger than morphine, and is normally used for palliative care or for cancer-induced pain. Fentanyl can kill.

Not incidentally, a recent study published in *The Lancet* said that more than half of the deaths caused by illegal drug use (in a global survey for 2010) were caused by prescription drug abuse.[31] The worst death rates were found in countries with harsh anti-drug regimes.

INTENDED CONSEQUENCES

The official, prohibitionist approach to plant-based illegal drugs (marijuana, cocaine, and heroin) has become basic to the world's approach to all illegal drugs. These three are significantly representative of the public's serious concerns as to the choices people make about their preferred high, or about their preferred medicine.

Any discussion of legalization or decriminalization of illegal drugs usually devolves into a discussion of marijuana, which is among the least harmful of all banned drugs.[32] The more difficult question, though, is what to do about those drugs that are regarded to be more harmful to individuals who use or abuse them (heroin, for example). On this question, the experts are divided. Some say that the least harmful model includes the outright legalization, control, and regulation of all illegal drugs, adjusting the details to recognize and deal with the differences among drugs. Others who might allow for some relaxation of the laws around marijuana are dead against the idea of similar treatment for heroin and cocaine, referring to the harms these can cause to individuals and families.

There are, however, well-documented consequences arising, not from the use of the drugs themselves, but from the fact that they are prohibited. An examination of these so-called "unintended" consequences of prohibition is important when it comes to deciding whether to continue the status quo of prohibition or adopt a new approach. It has to be said, though, that we are well past the point where we can call such consequences "unintended." They include the well-known damage caused by prison sentences and criminal records, the destruction to families and communities whose members are in prison, the health consequences of allowing crime bosses to distribute uncontrolled and unsafe products, the violence and corruption associated with organized crime, and the health consequences of spreading HIV, Hepatitis C, and other diseases to users and to the community. These are serious and devastating harms. They are easily anticipated and can be alleviated by policy changes that recognize the damage done by prohibition.

In addition to these, there are harms caused to offenders who are saddled with criminal records. In the United States, a felony conviction can result in the loss of the right to vote, to obtain public housing, federal education assistance, welfare benefits, food stamps, and other services.[33] In Canada, the ability to obtain employment and to travel freely is permanently impaired by a criminal record. In all cases, the shame and stigma of a record is very damaging. These consequences have been clearly recognized for years. Proponents of prohibition can therefore be said to both understand and "intend" the serious and debilitating consequences of the criminalization of drugs.

As one small example, I was once approached by a middle-aged woman — I'll call her Jane — to defend her on a simple possession charge. She had been arrested for possession of a small amount of marijuana, and intended to plead guilty and pay the fine. She also worked at a retail outlet downtown, and was most concerned about losing her job.

Jane told me that the night before she was arrested, she had been partying with a group of people, all smoking marijuana, and the group included members of the local RCMP. These turned out to be the same people who arrested her the very next day. She was, of course, at a loss as to why they would arrest her for smoking marijuana when they themselves had been partaking.

Despite our best efforts, Jane's employer soon learned of the conviction. Jane was laid off immediately. I expect she has not worked at a decent job since, much like thousands of others across the country, because her criminal record will be held against her. She will certainly have no faith in the justice system or the police who are bound to uphold it.

Another example of "unintended" consequences has to do with the effect of a criminal record upon travel opportunities. Recently, a resident of Victoria, B.C., won a contest to go to the Super Bowl in the United

States.[34] When he arrived at Pearson International Airport in Toronto, he was turned back by U.S. Customs because he had been convicted of marijuana possession in 1981 — thirty-two years earlier. Myles Wilkinson said he was nineteen years old at the time of his conviction. He was caught with two grams of marijuana, for which he paid a fifty-dollar fine. He never did get to the Super Bowl.

Crossing the border into the United States gets more perilous by the day if you make any mention of illegal drugs. It is the federal government that controls the border in the United States, so any disclosure a traveller might make about previous drug use or intentions can bar him from entry.[35] If you tell the border agent you are travelling to Washington State to take advantage of the new legal marijuana laws, you can be turned back. If you admit to having used drugs in the past, you can be turned back. You can also be banned permanently from entry. In order to cross the border in such circumstances, you will be required to apply for an expensive, renewable travel waiver. Such travel restrictions impair an individual's ability to seek employment, maintain contact with family and friends, conduct business, and live an ordinary life.

In order to start the process of reaching rational conclusions about illegal drug policy, it is important to consider the various risks, harms, and benefits provided by the main three plant-based drugs. The next chapter looks into the known characteristics of marijuana, cocaine, and heroin, both positive and negative. It also draws a very important distinction between public health harms caused by the use of the drugs and harms caused by the fact that they are illegal. The tension between these two should help determine our public policy approach to drugs.

Chapter Three

Heroin: Fear and Loathing

Direct Health Effects

Sometimes it takes the death of a celebrity to bring home salient points about drugs, and to dispel the myths that surround them. Cory Monteith, a Canadian actor who made his name on the television series *Glee*, died in July of 2013 in Vancouver of what was reported as a heroin overdose. Almost immediately, a *Calgary Herald* editor implied that he would be alive today except for Vancouver's ready supply of illegal drugs. She took particular aim at the city's safe injection site (InSite) in the Downtown Eastside neighbourhood.[1]

It was swiftly pointed out that InSite is not in the business of selling drugs of any kind.[2] It also became clear after the coroner had done his work that Cory Monteith did not die of a heroin overdose but of a combination of heroin and alcohol.

As a sidebar to the Monteith story, the day after his death, Abbotsford police sent out a public warning.[3] They reported, in response to a sudden rise in overdoses, that there was a surge of dangerously potent heroin in the area. They had found fentanyl in recent supplies of heroin, which greatly increases the drug's strength. As it turned out, there was no fentanyl found in Mr. Monteith's body, but the warning was a cautionary tale to all those in the area who might be using heroin.

More recently, Philip Seymour Hoffman, one of his generation's finest actors, was found dead in his apartment with a needle in his arm, and a large quantity of heroin in the room. There has been a similar outpouring of grief over Hoffman's early demise and much soul-searching over the fact that he was an admitted heroin addict who had been clean for years. The relapse was perhaps inevitable, but his death should not have been. Experts have noted that a relapse could have been triggered by prescription drug use.[4] As well, a former addict returning to heroin might overestimate his tolerance for the drug after many years. And even a change as to where the drug is used might be dangerous. For example, if an addict is accustomed to using the drug in his car, injecting in a different environment might trigger an overdose. This is known as "conditioned tolerance." As it turned out, the toxicology report showed several drugs were present in Mr. Hoffman's body, specifically heroin, cocaine, benzodiazepines, and amphetamine.

Simon Jenkins, a respected columnist for *The Guardian* newspaper, talks about the double standard that we have adopted toward drug use.[5] His comments are a direct reference to the classism that determines who gets punished for illegal drug use and who does not. He says, "The law … lumps Hoffman together with thousands found dead and friendless in urban backstreets, also with needles in their arms. It treats them all as outlaws…. Offices, schools, hospitals, prisons, even parliament, are awash in illegal drug use. Their illegality is no deterrent." Then he concludes: "So what do we do? We turn a blind eye to an unworkable law and assume it does not apply to people like us. We then relieve the implied guilt by taking draconian revenge on those who supply drugs to those who need them, but who lack the friends and resources either to combat them or to avoid the law." Jenkins expresses the hope that high-profile casualties like Hoffman will lead legislators to re-think their position on illegal drugs and change the law.

What is this drug that took the lives of Monteith and Hoffman? Why is it so feared?

Heroin is derived from the opium poppy, and today most of the world's supply comes from the Afghanistan, Burma, and Colombia. Opium was first synthesized back in 1874 as an alternative to morphine, after it was discovered that some people were becoming addicted.[6] In 1895, Bayer began producing the substance. The company called their new product "heroin" because soldiers (heroes) who used it would charge into battle in the face of live fire. Bayer promoted heroin as non-addictive and sold it as a substitute for morphine and as a cough suppressant. But as the twentieth century wore on, heroin was eventually prohibited in both the United States and Canada.

Heroin has a blood-brain permeability ten times that of morphine, from which it is derived.[7] This means that the drug causes depression in breathing and increased pleasure, and it can block pain signals from the spinal cord. Injection produces an immediate "rush" like an intense orgasm. Then the user feels four to six hours of a "high," which might include nodding off or periods of very busy, talkative behaviour. Alternatively, some high-functioning addicts show no abnormal behaviour at all.

As noted, it is possible to overdose on heroin, and to die, although by far most cases of death involve more than the one drug, usually a combination of heroin and alcohol. "While it is theoretically possible to die from an overdose of any of these [illegal] drugs alone, in practical terms this is extremely rare."[8] With respect to heroin, Dr. Carl Hart says, "In virtually every overdose death involving an opioid … some other substance is present. Most of the time it is alcohol." He recommends a mass media educational effort to inform people of the dangers of these combinations.

Heroin is a powerful painkiller that sedates the central nervous system.[9] It is addictive both physically and psychologically. Withdrawal symptoms include dysphoria (a combination of anxiety, depression, and restlessness), insomnia, muscle aches, and diarrhea. Some maintain that regular use can cause addiction, but others question this seemingly straightforward assertion. Dr. Bruce K. Alexander, retired professor at Simon Fraser University, for example, rejects the claim that all or most people who use heroin (and cocaine) beyond a certain amount become addicted.[10] He points out that when heroin was being used for therapeutic purposes in the nineteenth century, the incidence of addiction never reached 1 percent of the population, and was declining when the drug was banned.

Withdrawal from heroin is commonly depicted as extremely painful and long-lasting, although some say it is similar to a bad case of the flu. We know that heroin withdrawal can be relatively straightforward if the pressures that led to the addiction are relieved. A favourite example is that of Vietnam veterans returning stateside after the war. Soldiers took drugs to help them through the experiences they were enduring in combat. About 50 percent tried opium and heroin, and half of these showed signs of addiction.[11] Most of them, contrary to the fears of the American government, were able to withdraw from the drugs relatively easily upon returning stateside. The stressors that had led to drug use in the first place had been removed, so users were able to control or eliminate their drug use at home.

One common misperception about drug addiction is the notion that addicts are taking drugs for recreational purposes — to have a pleasurable experience, to get "high." While this may have been the rationale for their first experiment with drugs, once they have become addicted, attaining a "high" is the last thing on their minds. Rather, they are trying to ward off serious withdrawal symptoms so that they can function. As Dr. Nutt points out, "It is quite common for someone to start taking a drug for the enjoyable effects, but once they're addicted it becomes the only thing that can relieve the intense cravings and unpleasant physical symptoms of withdrawal."[12]

Dr. Lisa Lefebvre of Canada's Centre for Addiction and Mental Health (CAMH) made an educational video in response to the Hoffman overdose. In it she addresses the issue of an addict's ability to choose to use or not use heroin. "One of the biggest misconceptions is that it is a choice someone makes, and unfortunately that's not the case.... Heroin addiction is an illness.... Thinking of this as a sort of disease of choice has not been helpful in the past because it has put the onus entirely on that person to, with their willpower, treat what is really a medical illness that needs medical and psychosocial treatments in order to improve the outcomes."[13]

In a seminal ruling allowing the drug injection clinic InSite to continue operating in Vancouver, the Supreme Court of Canada (in a unanimous 9:0 ruling) said that "serious drug addiction is not a moral choice; it is an illness which essentially negates the notion of 'choice' altogether."[14] Chief

Justice McLachlin said many addicts "use multiple substances, and suffer from alcoholism.... [T]hese people are not engaged in recreational drug use: they are addicted."

American jazz legend Billie Holiday's riff on heroin explains it this way: "If you think dope is for kicks and thrills you're out of your mind. There are more kicks to be had in a good case of paralytic polio and living in an iron lung. If you think you need stuff to play music or sing, you're crazy. It can fix you so you can't play nothing or sing nothing." She went on to say that in Britain the authorities at least had the decency to treat addiction as a public health problem, but in America, "if you go to the doctor, he's liable to slam the door in your face and call the cops."[15]

NEGATIVE EFFECTS OF CRIMINALIZATION

A number of negative health effects are also caused by the fact that heroin has been criminalized. These effects can be profound, sometimes life-threatening, and all-but-impossible to alleviate because of the fear of prosecution. The suppression efforts of law enforcement drive the trade underground, where there are no controls over the quality of the drug or its potency. Users are thus consuming dangerously adulterated and dangerously potent heroin, both of which can kill. Users also inject in unhygienic conditions because of a fear of being arrested. Forced to hide from the law, heroin users may inject with dirty, shared needles, using water from puddles, in cold back alleys that make it more difficult to inject into constricted veins. These conditions encourage the spread of deadly diseases like HIV/AIDS and HCV.

One heroin addict in Moscow described the fear occasioned by aggressive drug law enforcement, and the negative effects it produces: "Fear. Fear.... And not only fear of being caught, but fear that you will be caught and you won't be able to get a fix. So on top of being pressured and robbed [by police], there's the risk you'll also end up being sick [from withdrawal]. And that's why you'll use whatever syringe is available right then and there."[16]

Safe injection sites are one way of providing a safe place and safe conditions for heroin addicts to use their drugs. These are places staffed by trained nurses and doctors. Users must buy their drugs from their usual illegal source, but are provided with sterile syringes and clean surroundings in which to inject safely. Should the heroin prove to be so pure that the user begins to show signs of overdose, medical personnel step in to help. Similarly, should the heroin be adulterated with a dangerous substance,[17] they are available to deal with the consequences. The spread of HIV/AIDS and HCV is substantially reduced by safe injection sites because of the hygienic conditions in which the injections take place. As well, used needles must be left at the location, and so are not discarded in public places where they can cause harm to the public.

In Canada, the only safe injection site (InSite) is located in Vancouver. It was established in 2003 in response to the epidemic of illness and death associated with large numbers of heroin-addicted people living in the Downtown Eastside neighbourhood. It was able to operate due to an exemption from criminal prosecution provided by the federal Liberal government. Despite the proven success of InSite, the subsequent Conservative government spent three years and substantial funds to oppose its continuation. Only a direct order from the Supreme Court of Canada in 2011 compelled the Harper government to continue providing the site with its exemption from prosecution.

This case represented a direct confrontation between the hard-line criminal justice approach of the Conservative government and the public health approach represented by InSite. In assessing the evidence presented by both sides of this argument, the Supreme Court concluded that "InSite has saved lives and improved health. And it did those things without increasing the incidence of drug use and crime in the surrounding area. The Vancouver police support InSite. The city and provincial government want it to stay open."[18] Chief Justice McLachlin noted that this tiny area of Vancouver is home to 4,600 intravenous drug users whose lives are on the line.

InSite said its staff had intervened in 336 overdoses since 2006, and that no deaths had occurred at the facility. It had supervised more than 1.8 million injections since it opened, and oversees an average of 587 injections daily.[19] In 1993, before InSite was opened, two hundred people were dying annually in the Downtown Eastside.[20] A recent peer-reviewed study reported in *The Lancet* showed that fatal overdoses dropped by 35 percent in the vicinity of InSite in the two years after it opened (from fifty-six deaths to thirty-three), compared to 9 percent in the rest of Vancouver during that same period. In 2011, there were sixty-six overdose deaths in the entire city.[21] Many others were contracting AIDS/HIV, Hepatitis C, and other serious illnesses. Today, British Columbia is the only Canadian province in which the rate of HIV infection is going down.

Importantly, InSite does more than just provide a safe place to inject drugs. Nurses attend to wounds, abscesses, and vein and skin conditions. Clients are treated like human beings and not like criminals. For some, it is the only place they can go where no one is judging them. And it is critical that the clinic provides a point of entry for treatment. There is a detox centre on its premises that claims a 43 percent completion rate for addicts who seek treatment — something addicts are otherwise reluctant to do because it means risking exposure to law enforcement. InSite also provides transitional housing for addicts who finish detox.

Critics of InSite say that "safe injection" is an oxymoron, and that programs like InSite "enable addictions."[22] Because the emphasis of such a program is on maintenance and disease prevention rather than abstention, many are unwilling to see its value. "Arguably, places like InSite are actually making addictions worse by enabling the drug use and sending the message that its 'okay' to use drugs, so long as it's done 'safely,'" says one critic. This statement flies in the face of evidence that clearly shows the number of addicts to be falling substantially from harm-reduction programs such as the one in Switzerland.

Critics often fall back on inflammatory language in rejecting the idea of harm reduction. For example, one says that InSite is a "spit-shined flophouse of momentary sobriety" where, "despite any lofty claims, for most addicts, InSite's just another place to get high."[23] This critic claims that there has never been an independent analysis of InSite, choosing to ignore the extensive analysis done by the Supreme Court of Canada, among others. He appears to be unaware that even the Vancouver Police Department approves of the program and urges addicts to use the location.[24] Police say that "injecting drugs without close supervision compounds the problem. InSite has been established to reduce that risk." Opened in 2003, InSite has been visited 1.9 million times and there have been no overdose deaths as a result of its services.

The Urban Health Research Initiative in Vancouver has recently reported some other remarkable improvements that can be largely attributed to harm-reduction programs.[25] For example, in 1996, 39.6 percent of drug users were borrowing needles. In 2011, only 1.7 percent were engaging in this risky behaviour. There have also been dramatic decreases in diseases over those years. In 1997, there were 8.1 cases of HIV per one hundred person years. In 2011, the number was down to 0.37. HCV experienced a similar decrease, from 37.1 cases to 1.1. Fewer people are injecting drugs and more are ceasing use. Incredibly, in 1996, the rate of cessation of injection drug use was 0.4 percent; in 2011 it was 46.6 percent.

Proponents of needle exchange programs like "Cactus" in Montreal (the first of its kind in North America) say that the Supreme Court decision on InSite will let them "stop being hypocrites" if it means that they will now be able to open a full-service safe injection site.[26] As Cactus community coordinator Jean-François Mary said, "For 22 years, we gave people clean tools, then sent them out into the street. We were doing half the work. Now they'll be able to shoot up in complete safety."

Unfortunately, it seems that the current Conservative government is trying to make setting up these safe injection sites in Canada a lot more difficult. Proposed new regulations will make it near-impossible to satisfy all the requirements for opening such a facility. Not only will new sites have difficulty meeting these new requirements, but InSite itself will now find it hard to renew its mandate. The federal health minister will now be able to block safe injection sites based upon his or her assessment of "the local conditions indicating a need," "the regulatory structure in place to support the facility," and "expressions of community support or opposition." The fact that the mayor and police chief in Toronto are both opposed will probably weigh more heavily with the current government than the expressions of support by public health officials.[27]

Other cities in Canada are planning to apply for an InSite-style exemption from criminal law so that they can operate safe injection sites as well. At the end of 2013, Montreal had approved four new supervised injection sites, including one mobile unit.[28] With start-up costs of $3.2 million and operating costs of $2.7 million per year, proponents said the program would pay for itself within four years. They claimed that the health care system would be the winner, with reduced incidences of HIV/AIDS, HCV, overdoses, and problems with dirty needles left in public places. However, nothing can happen until Health Canada provides an exemption from criminal prosecution — something that is by no means guaranteed under the new regulations.

Thousands of prison inmates who inject drugs like heroin are also at risk for disease and death. The government has steadfastly refused to allow for a needle exchange program in prisons despite repeated requests by the prison ombudsman.[29] Prison authorities provide bleach for cleaning needles, but this is not a wholly effective method of killing viruses. The resulting rates of HIV/AIDS and Hepatitis C are ten to twenty times higher in the prison population than in the general population. These are serious and even deadly diseases, which are later spread to the community as prisoners are released from incarceration.

Reasons provided by the correctional services for refusing clean needles have no foundation in fact. Prison needle exchanges do not lead to an increase in drug use, do not result in syringes being used as weapons, and do not result in an increase in accidental needle-stick injuries. These three myths have been rejected by the Public Health Agency of Canada.[30]

Needle exchanges are run inside prisons in many countries, including Spain, Moldova, Iran, and Kyrgyzstan.[31] These regimes are not known for their progressive ideas with regard to incarceration, but they do recognize the facts of life, one of which is that inmates will find ways to obtain drugs and inject them.

NAOMI, the North American Opiate Management Initiative, was a program that operated out of St. Paul's Hospital in Vancouver. NAOMI supervised the administration of heroin to 350 of the "toughest, most difficult to reach narcotic abusers," according to Dr. Keith Martin.[32] The randomized trial divided addicts into three groups and provided them with heroin, hydromorphone, or methadone. Hydromorphone is a very potent opioid, a derivative of morphine, used to treat chronic pain. It is anywhere from six to ten times as strong as morphine. Methadone is a synthetic opioid that is legal, has been approved for use as an alternative to heroin, and can be prescribed for addicts. In the remarkable results reported by the NAOMI project, users who were resistant to methadone, and to whom heroin was provided instead, were 62 percent more likely to remain in treatment, used less heroin, and committed fewer crimes.[33] They also showed improved employment satisfaction and social integration — all indicators of a return to some version of a normal lifestyle.

In practice, NAOMI patients attend at a facility like Vancouver's Crosstown Clinic at set times (two to three times a day) and sign in to receive their prescribed heroin. They are turned away if they have been using alcohol. The clinic provides them with a measured dose of pharmaceutical-grade heroin and sterilized equipment. The patients administer the dose themselves in a mirrored room, and then must sit in the lounge for twenty minutes for monitoring so that staff can deal with any negative reactions.

Dave Murray was one of the addicts who was treated with heroin.[34] He says he is living proof that heroin maintenance works. "After more than 20 years dealing and injecting drugs, Mr. Murray participated in the earlier NAOMI trial, where he regularly received doses of heroin without having to worry about his next fix. This new stability erased the stress from his life and prompted reflection, Mr. Murray said. 'My brain re-engaged, and I made a conscious decision to try detox. I failed at first, but about three years ago, finally I stopped using.'"

Health Canada sought advice from independent experts on the subject of prescription heroin.[35] These experts told Health Canada that this is the only "next step" available for some addicts, and that prescription heroin is a "promising treatment of last resort." They also said it decreases harm to individuals and to their families. The Health Minister of British Columbia calls prescription heroin "compassionate use of a medication."

A follow-up study to NAOMI, "The Study to Assess Longer-term Opioid Medication Effectiveness" (SALOME) has been designed to determine the effectiveness of providing hydromorphone to heroin addicts.[36] It involves 322 patients and will be completed by early 2015. It will attempt to show whether or not hydromorphone is as good as prescription heroin at treating the addicts who do not respond to methadone. Hydromorphone treatment currently costs $39 per day, a not-insignificant amount for patients.

The question then arises: why is the government going to such lengths to find a viable alternative to heroin when prescribed heroin itself appears to provide the best results? We know that methadone does not work for everyone, and that some addicts suffer from pain and craving when they take it.[37] As one pharmacist says, "Most addicts loathe it. It is a highly addictive synthetic opiate, more addictive than heroin and harder to withdraw from, but it survives the digestive system and so does not need to be injected."[38] In other words, addicts are being required to drink "green gunk" largely because legislators appear to have an aversion to the idea of injection, and especially to providing heroin as the best treatment. As Dr. Perry Kendall, British Columbia Provincial Health Officer, says, "In Switzerland and Germany, they don't have a problem with treating people with heroin, but here we do."[39]

Doctors in the SALOME project expressed concerns about an exit strategy for addicts who would be leaving the clinical trials. How would they survive if they could no longer rely upon heroin maintenance? The doctors made an application to Health Canada under its Special Access Program (SAP) to enable them to continue with heroin maintenance and Health Canada duly approved prescription heroin (for ninety days after exiting the program) for 21 of the addicts who would otherwise be facing serious, life-threatening conditions.[40]

When this came to light, the Health minister, Rona Ambrose, was swift in her response. She quickly banned what she called "dangerous drugs like heroin, cocaine, ecstasy, and LSD" from being prescribed to patients.[41] And she followed this up by stating that "the prime minister and I do not believe we are serving the interests of those who are addicted to drugs or those who need our help by giving them the very drugs they are addicted to."[42] She suggested that addicts try alternative approaches like acupuncture.

Five of the affected addicts, together with their health provider, Providence Health Care, and a legal advocacy group have now filed a lawsuit challenging the federal government.[43] The same arguments will be made as were successfully made in keeping InSite open. In that case, the Supreme Court of Canada found that the government's attempts to close the site were "grossly disproportionate because the potential denial of health services and correlative increased risk of death and disease to injection drug users outweigh any benefit that might be derived from maintaining an absolute prohibition on possession of illegal drugs on InSite's premises."

Larry Love is one of the patients named in the law suit. He describes his life before SALOME as "a life of hell" and claims that the heroin maintenance program has provided him with "vastly improved" health and well-being. He believes it can save lives and allow addicts to become productive members of society.

His voice "quivering with emotion," Dr. Scott MacDonald of the SALOME project responded to the federal government's opposition to the program: "As a human being, as a Canadian, as a doctor, I want to be able to offer this treatment to the people who need it. It is effective, it is safe, and it works.... I do not know what they [the federal government] are thinking." He claims that about 10 percent of those addicted to heroin require heroin maintenance. Of those, about half are able to move to less-intensive treatment or abstain altogether.

Other jurisdictions have already proven the value of similar maintenance programs. In Liverpool, England, for example, Dr. John Marks reported to work at a clinic that offered treatment to drug addicts.[44] This was back in 1982. At his facility, if users did not wish to work toward abstinence, and if they satisfied certain other criteria, they were offered a drug maintenance program instead. This meant that physicians gave users a prescription for their drug (heroin, cocaine, crack cocaine), which they could take to a pharmacy where it would be filled for free. As part of their therapy, they were expected to attend meetings to show they were otherwise healthy and crime-free. If they did not comply, they were dropped from the program.

Dr. Marks thought prescribing dangerous drugs to addicts was silly, and he planned to shut the clinic down and replace it with a psychiatric program that he believed would succeed. However, the success of the drug maintenance program was so convincing that Dr. Marks changed his mind. Addicts in the program remained free of AIDS, and most of them became healthier and obtained jobs. Police reported a 94 percent decrease in theft, burglary, and property crimes around the area of the clinic, and there was a reduction in drug use. Unfortunately, this program was shut down in 1995 despite its clear success. Dr. Marks put this down to the fact that the American television show *60 Minutes* aired an episode highlighting the clinic's work, and that this approach to addiction flew in the face of the American War on Drugs.

Dr. Marks explained his view of drug treatment (aimed at abstinence) versus drug maintenance (aimed at harm reduction and maintenance) this way: "If they're drug takers determined to continue their drug use, treating them is an expensive waste of time. And really, the choice that I'm being offered and society is being offered is drugs from the clinic or drugs from the Mafia.... [Giving them drugs] doesn't get them off drugs. It doesn't prolong their addiction either. But it stops them offending; it keeps them healthy and it keeps them alive."

Switzerland has also tried different approaches to drug addiction. After the failure of "Needle Park," a location where addicts could gather and use drugs without fear of arrest, the Swiss opened a number of safe injection sites, which resulted in a reduction in both the number of overdoses and the spread of AIDS. After visiting Dr. Marks's clinic in Liverpool, Swiss organizers went on to establish the "largest scientific heroin maintenance project ever attempted."[45] Addicts had to meet a number of conditions before being provided with drugs (either free or for a nominal fee). The final report of the Swiss government was so positive that citizens voted overwhelmingly in a nationwide referendum to continue the program. The report said that the "individual health and social circumstances [of users on the maintenance program, who were "hard-core" drug addicts] improved dramatically, usually in a very short time." Stable employment increased, unemployment decreased, users learned to function independently, criminal activities decreased dramatically, and costs of medical and social care and crime control dropped by about half.

The Global Commission on Drug Policy reported that in the Swiss program, between 1990 and 2002, the annual number of new heroin users dropped by 82 percent.[46] The overall population of users declined by 4 percent per year during that time, and several areas in Switzerland reported a decrease in injection drug use.

The advantages of a public health approach to heroin use are many. So are the negative effects of its criminalization. Addicts court disease and death by shooting up in back alleys to avoid the law. They must buy their drugs from criminals who specialize in violence, extortion, and corruption. They may commit crimes themselves in order to purchase heroin on the black market. The heroin, controlled by gangs and cartels, may be adulterated with unknown dangerous substances. The purity of the drug will be unknown, so overdoses can result. Members of the community as well as the addicts themselves may already suffer from family breakdown and community disruption caused by drug abuse. These problems are exacerbated by the criminalization of the drug, as addicts are further separated from their families and society by incarceration, and can contract diseases in prison that will then spread outside the prison walls when they are released.

THERAPEUTIC USES

Despite heroin's reputation for producing serious addiction and health problems, many credible voices have called for its use as an effective painkiller. As noted earlier, heroin works better for many addicts than methadone because it is more effective at eliminating the pain and discomfort associated with withdrawal. It has also been shown to produce better results in helping patients become drug-free: one study showed that only 1.2 percent of clients became drug-free after using methadone, while 12.5 percent succeeded using heroin.[47]

What about using heroin to treat pain in a therapeutic setting? While legislators and physicians and many members of the public reject the notion of prescribed heroin, in some cases it provides the best remedy for chronic, excruciating pain, particularly for patients who are terminally ill with cancer. The main opposition to the use of heroin comes from those who believe patients run the risk of becoming addicted. Others respond that this concern is not germane, especially if patients are suffering and have only a short time to live.

We also know that people are generally less likely to become addicted when taking the drug for therapeutic purposes rather than for pleasure. According to WHO documents, "research makes it very clear that addiction is a negligible occurrence among patients with no history of addiction who receive opioids for pain."[48] In one review of such cases, only seven out of twenty-four thousand patients became addicted. The authors say "cancer patients can stop taking opioids when the pain stops; i.e., they do not crave opioids when they no longer need them for pain relief." They further state that the number one impediment to the medical use of opioids, according to a recent survey of governments, is the confusion and misinformation disseminated on the subject.

Canadian doctor W. Gifford-Jones has been championing the use of heroin for pain relief in terminally ill cancer patients for decades. In 1984, the Ministry of Health finally did legalize the use of heroin for this purpose. However, many restrictions were attached to its use: doctors were required to present their reasons to a hospital committee before permission to prescribe heroin was granted, and the drug had to be kept in a secure location and transported by armed guards. Because the process was so difficult, few doctors prescribed heroin, and ultimately the pharmaceutical company that was licensed to import the drug stopped doing so.

In a recent survey, Canada and the United States were listed in ninth place as the "best place to die." England, which holds first place, allows prescribed heroin for end-of-life pain.[49] In fact, it has been using heroin for easing palliative pain since the early 1900s.[50]

When the Royal Canadian Mounted Police stated that there was a security risk associated with prescribed heroin, Dr. Gifford-Jones travelled to England to learn about the experience there and to assess these risks. He was told by Scotland Yard that there were few problems, and that hospital pharmacies were never broken into. Rural doctors even carried heroin in their bags for use in emergencies, and he was told that even children dying of cancer were given the drug because it gave them comfort and a "fuzzy" feeling.

Dr. Gifford-Jones emphasizes that the biggest fear of dying patients, especially cancer patients, is the fear of pain. His experience in England confirmed that terminally ill cancer patients do not become addicted to heroin. Why? Because they are taking it for pain relief and not for recreational purposes. Where remission of the cancer occurs, it takes only about three weeks to wean a patient off the drug. Those who claim that morphine is just as effective are mistaken, because heroin is stronger, passes through the blood-brain barrier faster, and provides a comforting euphoria.

Dr. Bruce K. Alexander, professor emeritus at Simon Fraser University, has also determined the efficacy of using heroin for therapeutic purposes. As he says, "conventional wisdom notwithstanding, administering large doses of heroin and other opiate drugs over long periods of time to medical patients does not cause addiction."[51]

Tom Carnwath and Ian Smith, authors of *Heroin Century*, also assert that heroin is a more effective drug than morphine in some contexts.[52] Heroin is less likely to produce nausea and itching. It is more concentrated, so less of the drug is needed, which is helpful when injections are required. It gets to the brain faster. Heroin is useful in treating terminal tuberculosis and heart failure, and it is good for treating the cough associated with cancer or influenza in the 15 percent of cases in which patients get very sick if they use morphine. It remains the drug of choice in the United Kingdom when subcutaneous treatment is required.

The authors cite some of the advantages of heroin in detail:

> Patients with severe cough and shortness of breath … were undoubtedly very frightened and uncomfortable.… Heroin slowed down the breathing rate and this in itself made patients calmer, even if it did not help their oxygen levels. It is also very effective in suppressing troublesome coughing. On top of this, it is matchless in producing a mental state of calm detachment. Patients remain aware of their pain and illness, but no longer feel it really matters. Much of the horror of illness lies in the fear it induces.

Clearly, the psychological effects of comfort and the easing of anxiety rank high among the advantages of using heroin. As the authors say, heroin, which "even after a hundred years … remains a medicine without superior," provides "a way of confronting with dignity the challenge of illness and death." American doctors who have lobbied to be able to prescribe heroin describe it as "the most potent, effective, soluble and rapidly active narcotic ever created."

Nonetheless, in North America heroin remains unavailable to most patients suffering from extreme pain. Although it is still technically legal to prescribe in Canada, it is in practice not an option. As a consequence, many terminally ill patients are suffering unnecessary pain, fear, and anxiety. Concerns expressed by those who reject the idea of therapeutic heroin should be allayed by the experience in England. As one pharmacist said, "Those politicians who, in the face of all contrary evidence, stubbornly see the drug as the problem are no less misguided than the addicts who see drugs as the solution."[53]

Chapter Four

Cocaine: White Lines

Direct Health Effects

Cocaine was first synthesized in 1850, and was even promoted by Sigmund Freud as a cure for depression and sexual impotence.[1] In 1886, it became the main ingredient in a new drink, Coca-Cola. Consumers found that it had euphoric and energizing effects. It was widely used up until the early 1900s as an ingredient in various elixirs, cure-all tonics, and beverages.

Cocaine was removed from Coca-Cola in 1903, and in 1920 it was banned in the United States under the *Dangerous Drug Act*. This prohibition was largely in response to racist attitudes. For example, the *New York Times* quoted Dr. Edward Huntington Williams denouncing "Negro cocaine 'fiends.'"[2] Congress heard testimony that "most of the attacks upon white women in the South are the direct result of a cocaine-crazed Negro brain."[3]

In Canada, cocaine was banned for use in medicines in 1908, and later was included in the list of drugs prohibited by the 1911 *Opium and Drugs Act*, preceding prohibition in the United States by several years.

Cocaine is derived from the coca plant, which is grown mainly in the high Andes of South America. Indigenous peoples living at high altitudes chew coca leaves to help them deal with cold, hunger, and fatigue. The mild stimulant improves their oxygen intake, a necessity at high altitude, and increases their stamina. Many indigenous peoples consider coca leaf to be sacred, and include it in their ceremonies and traditions.

Cocaine (the white powder processed version of coca leaf) is a powerful stimulant of the central nervous system that creates intense euphoria in the user.[4] It also affects the cardiovascular system, increasing both blood pressure and heart rate. It may be smoked (in its form as crack cocaine), snorted, or injected, and suppresses fatigue, appetite, pain, and the need for sleep. The drug may also induce feelings of agitation or anxiety or, by contrast, of physical and intellectual prowess in the user. Cocaine can be dangerous if mixed with alcohol.

Neuropsychopharmacologist Dr. Carl Hart is one of the few experts to have done clinical trials of human beings using cocaine. He himself believed popular misconceptions about cocaine and other illegal drugs until he began to do the science himself. "When I started applying my critical skills to what I thought I knew about drugs," he explains, "very little survived."[5] He uses as an example the hysteria around "crack babies" and how the ONDCP put out a statistic that "wildly overstated" the extent of this problem. He assembled "a mountain of scientific data to call into question some of the purported damaging effects of drugs like cocaine, heroin, and methamphetamine."

In the face of claims that crack is especially dangerous, Dr. Hart points out that powder and crack cocaine are "qualitatively the same drug." They are "identical pharmacologically." The fact that a user might experience more intense highs with crack cocaine than with powder has to do with the ways in which they are ingested. Injecting cocaine, for example (instead of snorting it, which is the more common method), will provide about the same intense response as smoking crack. Dr. Nutt of the U.K. agrees that it is the "route of administration" that determines the intensity of the high experienced.[6]

Dr. Hart also clears up some misconceptions around addiction to cocaine. For example, it is widely believed that after one hit of crack cocaine, a person can become addicted. As he points out, this is false, and even at the height of its widespread use, only 10 to 20 percent of crack users ever became addicted.[7] He also asserts that "physical dependence isn't the primary reason for continued drug use," and, unlike heroin or alcohol or tobacco (or even caffeine), cocaine withdrawal does not include physical symptoms. So any dependence or addiction to cocaine must be described as psychological. This is consistent with the WHO definition of addiction as a psychological dependence; that is, "compulsive use of a drug for its mood-altering properties, and continued use despite harm."[8]

Dr. Hart explodes other myths about cocaine, as well, and he does so through his own scientific research. Cocaine addicts are not hopelessly impulsive. They will not choose the drug inevitably over other available rewards. The craving is not their primary concern — they are more pre-occupied with the cost of housing and other essentials. They are not more paranoid than the non-addict, except in that they have much to fear from the police. He concludes that "the emotional hysteria that stems from misinformation related to illegal drugs obfuscates the real problems faced by marginalized people. This also contributes to gross misuses of limited public resources."[9] Dr. Hart came to these conclusions reluctantly. A child of "the projects" himself, he had grown up believing everything he was told about the evils of illegal drugs.

Over the years, the media have been largely responsible for spreading fears about the addictiveness and danger of crack cocaine. *Newsweek*, for example, quoted the director of a cocaine hotline stating that "*There is no such thing* as recreational use of crack. It is almost instantaneous addiction." He went on to say that "crack is the most addictive drug known to man right now."[10] Broadcaster Dan Rather called cocaine use "a deep sickness in our society." Drug use even apparently threatened U.S. competitiveness: "The scourge of drugs is now so widespread among adults that it threatens to sap the nation's strength.... No one has measured how all this pill popping, injecting, and inhaling has affected the national output," said the *U.S. News*. Not to be outdone, *Newsweek* reported: "Joint by joint, line by line, pill by pill, the use of illegal drugs on the job has become a crisis for American business." In reality, however, that same year (1983), American corporate profits hit record highs.

The role played by external stressors (like poverty and marginalization) in drug use, including cocaine use, has been well documented. So has the ability of users to withdraw relatively easily from their drug of choice when those stressors are removed. This phenomenon has also been noted among animals. In a pharmacological study from UCLA, Dr. Ronald K.

Siegel said it was in the nature of all mammals to use mind-altering drugs in times of stress.[11] He gave the example of water buffaloes in Vietnam. These large but normally very tranquil animals, Siegel explains, "when subjected to the stress of B-52 raids during the Vietnam War ... immediately headed for the local coca leaf plants and started chewing on them. When the raids subsided, they went back to their prior activities."

Many people will have heard about studies of rats that show them repeatedly pressing a lever to obtain cocaine until they die, choosing the drug rather than food and water.[12] What people don't know about these studies is that the rats were kept in isolated, unnatural environments with no social contact and little else to do. This was a stressful environment. When other natural rewards — like social and sexual contact and pleasant living conditions — were made available, the rats preferred those. One study showed that 94 percent of rats preferred saccharin-sweetened water to intravenous cocaine.

Some of the most reliable information on cocaine is contained in a report that was never published. In the largest study of cocaine ever, the World Health Organization (WHO) in the early 1990s examined cocaine use in 19 countries, including developing and developed nations.[13] The study was funded by the United Nations Inter-Regional Crime and Justice Institute (UNICRI). Its conclusions and recommendations, however, did not accord with the prohibition model preferred by the United States, which depended heavily upon a portrayal of cocaine as very dangerous and addictive — conclusions which the study did not support. Further, although the United States insisted upon severe law enforcement as the best response to cocaine use, the WHO report concluded that there was a "current over-reliance on law enforcement," and stated a preference for "more assessment of the adverse effects of current drug policies and strategies." Indeed, "[the over-emphasis on] punitive drug control measures may actually contribute to the development of health-related problems. An increase in the adoption of more humane, compassionate responses ... is seen as a desirable counterbalance to the overreliance on law enforcement measures."

The WHO research challenged current orthodoxies. As a result, the United States threatened to withdraw its funding from WHO research projects.[14] According to one source, here is what happened: Almost as soon as the briefing kit started to circulate in the U.N. corridors, U.S. officials used their full weight to prevent the release of the study. "The United States government has been surprised to note that the package seemed to make a case for the positive uses of cocaine," was the response of Neil Boyer, the American representative to the forty-eighth meeting of the World Health Assembly in Geneva. He said that the WHO program on substance abuse was "headed in the wrong direction" and "undermined the efforts of the international community to stamp out illegal cultivation and production of coca." He denounced "evidence of WHO's support for harm reduction programs and previous WHO association with organizations that supported the legalization of drugs." Then came a clear threat: "If WHO activities relating to drugs fail to reinforce proven drug-control approaches, funds for the relevant programs should be curtailed."[15]

The study itself was never published, but, as noted, the briefing kit had already been circulated and is still available.[16]

So, what were the more specific WHO findings that caused such concern among those countries that supported prohibition of cocaine? First, it found that social and health problems associated with cocaine use were "very rare and much less severe for occasional, low-dosage users." The briefing kit states: "In many countries, chronic problems related to poverty, hunger, infectious diseases, war and social disorder overshadow any health problems related to cocaine use. Most participating countries agree that occasional cocaine use does not typically lead to severe or even minor physical or social problems, though there is evidence of increasing cocaine-related health problems in some parts of North America."

The report went on to say that negative effects of cocaine use are restricted to heavy users, and include paranoia, memory loss, depression, anxiety, loss of cognitive skill/intellectual capacity, apathy, mood swings, aggression, social withdrawal, and low self-esteem. This would appear to be congruent with the conclusions drawn by Dr. Hart and others. Additional negative consequences of cocaine use were listed as: appetite and weight loss, sinus problems, perforated nasal septa, cardiopulmonary or nervous system damage, and scarring and collapsed veins related to injection. Importantly, the WHO report states it is not clear that any of these conditions is actually caused by the cocaine use. It emphasizes that the drug often exacerbates existing conditions in users rather than causing them.

Among the most heretical conclusions drawn by the WHO was that people who use cocaine should be encouraged to use it "as safely as possible" — not that they should necessarily be encouraged to abstain.

Canada participated in the WHO study, producing a Country Profile and a Key Informant Study conducted in Vancouver.[17] Dr. Bruce K. Alexander was principal investigator.[18] The research showed that the lifetime prevalence for powder and crack cocaine use (that is, those who have used at least once in their lives) was 3 percent for all of Canada. The report referred to "popular myths" that cocaine inevitably causes severe problems and that cocaine use is growing epidemically. It found that cocaine use does not typically cause even minor physical or social problems, and only a small minority of people use it. Recreational users reported positive results, mainly a boost in energy and increased creativity.

And in spite of enormous expenditures on treatment in British Columbia, most interviewees felt the lives of most users remained unaffected. The judge who participated said that people who are most likely to go for treatment fall into one of three categories: those who are rich; those who are in unionized jobs (whose unions can pay for the program); and prisoners (whose parole often depends upon their seeking treatment). There was strong opposition by users to compulsory treatment programs.

The interviewees felt that law enforcement efforts were not having any impact on cocaine use. Interestingly, "even the consultants who favour maintenance of hard-line enforcement see it as ineffective." Most informants favoured some mitigation of the current legal severity. Some recreational users recommended decriminalization or legalization. Those who worked with addicts also favoured some form of decriminalization (similar to the regime for alcohol). The judge in the study suggested making cocaine legal on prescription, somewhat like methadone. Many cited the negative influence of the black market as a reason for recommending a less severe response.

The Canadian Key Informant Study found that the media tend to exaggerate and lie about the dangers of drug use in general, and that efforts to counteract this in public school are fruitless, largely because schools will not allow this type of intervention. Thus, efforts must be concentrated at the post-secondary level. The report says that "we have ... found no indications that letting university students know that drugs like cocaine can be used in a rewarding and apparently harmless way leads them to experiment with cocaine." If young people are going to experiment with illegal drugs, they will do so as an act of rebellion against the orthodoxy and against the fact that the drugs are illegal.

The WHO/UNICRI report was generally very negative about international efforts to deal with cocaine use. It said that prevention and education programs generally "do not prevent myths but perpetuate stereotypes and misinform the general public." It claims such programs rely on "sensationalized, exaggerated statements about cocaine which misinform about patterns of use, stigmatize users, and destroy the educator's credibility." It also noted that "fear-based mass media campaigns" are being carried out in Bolivia, Brazil, Colombia, and Ecuador. Most information provided about cocaine use is "superficial, lurid, excessively negative and ineffective in reaching subgroups such as homosexual users, youths and pregnant women." Treatment programs exaggerate the dangers of cocaine use and are often politically motivated, and there is little effort to evaluate the effectiveness of such programs.

The WHO report also found that most users recover from problems associated with cocaine without undergoing treatment. Most of the available treatment programs emphasize abstinence rather than harm reduction, and most are poorly coordinated, under-resourced, and lack properly trained staff. The religious orientation of some programs is off-putting to many potential clients, and there is abuse within some treatment centres, further undermining their effectiveness. The twelve-step program of Narcotics Anonymous, for example, places heavy emphasis upon religion. And shocking abuses of those in treatment have been reported in over 25 percent of participating nations, including "financial and sexual exploitation, neglect, assault and psychological abuse."[19] Major psychiatric drugs, tranquillizers, and anti-depressants are reportedly overused by participants in many of these programs also.

This sad assessment of the world's efforts to deal with cocaine use and abuse could have provided a basis for an overhaul of attitudes and policies toward the drug. It appears, though, that the seemingly irreversible entrenchment of the War on Drugs has impeded efforts to change. It is about twenty years since the WHO research was done, yet our governments continue to rely upon law enforcement as the only reliable approach, and the public continues to regard cocaine as a highly addictive and dangerous drug.

Negative Effects of Criminalization

Cocaine causes serious problems for the health of users because it has been criminalized. For example, the drug may be contaminated with dangerous and unknown foreign substances by criminal traffickers or by accident. The main reasons for purposely adding adulterants are: to bulk or dilute the drug (adding to the profits to be made); to complement or enhance the effects of the active ingredient in the drug; or to facilitate the administration of the drug.[20] Contaminants may also be created through chemical reactions during processing, or accidentally while in storage.

Toxicologist John Ramsay described some of the substances regularly used to adulterate ("step on") cocaine:[21]

- Benzocaine: a local anaesthetic
- Caffeine: 14 percent of cocaine samples contain caffeine. While caffeine in a drink is relatively harmless, powder caffeine is not. As little as quarter to a half gram will make a user very sick. It can produce vomiting, and make the user feel "really unwell." One report claimed a party-goer died after ingesting two spoonfuls of pure caffeine powder.[22] The coroner in that case noted that this was the equivalent of seventy cans of a popular energy drink.
- Triacetin: a headache cure which affects the kidney and liver
- Lignocaine: a local anaesthetic
- Lactose; glucose: sugars
- Creatine: a supplement used by body builders
- Paracetamol (acetaminophen): a mild analgesic; headache cure
- Boric Acid: a household cleaner also used to kill cockroaches

Another source says that levamisole is present in 80 percent of the cocaine in the United States.[23] Levamisole is an anti-parasitic used in veterinary medicine that affects the white blood cells. Ritalin and methamphetamine have also been found in cocaine.

Ramsay points out that a user cannot tell what is in the cocaine by looking at it. And because cocaine is illegal, there is no way to ensure that no dangerous adulterants are being used. In Europe, some countries are setting up testing sites so that users can bring their drugs in and have them tested for toxic adulterants.[24] Otherwise, users are on their own.

Workers at drug testing sites begin by telling people about the risks of taking drugs. Then they test the drugs in order to determine what they are, how potent they are, and what other substances are present. Alerts can be sent out if dangerous drugs are found. In Bogota, Colombia, a testing site on the location of a huge music party — the only such testing site in the world — was set up to ensure, as far as possible, the safety of the partiers. These types of life-saving services are only necessary because the drug is illegal and thus unregulated. They are not being considered in Canada.

Other negative health outcomes can be attributed to the criminalization of cocaine. For users who inject, the concerns are the same as for heroin users — dirty needles spread diseases and cause death. Needle exchanges save lives, but people are nervous about having such programs in their neighbourhoods, and in Canada the government is reluctant to approve them. Many would be surprised to learn that an icon of conservatism, Margaret Thatcher — ever conscious of the economic bottom line — agreed to the establishment of needle exchange programs in Britain. They ultimately saved the treasury countless dollars as the United Kingdom achieved one of the lowest rates of HIV for injection drug users in Europe.[25]

Crack users face a similar dilemma. While there are crack smokers who can afford to buy small glass or Pyrex stems to use as pipes, others are making pipes from bottles, cans, or hollow car antennas, and many share.[26] Again, the risk is high of contracting communicable diseases like Hepatitis C, Hepatitis B, HIV, and even possibly tuberculosis.[27]

The Vancouver health authority wants to pursue a harm-reduction approach to cocaine users while enabling health-care and social workers to interact with otherwise hard-to-reach drug addicts (as they do with heroin addicts at InSite). Thus, a pilot project was launched in 2011 to distribute clean, unused crack pipes to drug users as a way of preventing the spread of disease through shared pipes. As Dr. Patricia Daly, medical health officer for Vancouver Coastal Health, says, "We use this as an engagement strategy like we do with our other harm-reduction initiatives. If you can deliver them [harm-reduction programs] in a way where you can get people into other services, that's very beneficial." The B.C. Centre for Excellence in HIV/AIDS reports that crack use in Vancouver has declined since officials began giving out free pipes and mouthpieces.

Crack pipe vending machines are the latest innovation in Vancouver aimed at reducing harms due to sharing pipes with users who have sores and lesions on their mouths.[28] Two such machines run by Portland Hotel Society (the non-profit organization that runs InSite) sell Pyrex 200 pipes for an affordable twenty-five cents each. Since existing programs limit users to one pipe per day, this allows them to purchase more if necessary.

These vending machines had been quietly operating for about eight months before they came to the attention of the public and the Conservative government was required to respond. Public safety minister Steven Blaney expressed his disapproval of the program, saying that his government is committed to reducing drug use rather than handing out drug paraphernalia to users. Ironically, the vending machines probably do reduce drug use, since they provide a point of access for users to seek help in treatment centres and detoxification programs.

Dr. Evan Wood and Dr. Julio Montaner of Vancouver — both experts in HIV/AIDS — emphasize that it is the War on Drugs, with its criminalization approach, that is causing much of the ill health associated with drug use. "You can't end AIDS unless you end the War on Drugs. It's dead simple."[29] They assert that the War on Drugs will never succeed in eradicating drug use; thus, we need to adopt means and measures for reducing risky drug use as far as possible, while educating the public as to its dangers. This means rethinking our whole approach to drug use. It particularly means replacing drug warriors with health and social professionals who will work to alleviate the conditions leading to drug use and to reduce the risk of harm to drug users.

Doctors Wood and Montaner launched an advertising campaign in 2012 that was endorsed by the 2010 Vienna Declaration, by former presidents of Brazil and Colombia, and by British billionaire Richard Branson (who is a founding member of the Global Commission on Drug Policy).[30] They called on world leaders to stop the spread of AIDS by ending the War on Drugs, which they say facilitates the spread of the HIV virus. The war forces addicts into hiding where health officials are unable to protect them from the dangers of intravenous drug use. And when addicts are sentenced to prison time, the disease is easily spread in the close living quarters, where needles are shared and conditions are unhygienic.

Cocaine users are prosecuted as criminals, but the law is not blind as to the type of user who comes to court. Users of white powder cocaine are less likely to be prosecuted than those who use crack, since consumption is largely by middle and upper-class people who can afford to buy powder, and who are not normally targeted by police.[31] On the other hand, users of cocaine paste and crack (the cheaper versions of cocaine) do end up in criminal court. The WHO report on cocaine says that this is mainly because such users are already poor and marginalized, living a precarious lifestyle. Civil rights lawyer Michelle Alexander, Dr. Carl Hart, and others have produced data to show that African-Americans are targeted disproportionately.

The discrimination by class represented by the 100:1 ratio of sentences between powder and crack users in the United States has already been mentioned. After the reduction of this ratio to 18:1, which was made retroactive, about 7,300 federal prisoners were released early. This occasioned a half-billion-dollar savings to federal corrections, and the recidivism rate for these prisoners was not appreciably different from other released prisoners.

Dr. Hart points out that it is particularly easy to continue vilifying drugs that are associated with a despised group — opium with the Chinese early in the twentieth century, marijuana and crack with poor, urban African-Americans, methamphetamine with gays and poor white rural people. The perpetuation of the War on Drugs thus relies upon the same prejudices that spawned it in the first place.

THERAPEUTIC USES

Coca leaf is reputed to have a number of therapeutic uses, including treating toothache, ulcers, rheumatism, asthma, indigestion, gastritis, constipation, motion sickness, laryngitis, cluster headaches, and even malaria.[32] It is also essential for dealing with altitude sickness. Users of coca leaf experience no negative effects of the drug.

The European Coalition for Just and Effective Drug Policies (ENCOD) reports that:[33]

> Use of coca leaves is reported to have antibacterial and parasital [sic] effects in the treatment of stomach pains, infections and diarrhea, it reduces fever, has anesthetic effects during childbirth, in case of head- tooth- and muscle aches, as well as irritations to skin and eye [and] … regulatory effect on blood circulation, heartbeat, lung diseases such as asthma, altitude sickness and emboly [sic], a stimulating effect in case of impotence and other forms of fatigue, and a calming and analgesic effect in case of central nervous [system] disorders.

The refined version of the drug, cocaine, also has recognized therapeutic uses. According to the World Health Organization, it has positive effects as an analgesic (especially for toothache).[34] It can alleviate menstrual pain. It helps workers remain alert and require less sleep. The WHO also reported that some people say cocaine has "an extremely positive influence on social interaction." Canada's contribution to the WHO study said that recreational users of cocaine reported positive results, among them more energy and creativity.

The American Academy of Otolaryngology — head and neck surgery — "considers cocaine to be a valuable anesthetic and vasoconstricting agent when used as part of the treatment of a patient by a physician. No other single drug combines the anesthetic and vasoconstricting properties of cocaine."[35] Thus, the drug is a popular anaesthetic in operations of the ear, nose, and throat, and it is used to alleviate the pain — both physical and mental — of terminal diseases. "Although cocaine has a high public profile as a drug of addictive potential, this drug has also had a long and distinguished history as a medicine and local anesthetic."[36]

Cocaine is used by health care professionals to "temporarily numb the lining of the mouth, nose and throat (mucous membranes) before certain medical procedures (e.g., biopsy, stitches, wound cleaning). It is an anesthetic that works quickly to numb the area about one to two minutes after application. Cocaine also causes blood vessels to narrow, an effect that can decrease bleeding and swelling from the procedure. Cocaine is also very useful for the treatment of dermal lacerations in children."[37]

Thus, cocaine has a number of therapeutic uses, as well as a number of advantages on the social front. People who use it cite a pleasant sense of euphoria and stimulation. They take it to improve their confidence, and some believe it leads to better sexual relations. The WHO says that most of the negative consequences of cocaine use are experienced by heavy users, if at all. It also says that many of the negative conditions cited are exacerbated by cocaine use, not caused by it.

Chapter Five

Marijuana: Sparking the Debate

DIRECT HEALTH EFFECTS

Marijuana is the third most commonly used drug in the world after alcohol and tobacco.[1] It is the illegal drug with which Canadians are most familiar, and we have one of the highest consumption rates in the world.[2] About three million Canadians per year use marijuana, including 17 percent of all citizens between the ages of fifteen and sixty-four.

Cannabis sativa (marijuana, hash, and hash oil) can be smoked, eaten in baked goods, or made into tea.[3] It can produce feelings of relaxation and drowsiness, or nervousness and paranoia. It makes the user hungry. Senses are heightened. Short-term memory can be impaired and users are often giddy. Long term use may make a user inattentive and dull — "burned out." There is no risk of death from overdose with marijuana,[4] but psychological addiction is possible.[5]

There are many claims made both for and against the effects marijuana produces. For example, the discussion around schizophrenia is fraught with contradictions and disagreement. Some experts say marijuana does not cause schizophrenia, some say it may exacerbate an existing condition, and others say it actually helps alleviate the symptoms of schizophrenia.

A recent study published in *Neuropsychopharmacology* suggests that a genetic susceptibility to schizophrenia might be exacerbated by marijuana use early in life.[6] Children may have a greater risk of permanent cognitive deficits (like the ability to plan or control impulses) if they use marijuana before age sixteen, and one source says they will also have a significantly higher incidence of schizophrenia. Meanwhile, scientists recently published a report in *The Lancet* saying that "evidence is consistent with the view that cannabis increases risk of psychotic outcomes,"[7] while others have concluded that "cannabidiol [a derivative of cannabis] enhances anandamide[8] signaling and alleviates psychotic symptoms of schizophrenia."[9] In other words, the authors of the *Lancet* study think marijuana may be a potential new treatment for schizophrenia.

More generally, and perhaps more significantly, many experts point out that the issue of causality has not been established. In other words, it is just as likely that people suffering from schizophrenia are self-medicating with marijuana as it is that marijuana is causing psychosis.[10] Dr. Lester Grinspoon, senior psychiatrist and associate professor at the Harvard Medical School, is skeptical that marijuana can be said to cause schizophrenia. As he says, there has not been even a "blip" in the incidence of schizophrenia in the United States over past decades, although millions of people have taken up marijuana smoking since the 1960s.

Dr. David Nutt agrees, pointing out that marijuana use has increased twenty-fold over the past forty years, but the incidence of schizophrenia seems to be dropping.[11] He says scientists have not found any link between marijuana use and schizophrenia, and worries that doctors and parents are effectively blaming patients for their medical condition, implying that they have brought it on themselves by their drug use.

Negative health effects can result from the act of inhaling marijuana smoke (for example, chronic bronchitis), but most users smoke far fewer marijuana cigarettes than tobacco users smoke regular cigarettes, so the risk is minimal. Also, long-term exposure is critical to the development of lung cancer from smoking, but those who smoke marijuana tend to stop using the drug in their thirties.[12] A 2006 UCLA study concluded that not even heavy marijuana use can cause lung cancer. The lead author of the study confessed that the findings were not at all what researchers expected, and that they had found "no association at all [between smoking marijuana and lung cancer] and even some protective effect."[13]

Findings that went somewhat further were reported to the annual meeting of the American Association of Cancer Research in April 2013.[14] Dr. Li Rita Zhang of UCLA found "no significant association between cannabis smoking and lung cancer." There was no increased risk of lung cancer among marijuana users as compared to non-users, and there was no increased risk among heavy users compared to casual users.

The British Lung Foundation (BLF, a charitable organization), however, insists that the risk of developing lung cancer is twenty times higher for those who smoke marijuana cigarettes than for those who smoke tobacco.[15] These assertions have been challenged by other experts, notably Kevin Williamson, author of *Drugs and the Party Line* and proponent of legalizing marijuana in the U.K.[16] He challenged the BLF's science, citing an earlier study of 2,200 people published in *Cancer Epidemiological Biomarkers and Prevention* that found "that the association of these cancers with marijuana, even long-term or heavy use, is not strong and may be below practically detectable limits." When asked to identify the science supporting the BLF's claims, the charity's representative refused to do so.

In the category of dubious research is another study that purported to follow forty-nine thousand men who were conscripted into the army in Sweden in 1969–70.[17] More than half of them said in their 1970 interview that they had smoked marijuana at least fifty times up to then. Forty years later (in 2009), these men were found to be more than twice as likely as the others to have contracted lung cancer. But while the researchers controlled for a number of other factors (alcohol use, respiratory disease, and socio-economic status), it turns out that these men were never interviewed again. Thus, there was no way to know how many of them had switched to smoking tobacco after 1970. Also there was no way to know if any of them ever used marijuana again after that time.

This kind of questionable research distorts the debate about marijuana's potential harms. The media, however, tend to report the findings uncritically, thus often misinforming the public. For example, the headline for the article on the latter study was "Heavy Marijuana Smoking May Double Risk of Lung Cancer, Canadian Study Finds." Fortunately, for those who persevered in reading the entire article, the counter-arguments were presented together with the findings of other scientists who conducted more legitimate research and found no significant risk of lung cancer from smoking marijuana.

Leaving the debate about potential respiratory problems aside, even if smoking marijuana were found to be risky, a simple solution is for the drug to be consumed in other ways, such as in baked goods and teas. No adverse effects have been identified with ingesting marijuana in these forms, unless the user over-indulges. In that case, the results can be upsetting, but not dangerous. They include dizziness, sweating, nausea, and so forth, but nothing that is injurious to organs.[18] For many people, smoked marijuana is the only way to obtain relief from various medical symptoms. For these people, any risk from the smoking is worth it, and they would like to have the opportunity to exercise their own judgment in managing their health care.

A recent study out of New Zealand had marijuana advocates and opponents alike buzzing in 2013.[19] This one claimed that smoking marijuana may double the risk for stroke in young adults. The response from the medical community was swift. The American Stroke Association (ASA) said that the study was small and that it failed to control for certain important variables. For example, it is well known that smoking cigarettes doubles the risk of stroke. The study, however, did not control for tobacco use. Not surprisingly, "all but one of the stroke patients who tested positive for cannabis use were smokers." Other variables that were not controlled for were diet, alcohol use, and head injury. The ASA also said that a much larger study reported in the *American Heart Journal* showed no link between marijuana use and heart attacks.

Another study from New Zealand followed a group of children for forty years and concluded that there was a link between teenage marijuana use and lower IQs.[20] This conclusion was also swiftly challenged by other scientists. Norwegian economist Ole Rogeberg said that the research did not rule out other explanations for lower IQs, such as lower socioeconomic status. According to Rogeberg, "we don't know how much of the change in IQ we can explain by differences in education, jail time, occupational status, etc. and whether this affects the estimates in the paper."

The criminalization of marijuana militates against further research being undertaken. In Canada, the Conservative government put a stop to a medical marijuana research program in 2006 when the government first came to power.[21] According to Health Canada, the current government believes clinical research is "best undertaken by the private sector, such as pharmaceutical companies." But obviously no drug company wants to evaluate smoked marijuana because there is so far no money to be made from it. (This may change now that medical marijuana is to be produced by commercial interests in Canada.)

Kevin Sabet is a strong proponent of marijuana prohibition and was President Obama's senior adviser at the Office of National Drug Control Policy until 2011. In the years previous, he also advised Bill Clinton and George W. Bush. In his argument for prohibition, Mr. Sabet refers to the negative health effects of marijuana on children, and says that we should not adopt the treatment of alcohol and tobacco as good models for our approach to marijuana.[22] While he approves of a prohibition model, he deplores the racial discrimination inherent in the enforcement of the laws, and would encourage efforts to reduce the negative effects of prohibition. For example, he does not believe that people should go to jail for using marijuana; nor should they lose their ability to find employment. He believes that the use of non-smokable (edible) marijuana would be an improvement for public health reasons.

Sabet also worries about the fact that today's marijuana is up to six times stronger than what was available in the 1960s. The THC content (the active ingredient that provides the "high") in marijuana has indeed increased over past decades, although by how much is a matter for discussion:[23]

> According to the federal Potency Monitoring Project, the average potency of marijuana has increased very little since the 1980s. The Project reports that in 1985, the average THC content of commercial-grade marijuana was 2.84%, and the average for high-grade sinsemilla in 1985 was 7.17%. In 1995, the potency of commercial-grade marijuana averaged 3.73%, while the potency of sinsemilla in 1995 averaged 7.51%. In 2001, commercial-grade marijuana averaged 4.72% THC, and the potency of sinsemilla in 2001 averaged 9.03%.

Canada's Senate Special Committee on Illegal Drugs concluded that the higher potency of the drug did not negatively affect the health of users anyway, since "THC ... does not cause physiological damage to organs or tissues."[24] In addition, marijuana smokers adjust for the increased potency by smoking less of the drug. The Senate committee stated that most users of marijuana are not at risk for their physical health, but that potential effects on cognitive and psychosocial functions suggest use by people under the age of sixteen is risky. Other recent studies have raised concerns about the safety of marijuana for young people, but (leaving aside some of the more alarmist submissions by the United States government and others)[25] it is generally accepted that marijuana is one of the least harmful of illegal substances.

The United Kingdom House of Lords Select Committee on Science and Technology has reported that "Tetrahydrocannabinol [THC] is a very safe drug. Laboratory animals (rats, mice, dogs, monkeys) can tolerate doses of up to 1,000 mg/kg (milligrams per kilogram). This would be equivalent to a 70 kg person swallowing 70 grams of the drug — about 5,000 times more than is required to produce a high."[26] The United States Drug Enforcement Administration (DEA)'s administrative law judge, Francis Young, says users cannot die from using marijuana:[27]

> In strict medical terms marijuana is far safer than many foods we commonly consume. For example, eating 10 raw potatoes can result in a toxic response. By comparison, it is physically impossible to eat enough marijuana to induce death. Marijuana in its natural form is one of the safest therapeutically active substances known to man. By any measure of rational analysis marijuana can be safely used within the supervised routine of medical care.

NEGATIVE EFFECTS OF CRIMINALIZATION

As is the case for heroin and cocaine, significant risks to users are caused by the criminalization of marijuana. A major difference is that, with marijuana, there are not the additional risks associated with injecting. Otherwise, like the other drugs, marijuana may be adulterated with unknown and dangerous products. Pesticides and herbicides may be involved in the cultivation process, subsequently contaminating the marijuana — paraquat (a common herbicide) is one example. Tobacco may also be added to marijuana to bulk it up for smoking.

Medical health officers in British Columbia, together with physicians, researchers, and consultants, say that while they do not assert that marijuana is "safe," "policy as it stands puts the public at even greater risk."[28] By this they mean that lives are destroyed by the intrusion of the justice system into what most people regard to be a relatively harmless pastime. The three million Canadians who admit to using marijuana are stigmatized as criminals. Criminal records result in an inability to secure employment or travel freely. Incarceration costs a staggering amount of money and produces no deterrent or other advantage. Organized crime continues to control the trade, with all of the attendant violence and corruption.

Crackdowns on drug use in Canada over the past few years have meant that between 1990 and 2009, arrests for marijuana increased by 70 percent. In 2012, for example, 109,000 drug-related incidents were reported by police.[29] Two-thirds of these were related to marijuana charges. The policing and court costs are immense. Meanwhile, marijuana use continues to rise.

THERAPEUTIC USES

Access to medical marijuana was first made available in Canada in 2001. Until recently, a licence to possess medical marijuana had to be granted by Health Canada and the drug was supplied by a government agency. This system was found to be unsatisfactory by patients and the government alike. A new regime was to be instituted, but raised concerns from doctors and patients.[30]

The new medical marijuana regime will offload the responsibility for licensing patients from the government to medical doctors. The Canadian Medical Association (CMA) has objected to its doctors being put in this position. Many of them are reluctant to prescribe a drug that has not undergone the usual clinical trials and testing. They want some assurances as to its safety and some guidance as to dosage.

Doctors say they do not want to be the gatekeepers. They don't know enough about the drug. It is a plant material that is so far unapproved. Some doctors have in the past encouraged patients to try marijuana, but when patients then show positive results and come back asking for their doctor's signature on an application for medical marijuana, "that's when the mood changes," remarks one such patient. "That's when they say, 'Get out. I'm not risking my practice over you.'"[31]

Doctors representing the CMA and the Federation of Medical Regulatory Authorities of Canada (FMRAC) have urged the federal government to "rescind the new marijuana regulation and replace it with a robust regulatory framework that treats marijuana as other drugs in Canada are treated."[32] They argue that marijuana is a complex substance and that much remains unknown about it, including what risks might exist for younger users, and that the health benefits need to be proven in rigorous, controlled scientific studies before doctors should be asked to prescribe it.

The CMA actually claims that there is "no clinical evidence" to back up the usefulness of marijuana as a medicine. But the prestigious Mayo Clinic says there is class-A scientific evidence — including randomized clinical trials — suggesting that it is effective for chronic pain and some of the symptoms of multiple sclerosis.[33] Based upon this type of evidence, there are doctors who are preparing to set up clinics in Canada that will help people obtain marijuana, even under the new, stricter regime. They are moving cautiously, though, ever cognizant of the legal implications of what they are hoping to do.

There are many other problems with the new medical marijuana regime. For example, patients will no longer have the right to grow their own supply of marijuana or to appoint designated growers. Users will now have to get their supply from licensed commercial growers instead, thus eliminating their ability to tailor plant strains to fit their particular ailments. Pharmacists will be removed from the loop, so patients will have to rely upon couriers or the mail to receive their medical marijuana.

The price of the marijuana is expected to rise to the point where many patients will not be able to afford it. For example, one user with arthritis and knee and hip replacements currently grows her own marijuana for five cents per gram. Her husband, who suffers from MS, uses about thirty grams per day. Health Canada estimates that the price in 2014 under the new regime will be $7.60 per gram, meaning her husband alone will have to pay well over two hundred dollars per day for his medication. People like this will have no alternative but to continue growing their own, risking prosecution and prison time.

The new rules allow only for "dried" marijuana, thus removing the option for foods, tinctures, oils, and other non-smokable versions.[34] Hashish is not allowed. As one expert says, raw, smokable buds are not good for everyone.[35] But patients will have to smoke their marijuana. Finally, there is no allowance for a dispensary model where patients can obtain their marijuana and also be provided with information about how best to use it. It is not yet clear what the full impact of these new rules will be if and when the government succeeds in convincing the courts that they are constitutional.

An additional complication arises from the fact that it is taking so long for the government to approve licences for the commercial growers. As of March 21, 2014, only thirteen companies had been licensed.[36] There was a backlog of four hundred applications.

One of the first marijuana providers to be up and running will be Tweed Inc.[37] Its CEO, Chuck Rific, purchased the abandoned chocolate factory in Smiths Falls, Ontario, and is swiftly converting it into a marijuana grow-op. It will employ two hundred staff and produce one hundred million dollars worth of marijuana per year. The five-thousand-square-foot vault will contain up to fifteen million grams of the drug, which will be sold at four to twelve dollars per gram (less than the street value but considerably more than the cost of growing your own). The operation will be under continual video surveillance. Workers will be clad in hairnets, shoe covers, and uniforms. The walls in the grow rooms will be covered in food-grade anti-mould panels. Tweed Inc. is expected to be listed on the Toronto Stock Exchange in short order. This is the new face of industrial marijuana in Canada.

The Canadian Consortium for the Investigation of Cannabinoids (CCIC) is a federally regulated non-profit organization consisting of basic and clinical researchers and health-care professionals that was established to promote evidence-based research and education on the therapeutic applications of endocannabinoid and cannabinoid agents (marijuana compounds).[38] The CCIC has taken on the task of educating and supporting doctors around the use of marijuana. The consortium regrets the government's decision to give grow licences only to commercial growers. It says it is easier and cheaper for patients to grow their own supply, and that the act of growing their own medicine can be therapeutic for patients in itself because it gives them a sense of control and ownership of their health and treatments. As to the government's suggestion that clinical research would be better undertaken by the private sector, Dr. Mark Ware of the CCIC says there is no incentive for pharmaceutical companies to pursue such research, because there's no money in it for them.

The CCIC lists the marijuana compounds that are legally available in Canada. Nabilone is an antiemetic. Dronabinol is used to treat AIDS-related anorexia associated with weight loss. Cannabidiol is used for treatment of spasticity (an uncomfortable and disabling condition in which the muscles become tight and difficult to control) and neuropathic pain in multiple sclerosis (MS) sufferers, and for treatment of pain in advanced cancer patients for whom opioids do not work. And herbal cannabis is controlled by the government's medical marijuana program for treatment of various conditions.

Looking at just one of these, we can see the wide variety of uses for marijuana compounds. The CCIC says that cannabidiol is a system modulator used in ten European countries to relieve cancer pain. The substance also recently became available in Mexico. A clinical trial is underway to investigate the usefulness of this substance for patients who find opioids inadequate to treat their cancer pain. Cannabidiol is also available as an oromuscular spray for the relief of MS spasticity, and there are new trials underway to evaluate it as a treatment for other MS symptoms related to gait, fatigue, and depression.

And then there is the case of Kaitlyn Pogson. As an example of how the prohibition of marijuana can have devastating effects on sufferers, this case stands as an indictment of current Canadian government policy.[39] Kaitlyn (currently only a year old) has Dravet syndrome, a rare form of epilepsy. It resists traditional medicine and gets worse over time. Kaitlyn was unable to eat because of the medications she was taking (morphine and three other drugs that are not normally given to children) and was being fed through a feeding tube. Some of her hundreds of seizures lasted four to five hours. The child was waiting to get a special strain of marijuana from Colorado, but despite a petition from the desperate parents, the Canadian government would not allow its importation.

Kaitlyn's parents solved their problem by moving to Colorado, where they are now able to buy this extract of cannibidiol mixed with olive oil. Kaitlyn's three hundred seizures per week are now reduced to one or often zero per week, according to her father.[40] She is more alert, and her appetite has returned now that she is no longer taking the other medications.

Another little girl in Colorado, Charlotte Figi, had suffered from the same syndrome. Her seizures were reduced by 99 percent with the help of a small dose of this marijuana taken three times per day. The response was instant. At age six, Charlotte now has two to three seizures per month, mostly in her sleep. Her doctor, who admits that Charlotte was a "guinea pig," says her response to the drug was "a remarkable and heretofore unprecedented change."[41] Charlotte's remarkable recovery has meant that desperate parents from all over the world are bombarding her doctor with emails, while up to sixty families per month — like the Pogsons — are moving to Colorado.

The marijuana strain that works for Dravet syndrome is high in cannabidiol (CBD, at 17 percent) but low in THC — the ingredient that makes you high (0.5 percent). Even if Kaitlyn had had a Canadian medical marijuana licence, the approved marijuana has too little CBD and too much THC. Also, Health Canada would have required that Kaitlyn smoke her marijuana. Recall that Kaitlyn is a baby. In addition, a more accurate dose can be administered by using the oil.

Arthur Schafer, a noted Canadian bioethicist, has serious concerns about prescribing marijuana for medical conditions because there have been no clinical trials, and the long-term effects upon children could be negative.[42] Nonetheless, he is crystal clear about cases like Kaitlyn's. He says it seems absurd and inhumane that the family had to move to Colorado, and asserts that the cannibidiol should be made available here — an easy matter for the Canadian government, since we have rules permitting special access. Kaitlyn's brain was being damaged and her life was threatened. Where patients have nothing to lose, we should go ahead and make the substance available.

Interestingly, medical practitioners have known about the use of cannabis tincture to relieve seizures for centuries.[43] One of the first mentions is in 1464 A.D. and the first formally recorded use was in 1839 in Britain. It appears that a few decades of prohibition have sufficed to obliterate all knowledge of this therapeutic use of marijuana.

Kaitlyn's situation represents the kind of real-life consequence that results from criminalizing marijuana. If we are to have a serious conversation about illegal drugs, we need first to suspend whatever moral stance we are accustomed to adopting, recognize the outcomes of criminalization, and then look hard at the evidence.

In the United Kingdom, cannabidiol is being used by some for relief of the symptoms of Huntington's disease. It has been found to improve some neuropsychiatric symptoms. It also improves intestinal microcirculation and reduces inflammation in acute experimental pancreatitis. Cannabidiol has also been found to alleviate the psychotic symptoms of schizophrenia, and studies are underway to assess its usefulness for the treatment of epilepsy.

Dr. Lester Grinspoon and Dr. James Bakalar, authors of *Marihuana: The Forbidden Medicine*, report some success in using marijuana to treat spasticity.[44] They also claim that the drug can be effective in combating glaucoma by causing "a dose-related, clinically significant drop in intraocular pressure that lasts several hours." Marijuana can "retard the progressive loss of sight when conventional medication fails and surgery is too dangerous." They also cite it as an appetite stimulant and a good antiemetic, and say it may slow weight loss in cancer patients, preventing the nausea and vomiting associated with chemotherapy.

Patients who use medical marijuana swear that it is the only thing that provides relief from a wide variety of ailments. Some find it relieves chronic pain and other symptoms of scoliosis, fibromyalgia (FM), and epilepsy.[45] Arthritis Care and Research reported that 10 percent of FM patients use marijuana for relief from widespread pain, fatigue, and insomnia caused by this chronic illness.[46]

Dr. Carolyn Bennett, a Canadian medical doctor and Member of Parliament, says marijuana provides comfort, restores appetite, and provides relief from pain and nausea for patients who are suffering from the symptoms of chemotherapy.[47] Painkillers often cause nausea and constipation, so marijuana is the better option. She says that marijuana has positively changed the lives of some of her patients.

American Justice Gustin L. Reichbach tells his own story.[48] Suffering from pancreatic cancer, and given only four to six months to live, he underwent rigorous chemotherapy that kept the disease at bay. However, the symptoms of nausea, lack of appetite, and insomnia resulting from the chemotherapy were extremely debilitating. He discovered that inhaled marijuana was the only medicine that gave him relief — an irony, considering that for twenty years or so he was required to imprison those who smoked marijuana.

Other countries are finding novel ways to use marijuana as therapy. For example, there is a new cocaine-derived drug called bazuco in Colombia.[49] It is a cheap cocaine alternative that is said to be as addictive as heroin. It is made from the residue after processing cocaine, and is often mixed with kerosene and sulfuric acid. The high is powerful and brief, and reportedly the drug is very hard to kick. The Colombian authorities have adopted an interesting approach to this new threat. In a reversal of the "gateway" theory, marijuana is being given to bazuco addicts as an effort to move them away from rather than toward the hard drug. Marijuana is used because it provides relief from the anxiety associated with withdrawal from bazuco.

The bazuco program is about mitigating harms, not about abstinence. It is meant to help people make the transition to a less dangerous drug so they can function in society. The treatment regime also includes counselling, job training, the provision of emergency shelters, and so on. As the proponents say, "For us, there's nothing more ethical than offering ... a solution [to someone] who has never been able to find one before."

Aside from this kind of exotic use for marijuana, though, there are many other uses that will be more familiar to readers. Sufferers from multiple sclerosis (MS) say that muscle tightness and pain are reduced by using the drug.[50] Spasticity can be controlled with other medications, but these also carry adverse effects such as drowsiness and muscle weakness. A new study from the Department of Neuroscience at University of California, San Diego, tested smoked marijuana and concluded that "using an objective measure, we saw a beneficial effect of inhaled cannabis on spasticity among patients receiving insufficient relief from traditional treatment." Those patients who smoked marijuana "experienced an almost one-third decrease on a scale of spasticity of 2.74 points from a baseline score of 9.3 compared with those smoking a placebo." This study was reported in the *Canadian Medical Association Journal*.

New research suggests that marijuana may also have a therapeutic application with respect to diabetes risk.[51] Respondents to a questionnaire (4,657 people) who said they used marijuana regularly were found to have fewer risk factors for diabetes, and better blood-sugar control. Those who had used marijuana in the past month had lower fasting insulin levels than those who had never used. They had better readings with regard to blood-glucose control, and used insulin more efficiently. They also had smaller waist circumferences and higher levels of good cholesterol (the opposite of which indicates a risk for type 2 diabetes), and their bodies were leaner even though they had higher caloric intake.

The researchers said there was also a "transient spike" in risk for heart attack immediately after smoking marijuana. That is, marijuana use caused the heart rate to rise, at least briefly. It was not clear whether this was due to the THC itself or to the act of smoking. The authors recommended more research, especially since a higher number of marijuana users today are older and some may have heart conditions. Researchers noted that "over time the age distribution of users has changed. In the past [marijuana] was used mostly by young people who had very low risks of cardiovascular problems and other chronic diseases. That has shifted and we have a large population of [older] individuals who continue to use marijuana." Another study agreed that marijuana smoking poses no problem for healthy users, but may pose problems for people with existing cardiovascular disease because the drug causes the heart to work harder.[52]

Some older Canadians are taking marijuana to alleviate insomnia.[53] Others use it for attention deficit disorder, arthritis pain, dementia, nausea related to chemotherapy, nerve pain, stimulating appetite, and for stomach problems. One new study suggests that marijuana may actually stop the spread of HIV.[54]

Sellers of medical marijuana are knowledgeable and try to find the right variety of marijuana for various symptoms: *Cannabis indica* for pain and insomnia; *Cannabis sativa* for energy and appetite. They teach their customers how to use it properly and consume it in the right way. Under the new Canadian regime, it is not clear that there will be sellers who are knowledgeable enough to provide such a service.

In the United States, to date, some twenty-one American states allow medical marijuana (and fourteen more are considering this option),[55] and two voted in November 2012 to legalize marijuana outright. Significantly, in 2009, the American Medical Association reversed its long-held position that marijuana should be treated as a substance with no medical value and instead recognized its value as therapy. However, the U.S. federal government has been unrelenting in its prosecution of medical marijuana dispensaries. One business owner was raided after having sought advice about the legality of his proposed enterprise from accountants and lawyers.[56] He opened his medical marijuana outlet and was prosecuted anyway. He pleaded guilty to ten charges of cultivation and distribution for a minimum five year sentence.

Raids on American medical marijuana dispensaries have been common. For example, on July 25, 2013, a number of such raids were conducted in Washington State.[57] In the past four years, the DEA has conducted 270 SWAT-style raids on medical marijuana providers in the United States, at a cost of eight million dollars.

Canadians can probably expect a similar level of enforcement when medical marijuana users discover that the new regime makes it impossible for them to obtain their medicine. The marijuana may be too expensive or not suitable for particular symptoms. Or patients may not be able to gain access to a legal outlet. Or their doctor may be afraid to prescribe the drug. In all of these cases, patients will be tempted to grow their own, or obtain it from a non-sanctioned source, leaving them vulnerable to arrest and prosecution.

Implicit in these discussions is the question of the cost to the treasury. The financial costs of prosecuting illegal drugs are considerably higher than the costs of adopting a public health strategy, and the positive results from the latter are arguably much greater. All three drugs under consideration here provide therapeutic values that are underutilized. All three may cause harms in and of themselves, but the harms caused by their criminalization appear to be much more severe and far-reaching. Not only individuals, but their families and communities are affected by prohibition and the heavy law enforcement approach and mass incarceration that results. But if the humanitarian arguments are not convincing, then perhaps the economic ones will be. This is the subject of the next chapter.

Chapter Six

The Economics of Illegal Drugs: Our Gift to Organized Crime

PUTTING A PRICE ON THE DRUG TRADE: THE CHALLENGES

Efforts to estimate the value of the black market in illegal drugs are constrained because the business is conducted underground and away from public scrutiny. Those who are best placed to know what the trade is worth — drug lords, gangsters, organized crime bosses — are not talking.

Thus, outlining the economic impact of the illegal drug trade is not as simple as analyzing OECD reports or Statistics Canada figures. Truly reliable data do not exist. At least four areas need to be considered when assessing the economics of this industry and how it affects citizens and taxpayers: the overall value of the illegal market; costs related to health concerns, loss of productivity, and crime; costs of enforcement and interdiction; and the potential value to governments of revenue generation and of savings in law enforcement, should the industry become legalized and regulated. With respect to each of these areas, economists tend to heavily qualify their assessments. They typically underestimate their calculations to compensate for the lack of precise information.

Because there are virtually no rules in the black market, the simplest calculations are fraught with difficulties. The cost of fighting the War on

Drugs varies widely from country to country, city to city, gang to gang, and even street corner to street corner. So does the number of people using the drugs. So does the price of drugs. There is little consistency with respect to the sale price of a given drug, much less its quality or potency from one day to the next. These factors all affect any final calculations about the value of the drug market.

The assumptions that underpin final estimates also differ from one economist to another. For example, when calculating the cost of productivity losses due to drug use, the *United Nations World Drug Report 2012* states that the main costs incurred are because of reduced labour participation and incarceration.[1] The Canadian Centre on Substance Abuse, on the other hand, also includes lost revenues due to illness and premature death.[2]

In addition, there is an entire category of costs which is largely absent from the research. The humanitarian costs — costs to individuals and the community in terms of suffering and loss, due both to the use of drugs and to the fact that they are criminalized — cannot always be quantified. However, costs to the welfare system and employment insurance must be significant, as would be the costs of extortion, violence, and money-laundering associated with cartels and gangs. Often, these costs do not appear in the final calculations presented by researchers. This can seriously skew any final conclusions.

Generally accepted theories of economics do not always apply to the illegal drug market. For example, simple "risk-price" models used by economists do not work for data related to drug offences.[3] According to orthodox models, the risks attached to the drug market (arrest, long incarcerations, violence, extortion) should push prices up, since the "cost" (risk) of doing business has increased. These higher prices should then, according to accepted economic theory, reduce consumption. The reverse should also be true: as prices drop, we should see increased consumption.

However, the data do not support this model. In the United States, the average inflation-adjusted and purity-adjusted prices of heroin, cocaine, and marijuana decreased by 81 percent, 80 percent and 86 percent respectively between 1990 and 2007.[4] But this was at a time when the United States had vastly increased law enforcement in an effort to drive risks and prices up, and consumption down. The authors of this study concluded that the global supply of illegal drugs had likely not been reduced in the past two decades, and that the supply of marijuana and opiates had increased. This prompted them to conclude that, although drug seizures had increased during this time, this was not an effective way to reduce supply.

Looking at cocaine use in the United States, Caulkins and Reuter found that the price of cocaine dropped dramatically in the 1980s, and then another 25 percent between 2000 and 2007, even as enforcement efforts increased. Despite the exceptional drop in price, total consumption did not rise.[5]

Marijuana use rates in the United States rose from 27 percent to 32 percent among grade twelve students between 1990 and 2008, and from 26 percent to 29 percent among nineteen- to twenty-year-olds, even though U.S. enforcement efforts had increased.[6] Canadian statistics show the same results: although between 1990 and 2009 police crackdowns resulted in a 70 percent increase in marijuana arrests, the use of the drug also increased during this period.[7]

Dr. Francisco E. Thoumi has written about the difficulty of making meaningful calculations of the value of the illegal drug market. He is a professor of economics and has written extensively about the drug trade, particularly in Colombia. In a paper cheerfully entitled "The Numbers Game: Let's All Guess the Size of the Illegal Drug Industry!" he sets out the problems encountered by those trying to provide an unbiased economic analysis of the drug market.[8] He has come to believe that the numbers are often exaggerated and unreliable.

Dr. Thoumi's central argument is that the basic data are being manipulated for political reasons. "Morals and ideology tend to play an extremely strong role in these debates. For this reason, illicit drug data can be manipulated for political gain." He says that most users of the data do not have a formal model in which to apply them. "It would be nice," he writes, "to have accurate data on the illegal drug industry, but it would be a lot nicer if the data were used with scientific rigor, with users acknowledging their limitations and avoiding political biases."

Data on drug use may be exaggerated by those — such as law enforcement agencies — whose budgets depend upon maintaining a level of public alarm about illegal drug use. On the other hand, data may be manipulated by those fighting for re-election claiming their government has been succeeding in the War on Drugs. Data relating to drug seizures and arrests may be highlighted to show that the drug trade is growing, or conversely shrinking, depending upon the political needs of the day and of the proponent.

In the United States, a substantial federal anti-drug budget has supported both the retention of prohibition and education directed at sustaining public support for prohibition. In fact, in a shocking revelation, the International Centre for Science in Drug Policy reported that the ONDCP had been found guilty by its own government of disseminating propaganda about marijuana: "The substantial U.S. federal anti-drug budget has allowed for a longstanding public education campaign targeted towards maintaining public support for cannabis prohibition. Of concern, the United States Government Accountability Office has reported that some of the media produced by the Office of National Drug Control Policy violated U.S. domestic propaganda prohibitions for several years."[9]

The U.S. federal government later spent $42.7 million to evaluate its National Youth Anti-Drug Media Campaign. It concluded that the $1.4 billion advertising campaign was ineffective at dissuading youth from experimenting with illegal drugs. It may in fact have encouraged a false perception that drug use among youth is more widespread than it actually is. The most widely used school-based prevention program (Drug Abuse Resistance Education, or DARE) also failed to reduce rates of illegal drug use.

Powerful vested interests have been encouraging an all-out offensive in the War on Drugs. For example, nine former U.S. drug czars (heads of the Drug Enforcement Agency) recently wrote to the current Attorney General, Eric Holder, to ask him to fight on.[10] In the face of state ballots proposing legalized marijuana, they asked Holder to continue to apply federal prohibition laws. Their reputations and legacies were, it seems, at stake. Having fought illegal drugs for decades, these drug warriors were not about to sit back while the war unravelled, potentially exposing their efforts as misdirected and ineffective.

Robert DuPont is a former United States drug chief and the founding director of the National Institute on Drug Abuse (NIDA). He is also a medical doctor who argues that "drugs produce a powerful brain reward."[11] He discourages the use of all drugs, particularly tobacco. He does not advocate the prohibition of alcohol or tobacco, but says, "That's not a reason to make the use of other drugs legal." DuPont denies the clear evidence that the world is moving away from the status quo: "I would be interested in somebody somewhere trying to legalize the drugs and seeing how they do. I just hope that nobody I know lives there when they do that, because I think the consequences would be bad." Little did he know that he would have the opportunity to observe this very thing in both Washington and Colorado within a few short months.

DuPont concludes his article with a ringing endorsement of abstention. "The goal is to have drug-free citizens. Drug-using citizens are an economic drag on society, and drug addiction is modern chemical slavery. Promoting drug-free lifestyles is a matter of emancipation." As with many other proponents of the status quo, DuPont appears not to accept that we can pursue the goal of a drug-free lifestyle at the same time that we act to remove organized crime and violence from the equation and provide treatment to those who have drug use problems while educating others to abstain. These are not mutually exclusive goals.

William J. Bennett is another American with a lifelong investment in continuing the drug war. As director of the ONDCP under President George H.W. Bush, he supervised the unrelenting prosecution of illegal drugs. He continues to defend that position today, misstating the facts about decriminalization regimes in the Netherlands and blaming just about everything except a recent soccer loss to that "experiment." He wrongly states that the Dutch program resulted in "an increase in drug addictions and dependency followed by illegal drug trafficking, human trafficking, and crime." He continues: "After a rapid influx of organized crime, the Netherlands has announced that it will ban foreigners from the country's pot shops starting in 2013." As a matter of fact, this move to ban foreigners had less to do with a sudden arrival of organized crime (which did not transpire, as far as the evidence goes) and more to do with lineups at the border on weekends. And many cities, including Amsterdam, opted to lift the ban and continue the marijuana business as usual.

As an example of the intemperate language often associated with the pro-prohibition stance, Mr. Bennett has opined that beheading drug dealers would be "morally plausible" if "legally difficult."[12] The fervour of his dedication is almost religious: "The simple fact is that drug use is wrong. And the moral argument, in the end, is the most compelling argument."

It might be mentioned that this crusader against illegal drugs has been described as an addict himself — to both tobacco and gambling.[13]

There are many negative effects of prohibition that are not commonly recognized by such drug warriors. The cost of corruption, for example, is a significant factor in looking at the economics of the drug trade. Dr. Thoumi says it is important to determine the ability of the drug trade to "alter social behaviours, increase corruption and crime, and fund insurgent and counterinsurgent guerrillas."[14] His research shows that this alarming influence reaches into governments whether the trade is flourishing or struggling.

Lest we think this type of corruption only happens elsewhere, the Auditor General of Canada recently found that organized crime (with drugs as its primary source of revenue) has intimidated police officers, judges, juries, and correctional officers here at home.[15] The Auditor General regarded this as a direct threat to Canada's commitment to peace, order, and good government. How should we put a price on that?

The corruption of democratic institutions does have an identifiable financial cost, as does widespread intimidation, extortion, and money laundering. This concern was echoed recently by the head of UNODC. Antonio Maria Costa was commenting on the meltdown in world economies in 2008.[16] He said that he had "seen evidence that the proceeds of organized crime were 'the only liquid investment capital' available to some banks on the brink of collapse last year." When lending seized up, inter-bank loans were funded by money from the drug trade, and some banks were rescued that way. Costa said that "a majority of the $352 [billion] ... of drugs profits was absorbed into the economic system as a result," and that this would "raise questions about crime's influence on the economic system at times of crisis." He added, "It is understood that evidence that drug money has flowed into banks came from officials in Britain, Switzerland, Italy, and the United States." The money has now been thoroughly laundered.

Dr. David Nutt says that the 2008 financial crisis grew to enormous proportions largely because "the people in charge of the banks had no idea where their money was coming from or where it was being invested."[17] He says that in 2010, a single bank, Wachovia, paid $160 million to settle a federal investigation into laundering illegal drug money through Mexican currency exchanges. Wachovia was unable to track about four hundred billion dollars to determine whether it was being laundered. The bank was fined forty million dollars for failing to monitor money used to ship twenty-two tons of cocaine. As Nutt points out, this kind of behaviour "undermines governments and is dangerous for the financial system as a whole."

These are alarming allegations, provoking concerns about money flowing to drug cartels and then possibly to what are considered legitimate institutions. Mexican journalist Anabel Hernández in her new book provides evidence of the corruption that drives the illegal marijuana industry in her country.[18] She says that the rules of drug trafficking are the rules of capitalism. "I met these people, the narcos. They have no scruples, they're cruel — but in the end, they're just businessman; all they can see is money." She says the HSBC took Chapo Guzmán's money (he was the notorious leader of the Sinaloa drug cartel) to "look after it." The bank claimed not to know where the money came from. Hernández says of the bank's protestations of innocence, "I have studied the laundering networks in depth, and I cannot believe them."[19] At the risk of her life, Hernández draws links between the powerful Sinaloa drug cartel and the Mexican government, and says the government is lying about its role in the drug trade.

Even the most conservative estimates of the value of the illegal drug market are staggering. Huge amounts of money are involved in the trade itself, both in costs to enforce the law and in paying for harms to society, no matter which set of numbers we accept. As taxpayers, we all have an intimate interest in this discussion.

How exactly are our tax dollars being spent in the War on Drugs? A young RCMP officer recently told me that, every now and then, his office would get word from "higher up" that the force had "not been in the news lately." This was his detachment's cue to go out and round up the usual drug suspects — not a difficult task, since everybody in the community knows who they are. It is like shooting fish in a barrel.

But the "sting" always makes the front page and garners good public relations for the police. Thus, despite the futility and expense of running the same gormless dealers through the court system over and over, sting operations are conducted repeatedly and predictably.

But, you say, is it not important to arrest people who are dealing in illegal drugs? Maybe not, if it means we are getting no returns or negative returns on our very significant investment. Evidence shows that it is rare for law enforcement to capture the high-end kingpins of the trade. On the contrary, the Global Commission on Drug Policy says that "the majority of people arrested for small-scale drug selling are not gangsters or organized criminals. They are young people who are exploited to do the risky work of street selling, dependent drug users trying to raise money for their own supply, or couriers coerced or intimidated into taking drugs across borders."[20] These "small fish" are easily replaced without disrupting the drug supply. Neither increased amounts of drugs seized nor higher numbers of drug arrests does anything to reduce the trade in illegal drugs.

VALUE OF ILLEGAL DRUG TRADE[21]

Global consumption of drugs has risen appreciably since the United Nations held its 1998 forum optimistically called *A Drug-Free World: We Can Do It.*[22] Despite the U.N.'s considerable efforts, consumption of marijuana and cocaine since then has risen by about 50 percent. Opiate use has more than trebled.[23] Additionally, there are new synthetic drugs coming on line at the rate of one per week.[24]

Calculating the value of this industry, as we have noted, is not a simple task. To illustrate the wide divergence among estimates of the global value of the drug trade, take as an example the U.N.'s figures. In 2001, it said that annual global sales of illicit drugs were between $450 billion and $750 billion.[25] Later in 2003, however, it said the number was much lower at $320 billion.[26] The U.N. does not explain why this figure dropped by more than half in two years. And in 2013, the number increased again when UNODC said that gangs were making about $580 billion from illegal drugs.[27]

A report for the United States Congress in 2008 estimated the value of the global illegal drug market in extremely broad terms — between one hundred billion and one trillion dollars per year.[28] The RAND Corporation calculated it at a good deal less the following year — $51 billion to $153 billion.[29] This huge range in estimates engenders despair in anyone trying to come to grips with evaluating the trade.

A serious attempt at calculating the value of the global market has been made by Peter Reuter using statistics supplied by the United Nations Drug Control Programme (UNDCP).[30] Reuter estimated the global market in the low range — between $45 billion and $280 billion.[31] It is alleged that Reuter's conclusions were never published because some of the nations at the U.N. needed the numbers to be higher. One assumes a political motive — that some nations required high numbers to justify their hard line and huge expenditures on the War on Drugs.

More recently, Reuter repeated that the actual size of the drug market is about half of that claimed by the UNODC.[32] Yet his numbers seem very conservative compared to estimates individual countries have been producing about the value of their national markets. Does this mean that nations are inflating the data for their own political purposes?

Estimates of the value of the U.S. drug trade also vary widely. Government estimates are consistently high when compared with independent assessments. For example, a 2006 ONDCP (U.S. government) report calculates the illegal drug market (heroin, cocaine, marijuana, and methamphetamine) in the United States at $101 billion.[33] Peter Reuter, however, emerges again as a skeptic of the official numbers, and put the United States' illegal drug market at half that — fifty billion dollars.[34]

Some U.S. states are calculating the value of the drug trade in their own jurisdictions, particularly the value of the marijuana industry. For example, the illegal market for marijuana in California is said to be worth fourteen billion dollars per year.[35] This dwarfs the value of the second largest agricultural commodity in California — milk and cream — which comes in at $7.3 billion.[36] And it makes the value of the revered grape industry — at a mere two billion — pale by comparison.[37] Washington State, meanwhile, expects that a fully functioning marijuana market in its new legal regime will generate over $1.9 billion over five years, based on 360,000 annual consumers.[38]

Attempts have been made to estimate Canada's drug trade in the last decade or so as well. The *Auditor General's Report* for 2001 calculated the sales of all illegal drugs at between seven and eighteen billion dollars.[39] With respect to marijuana sales alone, RAND Corporation's 2009 report (prepared for the European Union) estimated Canada's annual retail market at three billion to four billion dollars, based on a market of three million annual consumers.[40] Other Canadian agencies at about the same time, though, valued marijuana sales in Canada at nineteen to twenty-one billion dollars.[41] This is a huge discrepancy and is not easily explained.

The Canadian estimate appears to be closer to the mark if we accept estimates of marijuana sales in just one province — British Columbia. The province is recognized as a major grower of marijuana, so the value of this market has been studied more than most. In 2001, marijuana was B.C.'s largest commodity — not cash crop, but commodity — estimated at six billion dollars per year.[42] This makes the Auditor General's estimate look extremely conservative at seven to eighteen billion dollars for all illegal drugs for all of Canada for the same year.

In 2004, the Fraser Institute (a conservative Calgary think tank) released a research paper on marijuana growth in British Columbia.[43] Its author, Stephen T. Easton, calculated the value of the B.C. marijuana harvest, measured at "per cigarette" values. He arrived at a figure of $7.156 billion. These figures would have to be adjusted today, since the legalization of marijuana in Washington State has resulted in a precipitous price drop.[44] Dana Larsen, who operates a dispensary for medical marijuana in Vancouver, said in November 2013 that prices had already decreased by 20 percent (from ten dollars per gram to seven dollars) in anticipation of the new legal regime across the border. Demand was also down, and B.C. bud that used to sell for two thousand dollars per pound was now selling for half that.

The value of Canada's export market in drugs is significant, and is of great interest to the United States Drug Intelligence Centre (USDIC). The USDIC says that Canadian gangs make fifty-six billion dollars annually in overall drug sales to the United States.[45]

Again, this appears high compared to Canadian estimates. With respect to B.C.'s export market in marijuana, Stephen Easton said it was worth about two billion dollars a year in 2001.[46] Seven years later, in 2008, criminologist Darryl Plecas claimed that 80 percent of the marijuana produced in B.C. was exported, and that it was worth about seven billion dollars to the B.C. economy.[47] This significant increase may be accounted for by the fact that "B.C. bud" had become recognized as a premium product around the world. In Hanoi, Vietnam, for example, young people can be seen lighting up Canadian marijuana at a cost of forty-five dollars per gram (the average weekly wage).[48]

Whatever way we choose to estimate the value of the illegal drug market, it is clear that an impressive amount of money is involved. Proponents and opponents of the War on Drugs all agree that illegal drugs are a very lucrative business. The question arises — should such an industry be controlled by organized crime, with the profits going to cartels and gangs, or can we envisage a different model? If the money spent fighting the War on Drugs is failing to achieve its objective of reducing drug use, should we be looking for new solutions? How do we justify the loss of life, violence, corruption, and other negative spinoffs that are caused by a law enforcement model that is unable to control the trade? How much of the harm caused by illegal drugs is because of their innate harmfulness, how much is because they are illegal, and how can we best reduce these harms?

COSTS OF ILLEGAL DRUG USE IN CANADA

Calculating the costs of illegal drug use is just as difficult as calculating the value of the drug market. Differing assumptions, the opaqueness of the industry, and the political biases of the research all make it difficult to come up with reliable numbers.

What we can say with confidence is that the costs of drug use — both legal and illegal drugs — are very high. For example, in looking at the social costs of drug abuse in Canada in 2002, researchers concluded that tobacco use cost seventeen billion dollars, alcohol $14.6 billion, and all illegal drugs together $8.2 billion.[49] The breakdown of these costs is interesting, not least because it shows that the costs of just two legal drugs are about four times the costs of all illegal drugs. Yet $1.5 billion was spent on direct costs of prevention and research, and fully $5.4 billion on direct law enforcement costs (which would have been spent mainly on the illegal drugs). This report also notes that the direct social costs of tobacco are more than double the social costs of all illegal drugs taken together, and that the direct health costs for alcohol are forty-five times as high as for marijuana alone.

There is at least one worrisome bias built into the CCSA statistics. Researchers note in some cases that the figures relating to the costs of alcohol use are "net." That is, they have also taken into consideration the benefits of alcohol use. (They don't say what these might be, but we can assume they refer to something like the benefits of moderate amounts of red wine.) They have not done this for any of the other drugs, whether legal or illegal. The fact that they did so for alcohol alone has a distorting effect on the final estimates, making alcohol look less dangerous. Had they done a "net" calculation for, say, marijuana, the results would have shown it to cause less harm than the CCSA claims.

It is difficult to distinguish between the costs of actually using the drugs and the costs created or exacerbated by the pressure of law enforcement — that is to say, by the War on Drugs itself. In 2001, Canada's Auditor General estimated the economic costs to Canada of illegal drugs, including health care (for example, HIV/AIDS and Hepatitis C), lost productivity, property crime, and enforcement at more than five billion dollars annually.[50] The report also pointed out that only 5 percent of available federal funds (twenty-five million dollars) were available to deal with the social issues, while 95 percent ($450 million) went to enforcing the drug war, including police, prosecutions, and corrections.

The *World Drug Report 2012* breaks out statistics for just one of those areas — loss of productivity in Canada in 2002 (related to illegal drug use) — at $4.6 billion, or four times the sum of health-related costs.[51] As earlier noted, the *World Drug Report* includes reduced labour participation and incarceration as the main costs when estimating loss of productivity.

Looking at these assumptions, we have to ask ourselves some questions. Are people failing to participate in the labour force because of the problems caused by the drug itself, such as illness? Are people failing to find work because they have a criminal record for previous drug use?[52] What about the possibility that people who are chronically unemployed might resort to drug use as a way of dealing with their poverty and marginalization? Causality becomes an issue when dealing with the use of psychoactive drugs. Researchers have to ask themselves whether people are using drugs because of other problems in their lives, or whether they are developing other problems because of their drug use.

If we look at illness and premature death as the main components of lost productivity (as the CCSA does), questions are raised there as well. Are people getting sick and dying because of their drug use, unaffected by other conditions? Are they getting sick and dying because of other debilitating socioeconomic factors experienced by marginalized people? Or are they getting sick and dying because the pressure of law enforcement compels them to engage in risky behaviour, like using dirty needles, shooting up in unhygienic conditions, or sharing crack pipes?

There is one area of health costs that we can more readily assess, due to the excellent work done in B.C. on HIV/AIDS and Hepatitis C (HCV). These are the costs associated with the use of shared and dirty needles, and with the way addicts adapt to increased law enforcement.

The Canadian HIV/AIDS Legal Network describes the consequences of intensified enforcement upon drug users.[53] It says the additional pressure destabilizes the drug markets, resulting in increased violence, more theft and property crime, and quite often a shift by users from smoking to injecting (which can be done more quickly and discreetly, thus evading police). There is also an increase in high-risk injecting behaviour, including reluctance to buy or carry clean equipment, and an increased likelihood that users will skip safety steps. For example, users will be less likely to take the time to measure the dose or to "taste" the drugs for purity or to clean the site of injection, and more likely to damage veins and soft tissue because of the haste required to inject while evading police.

For these reasons, diseases are being spread among the injecting population. What are the estimated costs to the health care system of such diseases? Dr. Evan Wood, an expert in the field of HIV/AIDS, said in 2012 that it can cost the Canadian health care system about five hundred thousand dollars for each case of full-blown AIDS.[54] The average cost of an HIV infection to the health care system is about $250,000.[55] The total cost per year for HCV infections in Canada was five hundred million dollars in 2005, and this was expected to double by 2010.[56] The cost of a liver transplant (often the only solution for HCV) in 2005 was $120,000 to $690,000. These staggering figures represent only a small part of the overall cost to the health system of one set of consequences of drug use. And, significantly, according to the physicians and others who deal with these diseases every day, both the costs and the suffering would be greatly alleviated by taking a public health harm-reduction approach rather than an enforcement approach to the problem.

In 1999–2000, it was estimated that treatment costs for HIV/AIDS in British Columbia alone would total $72.3 million.[57] Much of the problem was centred in the Vancouver East Side, where a lot of people were dying from the disease. This was when concerned physicians and others obtained a federal exemption from criminal prosecution in order to open a safe injection site. InSite is funded solely by the province and in 2013 operated with only $1.45 million.[58] The ratio of costs to benefits is stark. InSite's record of success has already been noted, and has resulted in large savings in human and financial costs.

Governments in pursuit of ideological or "moral" objectives often make poor policy choices. The Canadian Consortium for the Investigation of Cannabinoids years ago received permission to conduct research into the potential medical use of marijuana, but this was abruptly terminated in 2006 when the Conservative government took power. The decision to terminate the research cannot be explained on financial grounds, since defunding the program saved the government a mere two million dollars per year.[59]

Marijuana is a particularly interesting case because the main, indeed virtually the only, costs associated with its use are the costs of law enforcement (police, courts, prisons) and with the violence associated with organized crime. There are no confirmed serious health consequences of using the drug, thus no apparent costs to the health care system. Marijuana does not drive users to commit violent crimes, so there is no cost associated with this. Indeed, a recent book even claims that, in British Columbia at least, there is little violence at all associated with the production and trafficking of the drug.[60] The authors, Susan Boyd and Connie Carter, obtained a 2011 Justice Department report that studied five hundred grow-ops in British Columbia. Results showed that, despite fearmongering by the police and the media, only 5 percent of these grow-ops had ties to gangs or to organized crime. As well, firearms were found at only 6 percent. The media and police have continually talked about "significant" dangers to public safety posed by grow-ops. Hydro authorities and municipalities have been drafted into the effort to crack down on grow-ops. Yet the evidence, say the authors, does not support the necessity for a harsh law enforcement response.

Boyd is critical of the Conservative government: "This study wasn't released by our federal government and you could see why.... It doesn't fit with their *Safe Streets and Communities Act*, which frames marijuana grow-ops as always being associated with organized crime and gangs." Since the "say-no-to-drugs" message does not seem to be working (she notes that half of Canadians say they have used marijuana), "one way to continue with the drug enforcement law-and-order mandate is to talk about the dangerousness of the growers." Boyd says the media and police have thus "routinely exaggerated" the dangers of the industry.

It is not possible to assess the analysis of the Boyd and Carter book, since it was not yet published at the time of writing. However, one organization taking a radically different view of the amount of violence involved in the marijuana trade is Stop the Violence BC. This is a coalition[61] that advocates for legalization of marijuana under a "strict regulatory framework."[62] Its objective is to educate the public so that people will understand the link between marijuana prohibition and gang violence in the province. The founding members of the coalition comprise high-profile experts in health, the academy, law enforcement (including a retire RCMP superintendent), and justice. Among them are experts who are noted advocates for an evidence-based public health approach to drugs: Dr. Dan Werb, Bohdan Nosyk, Dr. Thomas Kerr, Dr. Benedikt Fischer, Dr. Julio Montaner, and Dr. Evan Wood.

The B.C. coalition notes that police estimate 85 percent of the marijuana trade in B.C. is controlled by organized crime. Violence in the sector is growing, while gangs proliferate and fight deadly turf wars in communities. Ross Lander, a retired B.C. Supreme Court judge, says that continuing with prohibition is completely out of step with "what's going on in society today."[63] He continues, "The coalition's objects meet what I would personally want, that is stop the useless killings and the violence that attends this drug trade."

Police officer David Bratzer (Canadian president of Law Enforcement Against Prohibition — LEAP) from Victoria agrees. He thinks prohibition is "well-intentioned" but that "it has failed in B.C. and around the world." He says the huge criminal organizations running the drug trade are becoming more dangerous every day and that he "strongly support(s) controlled marijuana legalization as an effective way to fight crime and protect our communities." This is a statement against the interests of police departments everywhere, since their budgets depend largely on fighting the drug war. As such, it deserves our attention.

The International Centre for Science in Drug Policy (ICSDP) is dedicated to producing research on illegal drug policy that is based upon hard scientific evidence. Its research shows that there are clear links between violence and the illegal drug trade.[64] In a comprehensive review of 306 studies on the subject, it also found that increased enforcement did not reduce gang violence. This research did not specifically assess violence as associated with the marijuana trade, except to say that the extreme violence in Mexico is due to the export of marijuana and other drugs north. It also did not address the issue of whether British Columbia might represent an aberration, with less violence associate with the trade there. What we do know is that the organized crime gangsters who operate the drug trade are involved with all of the profitable illegal drugs, including marijuana, and that violence attends their activities irrespective of the drug involved.

We can quibble about the exact amounts spent enforcing the ban on particular drugs in particular locations, but what about law enforcement costs more generally?

Chapter Seven

Prohibition vs. the Alternative: The Bottom Line

It is estimated that the United States alone has spent $2.5 trillion on the War on Drugs over the past forty years.[1] Much is made of the amount of drugs and cash seized by law enforcement every year, but according to a 1999 United Nations study, in order to seriously impair the profitability of the illegal drug trade, some 75 percent of all drug shipments would have to be intercepted.[2] Current efforts only intercept 13 percent of heroin shipments and 28 percent to 40 percent of cocaine shipments. Further illustrating the futility of these efforts, 5.5 million trucks cross the Mexico-U.S. border annually, but the entire annual supply of drugs trafficked across that border would fit into just sixty trucks.[3]

One researcher tallied up the cost to all levels of government (federal, state, and local) of enforcing prohibition in the United States between 1981 and 2008.[4] For purposes of interdiction and enforcement, the total was $600 billion. When the costs of treatment and rehabilitation were included, the balance soared to $800 billion. The numbers continue to rise. In 2012, the United States administration asked Congress to provide $25.6 billion for all federal drug control programs for 2013.[5]

The results have not justified the expenditure. The National Center on Addiction and Substance Abuse at Columbia University reported that in 2005 the federal government spent $2.6 billion on interdiction internationally (that is, to disrupt the importation of illegal drugs).[6] The centre found no evidence that this had any impact on reducing substance abuse and addiction or its costs to government.

Between 1981 and 2011, the budget of the ONDCP increased by more than 600 percent. However, government data also show that there was "an approximate inflation- and purity-adjusted decrease in heroin price of 80 percent, and a greater than 900 percent increase in heroin purity between 1981 and 2002, clearly indicating that expenditures on interventions to reduce the supply of heroin into the United States were unsuccessful."[7]

The *Tools for Debate* report by the International Centre for Science in Drug Policy (ICSDP) in Vancouver assessed data on marijuana prohibition in the United States.[8] It found that anti-drug law enforcement costs related to marijuana alone had increased from $1.5 billion in 1981 to $18 billion in 2002. At the same time, potency of the drug increased 145 percent and the price dropped by 58 percent. Use among school-age children increased, and marijuana was very easy to obtain.

The concern that drug use would be higher without law enforcement measures is at odds with the science. For example, the lifetime rate of marijuana use (meaning that a person has used marijuana at least once in his or her lifetime) in the United States is more than double that observed in the Netherlands, where marijuana is all but legal (42 percent compared to 20 percent).

Finally, the United States has become notorious as the country with the highest number of incarcerated people in the world. China comes a distant second even though China has more than four times the population and a very harsh judicial system.[9] Most people convicted of federal drug offences in the United States receive mandatory minimum prison sentences. Between 1980 and 2013, the federal Bureau of Prisons budget rose by almost 600 percent in real terms.

The United States spends $12 billion per year incarcerating about 500,000 prisoners convicted of drug offences.[10] According to the Drug Policy Alliance, 1.53 million people were arrested on non-violent drug charges in 2011 in the United States.[11] Of these, 757,969 were arrested for marijuana offences and 663,032 of these for possession only. Two-thirds of those incarcerated for drug violations are Hispanic or black, although they use drugs at similar rates to Caucasians.

Readers might be interested to know how some of the U.S. enforcement budget is spent. Under the Narcotics Rewards Program, for example, the State Department offers up to $5 million to anyone offering information leading to the arrest or conviction of major drug traffickers.[12] As of 2012, at least nine of these rewards had been paid out.

Eradication programs also consume billions of dollars. It is estimated that the United States has spent $8 billion to help Colombia eradicate its coca fields.[13] The immediate response by drug lords was to move elsewhere — in this case, to Peru and Ecuador.

In Canada, the costs of enforcing prohibition are also significant. One report from the 1990s said that Canada was accustomed to spending more than four times as much on enforcement as it did on the health response to illegal drugs ($400.3 million versus $88 million).[14] This is one of the few budget areas to be increased since the Conservatives took power in 2006.

By 2002, according to the CCSA, Canadian federal, provincial, and territorial governments together were spending up to $2.3 billion policing and prosecuting illegal drugs and imprisoning offenders.[15] In the same year, the CCSA says as much as $8.8 billion was spent by all governments on direct health care costs related to illegal drugs.

In a report published in 2006, though, the Canadian HIV/AIDS Legal Network claimed that a high proportion of the available budget for Canada's Drug Strategy was spent on enforcement — a full 73 percent. Only 14 percent of the funds available were spent on treatment, with 3 percent going to prevention and 3 percent to harm reduction.[16] Research received the remaining 7 percent. It is hard to reconcile these figures with those of the CCSA.

In 2007, the Harper government launched its National Anti-Drug Strategy. The first thing the new strategy did was to move responsibility for illegal drugs from Health Canada to Justice, thus signalling a change in emphasis from treatment and prevention to enforcement. The budget of $500 million was spread across a dozen departments and over five years.

In 2012, this budget was renewed for another five years and the change in emphasis became even more evident. Health Canada's portion (to be spent on treatment and prevention) decreased 15 percent to $230 million. Funding for the RCMP targeted to fighting the War on Drugs, on the other hand, increased 22 percent to $127 million.[17] The Director of Public Prosecutions received an increase from $43 million to $61 million for the same period. There were at the same time deep cuts to treatment agencies across the board. For example, Health Canada's Drug Treatment Funding Program was reduced to $80 million from $122 million for the next five years. The shift away from any public health response and toward a more punitive, law-enforcement response is indisputable and appears to be the ultimate objective of the government.

In 2008, the Canadian government also launched a related mass media campaign costing $30 million. This was despite the fact that such public education efforts have proven not to be effective at convincing young people not to use illegal drugs.[18] More recently, the government announced over $11 million per year for a campaign to advertise the evils of marijuana.[19]

Dana Larsen has amassed the data relating to marijuana prohibition in British Columbia. He says that in the six years from 2005 to 2011, the number of charges for simple possession of marijuana doubled. He estimates the costs of prohibition will amount to $60 million over the next four years.

Huge amounts of money are spent in Canada incarcerating drug offenders. Budgets for federal corrections in Canada increased 86 percent between 2006 and 2011 — that is, in the few years since the Conservatives took power — according to the government's own numbers.[20] The cost of federal prisons in 2013–2014 was expected to increase from $2.98 billion per year in 2001–2012 to $3.147 billion. New mandatory minimum sentences for drug offences will continue to push these incarceration rates higher.

Most of those incarcerated for drug offences have been convicted of victimless, non-violent crimes. Canadian Rosie Rowbotham is the most famous example. He was first sentenced to fourteen years for importing large quantities of hashish into the country in 1977.[21] He was later charged with importing hashish and sentenced to twenty years. He served six years before that case was overturned on appeal, then was sentenced to another seventeen years after the new trial. It cost Canadian taxpayers millions of dollars to convict this non-violent, victimless offender, and millions more to incarcerate him for decades. Just one of the trials cost six million dollars. It would cost more than one hundred thousand dollars per year to incarcerate someone like Rosie Rowbotham today.

Rosie sat in prison, bemused, and watched bank robbers, child molesters, and rapists coming into the system and then being released ahead of him.[22] He was philosophical about his situation: "When the time's up and the joke's over, I can start moving on with my life."[23] He did not believe he was doing anything wrong by selling marijuana. He said, "I disagree with the laws and I think they're really, really wrong and I think right now that they [the government] can't admit that they're wrong because of what they've done to thousands and thousands of people.... I paid for my beliefs. I don't owe anybody an apology."

The Canadian people have a decision to make. Do we want to continue driving deficits up and building prisons in order to warehouse people like Rosie Rowbotham? Or should we do a careful accounting and find out whether the money would be better spent elsewhere? If it is important to get people to stop using drugs (or never start), would it not make sense to explore less expensive, more effective, and less harmful solutions than prison? In today's atmosphere, this is unlikely to happen. The current government's commitment to the criminal justice model is unshakeable.

Between 2010 and 2012, the number of inmates in Canadian federal prisons increased a full 6.8 percent.[24] These exceptional increases in the numbers of people incarcerated and the budgets for enforcement and interdiction require justification. Have the numbers of drug users in Canada been rising to such an extent that these expenditures are warranted? Health Canada reports, to the contrary, that illegal drug use has been declining in Canada. The latest survey from the Canadian Alcohol and Drug Use Monitoring Survey (CADUMS) for 2011 shows that drug use since 2004 has declined for virtually all illegal drugs.[25] The U.N.'s *World Drug Report 2013* also shows that the annual prevalence of marijuana use in Canada (among the population aged between fifteen and sixty-four) decreased from 12.65 percent to 10.90 percent in just one year (from 2010 to 2011).[26]

Yet Statistics Canada states that police-reported drug offences increased between 1993 and 2007.[27] Marijuana possession accounted for six out of ten drug-related crimes, and the number of youth charged had doubled between 1997 and 2007. It is hard to explain this increase in arrests in Canada at a time when marijuana use was decreasing of its own accord. Statistics Canada stresses that the statistics on offences like impaired driving, prostitution, and drug crimes may be influenced by police practices that focus more resources on these areas. In other words, the more money is budgeted for arresting drug offenders, the more likely that the number of police-reported drug offences will increase independent of the amount of actual drug use.

Juristat, a publication of Statistics Canada, confirms that marijuana possession offences for 2011 have increased back to about the same rate as in 2000. One source claims the number of Canadians arrested for marijuana possession has increased by 41 percent since the Conservative government came to power.[28] Meanwhile, the rate of offences for trafficking, production, and distribution have fallen by 11 percent. This appears anomalous, but could be accounted for by police practices that focus on easier targets — like young people and small-time street dealers, rather than the high-end drug dealers or producers.

Since the Conservative government was elected in 2006, there has been a long list of new and draconian laws taking aim at the illegal drug market with the intention of exacting harsh prison sentences. A suite of mandatory minimum sentences now sends small-time traffickers, growers, and users to prison for serious prison terms. Anyone growing six marijuana plants will serve a minimum of six months. Anyone growing six marijuana plants on rented property will be sentenced to nine months minimum. For more than 200 plants, the minimum is 18 months, and for more than 500 plants, three years (a federal prison term). The sentences rise with the perceived seriousness of the drug involved. This law took effect in November 2012, so the first offenders to receive these longer sentences were only beginning to show up in the prison system in late 2013. It is expected that prisons will soon be seriously overcrowded as a result of the new laws, and that additional violence and an increased spread of disease will ensue.

Perversely, these long prison sentences were mandated in Canada at the same time as mandatory minimums were being rejected as failures elsewhere in the world. Asa Hutchinson, former drug czar (head of the Drug Enforcement Agency) under George W. Bush, came to Ottawa to address parliamentarians in 2011. He told them that the legislating of mandatory minimums was one of the biggest mistakes they had made in the United States, not least because of the financial burden of incarcerating so many people. The Canadian government went ahead and instituted mandatory minimums anyway.

There are many members of the public who feel these long sentences are justified if it means that the trade in illegal drugs is reduced, or that drug users and dealers will be deterred from such activity. But the trade always bounces back quickly after strict enforcement measures remove some of the players. There are many new entrepreneurs eager to take over, and the promised deterrent effect is illusory.

One case involved an accused who went to court fully expecting to draw a long prison sentence for dealing in cocaine. When he was released on a technicality, he thanked his lawyer by palming him a deck of cocaine. At the time this happened, the county court house was full of people on similar charges, with dozens of witnesses and security. The halls were teeming with police officers — Toronto Police, RCMP, undercover officers. Yet this accused thought nothing of carrying cocaine into the courthouse and handing it to his lawyer under their very eyes. Deterrence was simply not a factor.

Another way of measuring the costs of enforcing prohibition is to calculate how much would be saved if some or all illegal drugs were dealt with by regulation rather than prohibition. Dr. Jeffrey Miron and Dr. Katherine Waldock produced a report for the Cato Institute (a Conservative think tank) on the budgetary impact of ending drug prohibition in the United States. They estimated that "legalizing drugs would save roughly $41.3 billion per year in government expenditure on enforcement of prohibition," and that "approximately $8.7 billion of the savings would result from legalization of marijuana and $32.6 billion from legalization of other drugs."[29] Other estimates claim that national regulation of marijuana alone would save much more in enforcement costs — more than $44 billion per year.[30]

Individual states, in their drive to decriminalize (not legalize) marijuana, have calculated the likely savings to their coffers. The state of Connecticut, for example, estimates it would save $885,000 on law enforcement if it decriminalized.[31] Rhode Island estimates it would save $12.7 million per year in costs relating to the criminal justice system if it ended marijuana prohibition.[32]

RAND Corporation did a study on legalizing marijuana in California, estimating the savings in arrests and imprisonment at $300 million per year.[33] RAND notes that other studies have estimated the savings at $1.9 billion, but stands by the more conservative estimate. Either way, the savings would be substantial.

This gives a general overview of how much money is being spent fighting the War on Drugs in Canada and the United States, including costs of policing, prosecuting, and incarcerating drug offenders. The question arises whether this is the best use of taxpayer funds, or whether a different approach might yield better results for less money.

ECONOMIC BENEFITS OF LEGALIZATION

An alternative model to prohibition would be a system in which governments take control of the drug trade away from organized crime by legalizing, regulating, and taxing the drugs. One advantage of this model is that it presents an opportunity for the state to increase its revenues by taxing the substances, as it does alcohol and tobacco. Thus, it makes sense to determine what level of tax revenues the drug market might provide to governments if drugs, or at least some drugs, were to be legalized, regulated, and taxed.

In Canada, estimates have been made as to the value of taxing marijuana if it were to be legalized in British Columbia.[34] A recent research paper concluded this would generate $2.5 billion in government tax and licensing revenues over five years — based on a domestic provincial market of over 400,000 annual consumers. Stephen Easton added his voice, saying that, if there were a federal sales tax on legalized marijuana, the revenue would amount to approximately $2 billion per year, just for the domestic trade.[35]

A recent Liberal Party policy paper advocates legalizing marijuana. It concludes that Canadian tax revenues in a legal regime would amount to about $4 billion per year. Canada is currently budgeting for a deficit. If the government were to legalize drugs, the savings in law enforcement and the added revenues from taxation would provide a significant reduction in that deficit. The savings could also fund evidence-based programs of harm reduction to battle the scourge of addiction and illness, while eliminating the violence and mayhem of a gang-controlled marketplace.

In the United States, the Miron and Waldock report for the Cato Institute also estimated potential tax revenues in a post-prohibition world. They found that "drug legalization would yield tax revenue of $46.7 billion annually, assuming legal drugs were taxed at rates comparable to those on alcohol and tobacco. Approximately $8.7 billion of this revenue would result from legalization of marijuana and $38 billion from legalization of other drugs."[36]

Some individual states in the U.S. have also calculated the potential income generation from a legal regime. The Connecticut Office of Fiscal Analysis says that decriminalizing marijuana would add $1.4 million to its general revenues.[37] These revenues would result from an increase in the numbers of fines imposed (not strictly speaking from taxes). Some have argued that merely ticketing users will lead to higher rates of drug use. However, Australia learned years ago that this is not the case. Researchers concluded that regions that gave on-the-spot fines to marijuana users rather than harsher criminal penalties did not cause marijuana use to increase.[38]

California's government estimates that an excise and sales tax on marijuana would bring in about $1.4 billion per year to the state's coffers.[39] The potential for balancing budgets, or boosting health and education coffers, or both, is readily apparent to elected officials.

Colorado threw its doors open to legal marijuana on January 1, 2014. Users paid high prices (nearly double the cost of medical marijuana) at $50 to $60 per 1/8 ounce.[40] They did so in order to avoid the risk of buying on the black market. Sales surpassed $1 million on the first day.[41] The state expected tax revenues to amount to $67 million, but recent estimates suggest the total will be double that. Nationwide, it is expected that legal pot (both medical and not) should bring in $2.34 billion in 2014.

In addition to taxes, a marijuana industry has the potential to create thousands of jobs.[42] Although Stephen Easton says the number of jobs would not be "particularly important," he appears to be considering only the impact on agricultural jobs.[43] As he points out, agriculture today is highly mechanized and does not employ a lot of people. As well, the outlets that will control the distribution of the product will probably be liquor control boards, which already have their full complement of employees. He does not, however, consider the multiple spin-off industries that will be positively affected by legalizing the drug.

For example, we already have estimates of what the medical marijuana industry provided by way of jobs and incomes in one U.S. state. Montana was in dire financial straits after the housing crisis in 2008 when medical marijuana was first legalized. The medical marijuana industry swiftly became one of the biggest job-creators in memory.[44] It was estimated that, in a population of 975,000, 1,400 jobs were created. Growers spent $12 million per year in the state, and one grower spent $25,000 per month just on electricity for his grow-op. Everything from gardening supplies companies to mainstream bakeries to the state's biggest utility benefited greatly from the medical marijuana industry. In addition, marijuana grow-ops were one of the few year-round industries in the northern state.

Montana recently elected a Republican majority, though, and it has cracked down on medical marijuana grow-ops. A number of growers have been sent to federal prison and ordered to pay hundreds of thousands of dollars in fines. Montana is still one of the twenty-one states that continues to permit legalized medical marijuana, and advocates are working to change recent restrictions that have resulted in prosecutions.

Among the many experts who have advocated for legalization of marijuana are some of world's most high-profile economists. Three Nobel laureates were among the 530 signatories to a letter addressed to President Bush and the American government advocating for this change in the law.[45] All of them were economists, including Chicago School guru Milton Friedman. Friedman says, "If you look at the drug war from a purely economic point of view, the role of the government is to protect the drug cartel."[46] In other words, prohibition is a gift to organized crime, allowing drug kingpins to benefit from the industry, aided and abetted by government.

Legislators are not yet ready to end prohibition just because it promises to provide significant tax revenues. It is helpful, therefore, to look at some of the cost-benefit analyses that have been produced by researchers who compare prohibition to public health and harm reduction models.

The UNODC recently published a discussion paper in which it recommends a health care approach rather than a punishment model for dealing with drug dependence.[47] It recommended making drug courts available as an alternative to the normal criminal process, saying:

> Treatment as an alternative to criminal justice sanctions is specifically encouraged in the international drug control conventions and it has been found to be more effective than imprisonment in encouraging recovery from drug dependence and reducing drug-related crime. It can be provided in ways that do not violate the rights of the patients, provided that the decision to refuse treatment remains in the hands of the drug user and the patient's autonomy and human rights are respected.

The report then cited some figures by way of a cost-benefit analysis that lend support to this approach. The most rigorous and conservative scientific estimates from five meta-analyses have all concluded that drug courts significantly reduce crime by as much as 35 percent compared to imprisonment.[48] In addition, drug courts produce $2.21–$3.36 in avoided criminal justice matters for every dollar spent on them. Up to $12.00 (per one dollar invested) are saved by the community on reduced emergency room visits and other medical care, foster care, and victimization costs such as property loss.

One American study found that every dollar spent on drug treatment in the community returned $18.52 in benefits to society.[49] Another found that for every dollar spent on treatment, the costs of crime and lost productivity were reduced by $7.46.[50]

Statistics from a 1996 RAND Corporation research study confirm that there are many financial benefits in adopting alternative approaches to illegal drugs. In an effort to determine the most cost-effective way to reduce the flow of cocaine, for example, it found that one dollar spent on treatment achieves the same reduction of flow as $7.30 spent on enforcement, $10.80 spent on border control, and $23.00 spent trying to persuade Colombian farmers to grow alternative crops to cocaine.[51]

About fifteen years ago, Judge James P. Gray, a libertarian who supports the legalization of drugs, compared the relative annual costs of treatment models in the United States against the law enforcement/incarceration model.[52] Regular outpatient treatment cost $1,800 annually, while intensive outpatient treatment amounted to $2,500. Methadone maintenance cost about $3,900 annually. Short-term residential programs could be provided at a cost of $4,400 per year, while long-term residential treatment was in the range of $6,800. By contrast to all of these, incarceration of an individual cost the treasury fully $25,900 per year — almost four times as much as the most expensive of the alternative treatment programs.

A study by NIDA in the United States estimated that in 1991, the cost of one year of methadone maintenance treatment (MMT) for a heroin addict was only $2,400.[53] Meanwhile, the Lindsmith Centre claims that even the $2,400 estimate is high, since only about 5 percent to 10 percent of the cost of methadone treatment is actually used to pay for the medication itself. It said methadone could be prescribed and delivered even more cheaply. Either way, MMT costs a fraction of what it costs to prosecute and incarcerate a heroin addict.

In Canada, it can cost upwards of one hundred thousand dollars to incarcerate an addict for one year. Meanwhile, the current government is cutting back on funding for prison programs such as drug treatment. As well, the Canada Health Act does not cover prison inmates, so the availability of treatment for HIV/AIDS and HCV is restricted by the limitations of the corrections budget. Both diseases are being spread at shocking rates in prisons because the authorities refuse to establish needle exchanges. And it goes without saying that heroin and drugs are readily available in prisons despite the best efforts of Corrections Canada.

Methadone is the drug of choice to help addicts get off heroin, but methadone itself is highly addictive. It is estimated that 20 percent of inmates in Canadian prisons are hooked on methadone.[54] In these circumstances, an inmate is likely to be released from custody still addicted to one substance or another, making him (or her) more likely to reoffend than if he had received appropriate treatment, further adding to the costs to society.

CONCLUSION

The least one can say is that, from the point of view of economics, we should be looking at alternative models to strict prohibition. From a financial perspective, taking the drug trade away from organized crime and dealing with drug abuse in a measured, evidence-based way would be sensible. The most appropriate alternative to prohibition is likely to be a public health model, with features of harm reduction. Such an approach would remove the stigma of drug abuse, and would treat addicts in an holistic way that would reap rewards — economic and otherwise — not only for the individual, but for his or her family and the community.

Many nations around the world are considering different versions of a public health approach. Some have already stepped out and started the experiment. The results are promising. The next chapter will canvas these efforts around the world, and the changing attitudes that have given rise to a new approach to drug abuse.

Chapter Eight

A Shifting International Consensus

A Slow Recognition of the Damage Done

The international community is struggling to revise its position on illegal drugs. Different systems of decriminalization (allowing the possession of small amounts of illegal drugs without criminal penalty, while continuing to prosecute trafficking and production) have been adopted by various countries, and these seem to share a number of difficulties. For example, it is hard to ensure that the rules are interpreted evenly across jurisdictions; biases intrude into their implementation, resulting in injustices. Decriminalization systems often continue to allow for criminal penalties in the event of default on a fine or failure to complete a program. The administration of prohibition can be haphazard, and the same is true for that system of "prohibition lite" we call decriminalization.

Discrimination is rife in the exercise of discretion around drug charges. There is ample evidence that some prosecutors and judges treat African-Americans and Latinos differently from Caucasians when it comes to drugs. Discretion may also be exercised differently from jurisdiction to jurisdiction. In Canada, for example, a drug user in one location will be convicted of simple possession of marijuana and suffer the consequences of the resulting criminal record. In a different location, there are judges who will dismiss simple possession charges automatically, leaving no criminal record.

In Canada, we know that visible minorities, particularly Native people, are treated differently by the justice system. Under the current government, the number of blacks in prison has increased by 75 percent, while the number of Native inmates is up 45 percent.[1] Other types of discrimination are also apparent, netting prison sentences for people who are marginalized by socioeconomic status or mental ability, to cite just two examples. There is even an urban/rural divide created by some prosecutors. An amount of marijuana sufficient to attract possession-for-the-purpose-of-trafficking charges (entailing prison sentences) in a rural area may, unaccountably, only attract the lesser charge of simple possession (entailing a fine, probation, or an absolute discharge) in a nearby city.

In a misguided effort to compel courts to act with consistency, the Canadian government has recently legislated mandatory minimum sentencing. These sentences can and do themselves result in gross injustices, removing discretion from judges and placing it in the hands of police and prosecutors. In some jurisdictions — but, importantly, not in all — police and prosecutors may decide to adjust the facts of a case in order to avoid the most draconian sentences. For example, they may decide to ignore the fact that an amount of marijuana found growing in a student's basement was six plants, and call it five. This decision will be made before the case ever reaches a judge because, once the facts are before the judge, he or she has no ability to deviate from the mandatory minimum six-month prison sentence.

This places new and powerful authority in the hands of police and prosecutors, who should not be obliged or permitted to operate essentially as judges. Ironically, the ill that the government seeks to avoid — inconsistency with respect to sentencing — is propagated under this system in a way that distorts the dispensation of justice. It will not be applied the same way in all cases or all jurisdictions, or by all police and prosecutors. It results in unfairness and produces a public perception that the system should not be trusted or respected.

The other objective of mandatory minimum sentences, according to the government, is to act as a deterrent. Yet there is ample evidence that prison sentences do not deter offenders or potential offenders. There is plenty of evidence, though, that they cause extensive damage to those incarcerated and their families and neighbourhoods.

In an effort to avoid the injustices, and to treat drug users with more humanity, other countries are approaching the problem by decriminalizing illegal drugs. They instruct the courts that a user may possess a specified amount of drugs without incurring criminal sanctions. This represents a genuine effort to move away from the War on Drugs. However, in these decriminalization regimes, a system of prohibition continues to operate. First of all, possession of the drug is still regarded to be a criminal offence, and criminal sanctions may still be applied if the accused fails to pay the imposed penalty. Second, trafficking and production remain strictly prohibited. As to these offences, bias, inconsistency, the inability to control the product, and the influence of organized crime continue to present serious problems.

Countries trying to decriminalize do so in the shadow of the international community's organizations, mainly those of the United Nations. The U.N. has long been in the vanguard of prohibiting illegal drugs and encouraging nations to be drug warriors. It has directed its member nations to impose criminal sanctions upon drug offenders.

Recent publications of the United Nations Office on Drug Control (UNODC) insist that alternatives to imprisonment have always been available to its member states, but the international conventions unquestionably emphasize a law enforcement model. All three conventions use identical language.[2] They say that "serious offences shall be liable to adequate punishment *particularly by imprisonment or other penalties of deprivation of liberty.*" (Emphasis added.) All of them encourage parties to adopt more "strict or severe measures."

However, by the time the U.N. ratified the 1988 convention (in the midst, it must be said, of the ramping up of the drug war in the United States), its language had become truly alarmist. It said the parties were "deeply concerned by the magnitude of and rising trend in the illegal [production, manufacture, trafficking and use of illicit drugs]" and spoke of "a danger of incalculable gravity." International criminal activity had increased to the point that "suppression ... demands urgent attention and the highest priority."

The 1988 convention established a very long list of criminal offences related to illegal drugs, including possession for personal use. It added fines and confiscation as additional possible penalties, urged parties to eradicate illegal crops, and recommended the maximization of "the effectiveness of law enforcement measures … with due regard to the need to deter" — a reference again to incarceration.

After decades of tough law enforcement failed to control the drug trade, though, the U.N. changed its tune. In 2010, the discussion paper by the UNODC entitled *From Coercion to Cohesion: Treating Drug Dependence Through Health Care, not Punishment*, sets out the scientific case for dealing with drug abuse through treatment measures as an alternative to criminal justice sanctions.[3] It suggests that possession, purchase, or cultivation for personal use can be dealt with by alternative measures "as complete alternatives to conviction and punishment." In a classic example of "leading from behind," this report picks up on the momentum created by nations from Latin America and elsewhere as they agitate for an alternative to the War on Drugs.

The International Narcotics Control Board (INCB) of the United Nations, though, continues to emphasize law enforcement above all else, and operates in isolation from other U.N. agencies, including those involved with health issues.[4] The INCB is continually chastising nation members for not doing enough to prosecute the War on Drugs. It has expressed grave concerns about the legalization votes in Washington and Colorado states. It has even criticized the Supreme Court of Canada for instructing the federal government to provide InSite with its necessary exemption from prosecution.

International conventions notwithstanding, the drug trade continues apace. Drug use is not abating around the world, but is moving toward developing countries. The methods and routes of trafficking are moving as well.[5] More traditional methods of trafficking drugs have given way to a new dependence upon container traffic, air traffic, and trafficking over the Internet (for example, the Silk Road).

Organized crime gangs are beginning to traffic drugs as a means of funding terrorist organizations and related arms smuggling.[6] Today, about a quarter of all European cocaine transits through Africa. A common route is from Guinea-Bissau to Mali and Niger, then to Libya and Egypt.

Large parts of this terrain are controlled by extreme Islamists. They work with drug smugglers to finance their battles. In 2009, a burned-out Boeing 727 from Venezuela was found in northeastern Mali. "It had been stuffed to the gills with cocaine." In 2010, another two tonnes of cocaine were found in the Gambia. In 2012, a coup in Guinea-Bissau removed the democratic regime and replaced it with a corrupt army, after which drug trafficking spiked.[7] Today, West Africa is a production and distribution hub, as well as a trafficking route for illegal drugs.

UNODC executive director Antonio Maria Costa says of the situation in Guinea-Bissau that the country is "under siege. The threat posed by drug traffickers is so great that the state is on the verge of collapse.... So much drug money flowing in so easily, is a true curse: it is perverting the economy and rotting society."[8]

Algeria, Tunisia, and Egypt are all experiencing more drug use and smuggling.[9] It is alleged that drug and cigarette money financed the equipment used by al-Qaeda to attack a gas plant in Algeria in January 2013. The front man for this attack is nicknamed "the narco-jihadist." Corruption and poor policing are part of the problem, with officials and businessmen playing "a bigger role in the [drug] trade than terrorists." This makes it difficult to deal with organized crime, even though Algeria, Libya, and Tunisia have signed a co-operation agreement to tackle drug trafficking.

Most people are aware of the ongoing turmoil, violence, and corruption associated with the drug trade in Latin America, but who knew that it extended to tiny nations like Trinidad and Tobago? Its president recently came to Canada to buy Canadian planes to monitor drug traffickers' boats off the shores of her country.[10] She said that trafficking had moved to her waters because of the crackdown in Colombia and Mexico. She also noted that there was a regional agreement by which nations were to share information about the drug trade with each other, but that it was a one-way street — the United States is not required to share its information with other nations.

Corruption and other kinds of interference with national governments follow the drug trade wherever it goes. The Transform Drug Policy Foundation (TDPF) in Britain says that problems created by prohibition include: policy displacement, since funding is diverted to fight the drug war; distortion of development interventions; exacerbation of conflict (as drug money goes to fund insurgents and corrupt governments); the sidelining of underlying issues that affect the well-being of citizens; and environmental destruction as a result, for example, of deforestation in Colombia (which is done to facilitate detection of illicit crops). Further environmental degradation is caused by the fact that illegal coca growers are necessarily unregulated, and themselves often use herbicides and pesticides that are detrimental to the environment, and may discard other substances like ammonia, gasoline, sodium bicarbonate, and so on.[11]

As the TDPF points out, oil and diamonds have also caused mayhem among nations and created and fuelled conflicts. The difference is that oil and diamonds are innately valuable, while drugs are only valuable because they are illegal. Once they become legal and their value plummets, they will have little or no power to contribute to corrupt and vicious regimes.

The Summit of the Americas concluded in 2012 that the U.S.-led War on Drugs had been a dismal failure.[12] As a *Globe and Mail* editorial pointed out, the war is unwinnable and has led to "weakened states, staggering levels of violence and continued drug consumption." The United States spent $8 billion to help Colombia eradicate coca fields, only to have coca production move to Peru, Ecuador, and Bolivia. Cartels have set up new smuggling routes in weaker states, so that "Guatemala and El Salvador now have the highest homicide rates in the world, while 50,000 people have been killed in Mexico since 2006."[13]

The number of homicides related to the drug war in Mexico has now exceeded one hundred thousand, with tens of thousands more counted as "disappeared."[14] Between 25 and 40 percent of the drug cartels' revenues come from marijuana. Thus, one of the least harmful of illegal drugs is responsible for a shocking proportion of the violence. At the Summit of the Americas, Canadian prime minister Stephen Harper asserted that "everyone believes … that the current approach [to the War on Drugs] is not working, but it is not clear what we should do."

THE MOVE TO DECRIMINALIZATION

On the contrary, a number of Latin American and other countries already know what to do. Led by former military strongman and now president Otto Pérez Molina of Guatemala, the Summit of the Americas concluded that, despite decades of big arrests and seizures of tons of drugs, consumption and production were still booming.[15] Pérez Molina pronounced that drug consumption was a public health issue, and that leaders needed to stop being ideologues. He added pointedly that acting on ideological grounds "is pretty much customary in most government circles these days." He wrote that drugs cannot be eradicated, and recommended legalization with limits and conditions.

There are, in fact, a number of countries around the world that have stopped short of legalization but have adopted alternative approaches. They have all endorsed different forms of decriminalization. Uruguay is the exception. It is the only nation to have legalized marijuana fully, and it did so in 2013.

Almost all of the countries working with a decriminalization regime have done so by adopting "thresholds."[16] That is, they have identified in the case of each drug the maximum quantity that a person may possess without fear of prosecution.[17] These thresholds vary widely from nation to nation.

Even within countries, jurisdictions have established different thresholds. Australia is a good example. In South Australia, you may possess up to one hundred grams of marijuana for which you may be fined by police, who issue Cannabis Expiation Notices. If the fine cannot be paid, then a user may still be prosecuted. In Western Australia, the limit was thirty grams up until the election of a centre-right Liberal government, which toughened the laws by reducing the amount permissible to ten grams. Between 2004, when the limit was established at thirty grams, and 2008, when it was lowered, there was a significant decline in marijuana use.[18] After 2008, more drug users were being prosecuted. In 2011, the decriminalization law was repealed altogether. Full prohibition is again the law. In the Northern Territory, the limit permitted has been fifty grams since 1996, and in the Australian Capital Territory, twenty-five grams. That is a very broad range within which criminal sanctions have been established, and shows how difficult it is for any jurisdiction to decide what is appropriate. It can be confusing for the average recreational marijuana user, and it is decidedly and irrationally inconsistent. This is largely because the states rather than the federal government have jurisdiction over the prosecution of illegal drugs. It creates a patchwork of laws.

A comparison among nations proves even more confusing. Looking at marijuana laws, as of 2012, you could safely possess the following quantities: up to three grams (Belgium), twenty grams (Colombia), fifteen grams (the Czech Republic), five grams (Mexico and the Netherlands), ten grams (Paraguay), eight grams of THC — the active ingredient in marijuana — (Peru), six grams (the Russian Federation), and two hundred grams (Spain). So depending on where you were in the world, you could possess as little as three grams or as much as two hundred grams of marijuana without fear of prosecution.

What about illegal drugs other than marijuana? Some countries have established specific thresholds for these as well: twenty grams of cocaine (Colombia), 0.5 grams of cocaine and fifty milligrams of heroin (Mexico), five grams of cocaine paste, two grams of cocaine, and two hundred milligrams of heroin (Peru), and one gram of cocaine and 1.5 grams of heroin (the Czech Republic).

The Russian Federation's laws were always notoriously harsh when it came to drug use, but it too moved to decriminalize small amounts beginning in 2004. Limits were very low at 0.5 grams of either cocaine or heroin. In 2011, Russia re-established itself as a drug warrior and passed very harsh laws. This has been, in the words of some observers, an "unmitigated disaster," with extremely high HIV and Hep C rates, and widespread human rights abuses.

Another way of decriminalizing drugs is to allow possession of an amount based upon the average daily dose. Thus, Spain's thresholds (7.5 grams of cocaine and three grams of heroin) represent five days' worth of drugs.

In some jurisdictions, it is up to the discretion of the authorities to determine how much of the drug constitutes a "daily dose." So when Estonia (in 2002) and Portugal (in 2001) said that you may possess up to ten times the average daily dose of any given drug, there was no precise amount stipulated.[19] The Netherlands, meanwhile, allows for possession of only one dose of "hard" drugs. It is easy to see how inconsistency and unfairness can arise as different courts and individual judges establish their own views about quantity.

Finally, some countries allow possession with no thresholds at all, whether specific amounts or a "daily dose." Thus, Chile has permitted since 2007 the possession of all drugs for personal use, Armenia has done so since 2008, and Germany did the same in 1994. In Uruguay, possession of drugs for personal use was never criminalized. Argentinean courts decided in 2009 that criminalizing possession of drugs for personal use was unconstitutional. The definition of "for personal use" is, of course, open to interpretation.

In North Africa, Morocco is considering changes to its laws.[20] Until the 1950s, marijuana was legal by order of the king. Today, the country is trying to legalize the drug for medicinal and industrial uses in order to help small farmers who depend upon the crop and are currently under the heel of drug lords.

Interesting changes are taking place on the other side of the globe, too. The Chinese province of Guizhou, for example, has adopted a liberal approach to drug addiction. Not generally known for its leniency in such matters, the Chinese are providing methadone and emphasizing employment rather than incarceration for its heroin addicts.[21] The result? Police are reporting less crime, lower unemployment, and fewer HIV infections among drug users.

In North Korea, too, it appears there is either no law against using marijuana, or the law is not enforced.[22] One English freelancer bought a bag full (for eighty cents) at an indoor market in rural North Korea and smoked it in bars and restaurants, without repercussions. He reports that the government itself sells marijuana to obtain foreign currency. It grows wild, and citizens also grow it in small gardens and use it as medicine.

Looking at the variety of approaches, it is hard to tease out any viable explanation for the way different countries treat drugs. Neither ideology nor political culture seems to account for the wide divergence of views. Why, for example, is Australia well on its way to decriminalizing marijuana when Canada, the U.K., and the United States are not? Why has the EU not adopted a pan-European alternative to the War on Drugs rather than the patchwork that currently exists? Why have Latin American countries emerged as leaders in demanding change? Why should North Korea turn a blind eye to marijuana use while Canada incarcerates users?

Whatever the reasons for these anomalies, it is important to note that systems decriminalizing the use of drugs continue to have problems similar to those that prohibit drugs outright. For example, in Peru, police routinely jail people until it is decided whether or not the quantity they possess qualifies them as traffickers. Drugs are the third leading cause of imprisonment there, but one-third of the twelve hundred people imprisoned for drug offences have either never been charged or not yet convicted. In Argentina, despite the court decision that criminalization is unconstitutional, police have not changed their practices, continuing to arrest people as usual. Interestingly, Argentina's new drug czar, a Catholic priest, argues that there should be a debate in his country about the new Uruguay law.

There are other problems. In Armenia, fines are extremely high and often cannot be paid by the individuals, resulting in incarceration. In South Australia, too, police found it so easy to issue the Cannabis Expiation Notices (like a traffic ticket) that there was a net-widening effect. Police tended to issue lots of tickets. Many of the individuals were then jailed and convicted because they could not afford to pay the fines. In the United Kingdom, too, marijuana possession was effectively decriminalized in 2004, but this had the effect of widening the net so that there were almost the same number of people under criminal sanctions in 2010 as there were in 2003.

In New York City, the law says you are allowed to possess up to one ounce (twenty-nine grams) of marijuana, but not if it is "burning or in open view." This turned out to be an invitation to police to trick young people into revealing their marijuana so that they could subsequently arrest them. As a result, there was a significant increase in the number of arrests, from 33,700 in 1981 to 50,300 in 1995.

Legislated precise thresholds produce problems of their own. Like mandatory minimum sentences, thresholds remove a judge's discretion to decide how to deal with a particular drug user as an individual. If users possess a trace amount over the threshold, they may be treated like criminals, fined or imprisoned, and saddled with a criminal record. If they possess a trace amount under the threshold, on the other hand, they will be eligible for diversion with no criminal justice consequences. Thus the result smacks of arbitrariness, rather than the certainty and consistency that appear to be the objective.

SUCCESSFUL ALTERNATIVES: THE NETHERLANDS AND PORTUGAL

Critics of decriminalization say it will lead to an explosion of drug use. The foregoing survey of countries that have stepped into the arena of decriminalization should serve as reassurance. For those countries that have kept reliable statistics, it is clear that this is an unfounded concern. For example, the Czech Republic noted no rise in drug use after changing its policies to allow possession of small amounts of cocaine and heroin. And although the United Kingdom Drug Policy Commission (UKDPC) claims that the Australian experiment produced negative results, the evidence does not, in fact, support this conclusion.[23] With the exception of one analysis, studies show that decriminalization had no impact on marijuana use, but it did keep a lot of people out of the criminal justice system.

The UKDPC is clearly supporting its government's approach, which continues to be one of severe suppression. Marijuana use, for example, has historically been harshly treated in the U.K. Yet marijuana use there in 2008 was 114 percent higher than in Belgium, whose regime is much less punitive.[24] Uruguay also has a lower rate of use of opiates, cocaine, and marijuana than the U.K., although possession of these drugs has never been prosecuted in Uruguay.

Italy adopted new harsh prison sentences in 1990 and then found that it had the highest rate of problem drug users in the European Union by the early 1990s. Today, high numbers of Italians are still going to prison while drug use rates are among the highest in Europe.

The Netherlands and Portugal are well known as trailblazers in providing for lesser penalties. The former decriminalized marijuana in 1976 and provided for its famous "coffee shops," where people can smoke marijuana with impunity. There was no resulting impact on drug use rates. In fact, hard drug use dropped from 15 percent to 2.5 percent between 1979 and 1994, and most drug harms have been reduced. For example, the Netherlands has low numbers of deaths from heroin and methadone use compared with the rest of the globe. It also has a low prevalence of injecting drug use, and there has been a decrease in the number of young people who become problem offenders. Marijuana and cocaine use rates also fell below those of the United Kingdom during that time.

The Netherlands' approach has not been without its hiccups. As mentioned earlier, there were concerns about the large number of foreigners entering the country to buy marijuana. Friday nights produced long line-ups at the border as people from other countries arrived to purchase their weekend supply of marijuana. One observer claimed that the Netherlands did not actually have a drug problem — it had a parking problem.

As a result, new rules in May 2012 banned foreigners from entering "coffee shops" in the southern provinces of the Netherlands and were to take effect in the whole country on January 1, 2013.[25] Marijuana would then only be available to Dutch residents who registered to obtain a "weed pass." As a result, about half of the Dutch "coffee shops" were promptly forced to close due to the loss of business, and four hundred people lost their jobs.

A newly elected Dutch government then pronounced that each city could decide for itself whether to permit foreign buyers. The city of Maastricht swiftly rejected this option and voted to keep the weed pass. Since then it has foregone about $185 million in revenues as a result. The complaint in that city was that 1.6 million "rowdy foreign youngsters" were a nuisance. Weed passes, though, were also scaring away Dutch customers, so the city eventually relented, and now customers only need local residency papers to buy marijuana in Maastricht.

Amsterdam, meanwhile, remained open for business to foreigners, as have about half of the local authorities in the Netherlands.[26] This is partly because the weed pass restriction led to an "explosion" of illegal street dealing and more aggression on the street. Also police began to crack down on the street trade. This new spate of illegal street dealing and police activity has prompted ten local councils to lobby for the commercial production of marijuana (legalization and regulation) in order to remove organized crime from the equation. And some thirty-five city mayors are calling for the legalization of marijuana.[27]

Portugal decriminalized small amounts of all illegal drugs in 2001 in response to a serious problem of drug abuse. Illegal drugs had been rated in 1997 opinion polls as one of the country's biggest social problems.[28] The new approach provided for diversion to treatment instead of criminal prosecution, as well as for a number of significant improvements to the social welfare system. Twelve years later, polls showed the public judged illegal drugs to be thirteenth on the list of the country's most pressing social problems.

Portugal's "dissuasion boards" are made up of doctors, psychologists, and other specialists. Drug users are diverted to these boards, which are designed to get addicts into treatment and to prevent recreational users from becoming abusers. Fines and community work may be imposed. One of the objectives is to remove the fear and stigma of criminal punishment, which is one of the most debilitating aspects of prohibition.

A recent study by the Home Affairs Committee in the United Kingdom reported that the Portuguese program had resulted in reduced public anxiety about drug use.[29] It noted that the program was supported by all political parties and by the police. The report concluded that the treatment programs were not less expensive to run than the incarceration model, but that society would generally prefer to spend their funds on treatment than on prisons.

Glenn Greenwald lauded the Portuguese program in a 2009 report for the Cato Institute.[30] He proclaimed the program to be a "resounding success" in every way, saying that very few Portuguese would now wish to return to the former system of prohibition. He pointed out that two of the greatest concerns of early opponents had not materialized: there was no rampant increase in drug use by youth, and the country did not become a haven for drug tourists. Drug-related pathologies (overdoses and disease)[31] decreased dramatically under decriminalization, while drug use rates were among the lowest in the European Union, especially when compared with the harshest regimes.[32]

Greenwald found that addicts in Portugal were no longer afraid to seek treatment, because the threat of law enforcement had been removed. There was a 147 percent increase in the numbers of people in drug substitution programs. Greenwald concluded that decriminalization "has enabled the Portuguese government to manage and control the drug problem far better than virtually every other Western country does."[33]

Arguing against the Portuguese model is Dr. Manuel Pinto Coelho, president of the Association for a Drug Free Portugal. Described as "the last great opponent" of Portugal's decriminalization program, Dr. Pinto Coelho wants to return to a tough War on Drugs, with the goal of a drug-free world.[34] He believes that deterrents (like prison) are the best form of prevention, and that cold turkey withdrawal is the best treatment method for addiction. He argues against the methadone program.

Dr. Pinto Coelho travels the world speaking in support of the War on Drugs. A drug warrior outsider in his own country, he is in demand elsewhere in the world. He insists that decriminalization has not worked, and that "there is now in Portugal a trivialisation [of drug use]. It is more trivial than before. I'm not happy with this."[35]

Dr. João Goulão, who is the head of Portugal's national anti-drug program, disagrees with Dr. Pinto Coelho's interpretation of the data.[36] Dr. Goulão maintains that "drug users aren't criminals, they're sick." He says modestly of his very successful program that decriminalization is not "a miracle cure" but it has not made matters worse.

The European Monitoring Centre for Drugs and Drug Addiction (EMCDDA) is located in Lisbon. Frank Zohel works there as an analyst of various approaches to the drug problem. He says that the greatest innovation in drug policy is right outside his door, in Portugal. "This is working," he says. "Drug consumption has not increased severely. There is no mass chaos. For me as an evaluator, that's a very good outcome."

An extensive analysis of the Portuguese case by Dr. C.E. Hughes and Dr. Alex Stevens is in accord with this assessment, providing a more balanced view than any of the others.[37] These authors conclude from the data that there was a slight increase in lifetime drug use (that is, an increase in the number of people who say they have used drugs at least once in their lifetimes). Importantly, though, there was a drop in the number of users between the ages of fifteen and twenty-four from 2001 to 2007. There was also a 50 percent drop in the number of problem drug users and injecting users. Large numbers of drug users went into treatment. HIV rates were down, drug-related deaths were down, and offences and rates of incarceration were down. Some refer to an increased murder rate as evidence that the Portuguese program is not working, but the analysis by Hughes and Stevens shows that the two are unrelated.

Dr. Stevens emphasizes that in addition to decriminalizing the possession of small amounts of drugs, there were other factors that played a significant role in Portugal's success, including the expansion of drug treatment options such as methadone treatment. It also expanded its welfare state and established a guaranteed annual income. Dr. Stevens could find no link between levels of punishment and rates of drug use or drug problems. He did, though, identify a relationship between the rate of drug injection and the availability of welfare state options.

Dr. Stevens notes that since the 2007 recession in Portugal, with funding being removed from social welfare programs, some of the progress made on drug use has been eroded and even reversed. Drug use by children since 2007 is up (although alcohol use is down), and the prison population is creeping up again. Nonetheless, Portugal is now considering going further with its decriminalization regime. It intends to allow marijuana users to grow up to ten plants, and to pool this allowance with other users, as is currently being done in Spain's cannabis clubs.

The kind of austerity program undertaken in Portugal in the wake of the 2008 economic meltdown was also imposed upon Greece by the IMF and the EU. This resulted in an economic crisis that produced countless homeless people, a decrease in incomes of 40 percent, an increase in prostitution and suicides, an HIV epidemic, an increase in crime, and 64 percent youth unemployment.[38] Another result was the appearance of a new "austerity drug" — shisha.

Shisha (not the flavoured tobacco commonly smoked in a hookah) is a type of crystal methamphetamine. It is easy to make and cheap. Ever-responsive to changing conditions, dealers developed this drug for customers who could no longer afford heroin and cocaine. It is much in demand by the depressed and debilitated population, and the product is mixed with everything from battery acid to engine oil and shampoo. The prevalence of this drug is spreading fast, even while austerity budgets have slashed anti-drug and treatment organizations by as much as one-third. Every euro invested in such treatment programs saves the state six euros on health care and criminal justice, but austerity programs tend not to take into account the long view.

Iran is another country where economic hardship has produced a serious drug use problem. Under U.S. and European sanctions, the official youth unemployment rate is 28 percent, and inflation is running at 42 percent per year.[39] These hardships, added to the fact that opium is cheap and readily available, have produced high addiction rates. Iran's own figures show that two million of its people out of seventy-five million are addicted — the highest incidence in the world. Most are using what they call "crack," a cheap, highly addictive derivative of heroin unique to Iran.[40]

Others use the homemade crystal meth, called "shishe" or "glass" in Iran. Funds for outreach and rehabilitation programs have been frozen, largely thanks to current sanctions.

Iran has in some ways been very forward-looking in its handling of drug problems. It provides methadone clinics and needle exchanges, and is making other efforts to tackle drug addiction. The criminal justice system, however, is very severe. Dealers and smugglers are hanged. Some six hundred people were executed for drug offences in 2010.[41] Again, the severity of the law enforcement response does not appear to have reduced the number of problem users in Iran.

There is plenty of evidence that health and social policies need to be central to any discussion of alternative approaches to drug use. It is critical that the discussion not revolve mainly around the availability of criminal sanctions. Those countries that are considering alternatives to the War on Drugs would do well to observe the lessons provided by Portugal, and to avoid the mistake of slashing social programs.

Some of the most determined and radical changes are occurring in Latin America. With statements like "the U.S. provides the arms and we provide the dead," its leaders are rejecting prohibition on a large scale. It remains to be seen whether they have in mind a more holistic approach, as suggested by the Portuguese model, whether they will simply stop criminalizing drug users, or whether they will go all the way and repeal prohibition.

Chapter Nine

Stepping Out in Front: The Americas

Latin America

In recent years, Latin American countries have been among the primary advocates calling for an end to the War on Drugs. There was a time when political leaders waited to retire from office before speaking out on the subject (Cardoso of Brazil, Gaviria of Colombia, and Zedillo and Fox of Mexico).[1] Lately, though, sitting presidents have been vocal. Thus, Felipe Calderón of Mexico was calling for a national debate about legalization even while seventy to eighty thousand people were being tortured and murdered in the drug war under his watch. He said that if the United States was going to continue importing drugs, then it should seek "market alternatives" and "clear points of access other than the border with Mexico." Nonetheless, Calderón completed his six-year term while engaged in a continued vicious war against drug traffickers.

In late 2012, Colombia's president, Juan Manuel Santos, said "If [taking away traffickers' profits] means legalising, and the world thinks that's the solution, I will welcome it." Similarly, a group of Latin American countries jointly declared that if cutting demand is impossible, then consumer countries must "explore all possible alternatives … including regulatory or market options."[2] This would be diplomat-speak for legalization.

Colombia knows a good deal about the War on Drugs. In addition to the murder and mayhem among its competing cartels, there is a coca eradication program being conducted against the nation. The United States has been trying to get farmers to switch from coca to legal crops as part of the anti-drug campaign.[3] However, efforts to get farmers to grow, for example, cocoa as a replacement crop are failing for a number of reasons. Police and growers say that the price of cocoa beans dropped 40 percent in 2012, while the price of coca leaves held steady. Cocoa is bulky and hard to move to market from remote areas, while coca is portable and there are plenty of willing carriers. Guerrilla groups including the Revolutionary Armed Forces (FARC) and crime gangs help farmers pay for coca seeds and fertilizer, and pay cash for the leaves. The likelihood of getting caught by law enforcement is low. And coca can be harvested four times a year, more often than cocoa, making it a more profitable crop. Coffee, oranges, and cotton — all suggested alternative crops — also do not equal coca for profitability. Thus, farmers are making a straightforward economic decision to grow coca leaves.

An aerial spraying program designed to destroy coca crops started in 2001 and continues today. But no matter how much effort is put into eradication, the coca crops always seem to reappear.[4] Although the United States threatens to withdraw all assistance to Colombia under the United States Agency for International Development (USAID), 84 percent of eradicated crops are replanted.[5] Ironically, "there has been a massive increase in production" since the start of the program.

The spraying programs also have shocking repercussions for the environment. A stronger than normal version of Roundup (Roundup SL, which is not approved for use in the United States) is sprayed on the crops with less-than-accurate coverage.[6] It kills almost everything that is green. Peasant farmers claim the glyphosate harms the environment, the livestock, and the people. It also drifts onto legal crops, destroying them, and into neighbouring countries.

Colombia's top human rights official, ombudsman Eduard Cifuentes, says the program should be suspended because it endangers human health and damages the environment. In the summer of 2013, thousands of Colombian peasants were blocking roads, demanding an end to eradication programs.[7] For many, coca is their only source of income. Complicating matters, the FARC is promising peasants assistance in the form of weapons and fighters. The drug trade is a major source of income for both the FARC and the smaller National Liberation Army.

Next door in Bolivia, most of the twenty-eight thousand hectares of coca fields were brought within the law in 2004. State-controlled markets can account for eighteen thousand tonnes of the product.[8] Most of the rest is presumed to end up in the illegal trade, although this is not clear. In 2008, in response to perceived interference, President Evo Morales (who used to be the head of the Chapare coca growers union, and in 2012 negotiated the partial opt-out clause from the 1961 U.N. Convention for traditional use of cocaine) expelled the U.S. ambassador and its DEA officials from the country.

After the 2004 relaxation of cocaine laws in Bolivia, there was a slight increase in supply, which levelled out in 2008 and dropped by 12 percent in 2011 to a level below that of 2004. Bolivians say that this has enabled them to focus law enforcement on organized crime while allowing farmers to go ahead and earn a living. The abuses that were part of the military-led eradication programs of the 1990s have been reduced. At the same time, in 2011, Bolivian authorities destroyed more than five thousand cocaine processing factories (five times more than a decade earlier), thus demonstrating a genuine intention to fight the cartels.

In Guatemala, President Otto Pérez Molina is another current leader looking for alternatives. He is a former general who campaigned for office promising an "iron fist" against crime.[9] More recently, though, he has been advocating for the decriminalization of drug trafficking (not just drug possession), saying "you would get rid of money-laundering, smuggling, arms-trafficking and corruption." He wants to see global legalization and regulation of all drugs, from hashish to heroin, with strict controls.

Costa Rica's leaders have also called for a debate about legalization.[10] Meanwhile, Brazil and Argentina are considering the decriminalization of personal use of all drugs.

But Uruguay's regime is the most daring in Latin America. While possession of all drugs for personal use has never been a crime in that country, it has just legalized marijuana completely. President José Mujica backed the recently adopted legislation.[11] He is a seventy-eight-year-old former guerrilla who spent many years in prison, and has been described paradoxically as both "leftist" and "neoliberalism's booster-in-chief."[12] He says that "nowhere in the world has repression yielded results [in the War on Drugs].... We know we are embarking on a cutting edge experiment for the whole world."

The congressman who drafted the Uruguayan legislation legalizing marijuana, Sabastian Sabini, says simply of the War on Drugs: "The U.S. provides the arms and we provide the dead."[13] Sixty-three percent of the Uruguayan public still opposes the law,[14] but education is ongoing and has been undertaken by a group of non-profits, assisted by the U.S. Drug Policy Alliance (DPA). George Soros's Open Society Foundation also helped fund the media campaign. Other countries considering legalizing marijuana include Jamaica, Chile, and Trinidad and Tobago.[15]

Peru appears to be bucking the trend in Latin America. It is now the largest cocaine exporter,[16] and when Ollanta Humala became president in 2011, his first anti-drugs chief announced a "surprise suspension" of coca eradication efforts. Unfortunately, he did so without proposing any replacement policies. He was summarily fired and replaced by someone who had previously worked for an anti-drug organization funded by the United States. There are no current calls at an official level for decriminalization of drugs in Peru.

Among the countries closely watching the experiment in Uruguay and the conversation throughout Latin America is Mexico. There has been so much violence in Mexico because of the drug war that it is seeking alternative approaches.[17] Ciudad Juarez, for example, was one of the most notorious border towns, with a shockingly high murder rate.[18] The number of homicides, though, has fallen dramatically in the wake of additional federal expenditures on security and social development ($390 million in 2010 and 2011). Jobs are seen to be key, and the city is now held up as a model by the federal government. On the other hand, there are those who claim that all is explained by a deal that was struck between the cartels. "There was an informal agreement [among the cartels] to reduce violence, because it attracts the attention of the media, the military and the [U.S.] Drug Enforcement Agency," says the head of an NGO called the Binational Centre for Human Rights.

Mexico's new president, Enrique Peña Nieto, has responded to the carnage by promising to add forty thousand soldiers to his federal police force.[19] However, widespread corruption hampers the War on Drugs.

Poorly paid police, mayors, and others find the huge revenues too tempting. Although the prison system is straining at the seams, the drug trade continues virtually unimpeded. "As long as America imports billions of dollars-worth of drugs that it simultaneously insists must remain illegal, Mexico's gigantic criminal economy is unlikely to disappear," says one commentator. One analyst says "countless 'legal' businesses here, in the U.S., and elsewhere are doing business with the cartels. Cartels patronize hotels, restaurants, clubs, casinos, race-tracks, malls, a slew of businesses, including agro-industry and high-end real estate. All are laundering cartel money with the government protection. And a mere fraction have been prosecuted.... Chinese firms do business with the Knights Templar [a cartel], buying huge shipments of iron ore from cartel controlled mines. In return it sells them precursor chemicals for crystal meth and cocaine."[20]

Aside from the infusion of fresh troops, it is not yet clear what position the new president will finally adopt. American officials have expressed concern that Peña Nieto's government, having learned how deeply embedded American agents were in Mexico's War on Drugs under Calderón, will begin to rein in its anti-drug co-operation with the United States.[21]

What we do know is that a large portion of the illegal revenues flowing to drug cartels in Mexico come from the marijuana trade. These gangsters supply between 40 percent and 70 percent of America's marijuana.[22] The profits are in the order of two billion dollars, according to The Mexican Institute for Competitiveness (IMCO), a Mexico City think tank. Cocaine profits provide another $2.4 billion. Now that Colorado and Washington have legalized marijuana, it is estimated that Mexicans could lose up to three-quarters of their American customers.

The possession of small amounts of all drugs has been legal throughout Mexico since 2009.[23] New proposals are being considered by Mexican legislators that would increase the allowed marijuana possession limit to thirty grams from the current five grams.[24] They would also allow stores to sell up to five grams of the drug. In addition, there would be a possibility of defining marijuana as medicinal. Proponents are offering these changes as a way of "draining the black market." While only 16 percent of the Mexican public in a recent poll support the new limits, more than half like the idea of regulated dispensaries. The biggest opponent to any such changes is the Catholic Church.

The United States

In the United States, the glacial speed of reform is beginning to increase. Vermont just became the seventeenth state to decriminalize marijuana for personal use, allowing up to one ounce of marijuana or five grams of hash, for which tickets will now be issued.[25] People under the age of twenty-one are to be treated the same way they would be for alcohol use.[26] Vermont's governor says that limited resources should instead be used to reduce abuse and addiction by heroin and methamphetamine users.

Alaska is about to test the proposition of decriminalization at its next election.[27] A ballot initiative will make it legal for adults (over the age of twenty-one) to possess up to one ounce of marijuana, though not in public. It will make Alaska the eighteenth state to decriminalize marijuana.

Washington and Colorado voted unilaterally to legalize marijuana in 2012. Growers and users have been worried about what, if anything, the federal government will decide to do about this, since it still has the last word on whether or not to prosecute. Entrepreneurs who would like to get into the business in Colorado and Washington were understandably afraid to set up shop.

They had reason to be concerned. Although medical marijuana has been legal in twenty-one states for years, the DEA has continued to arrest people who grow or sell marijuana for medical purposes. As recently as July 25, 2013, raids were conducted on a number of medical marijuana dispensaries in Washington State.[28] In the past four years, the DEA has conducted 270 SWAT-style raids on medical marijuana providers in the United States, at a cost of eight million dollars.

In an effort to encourage the federal government to rethink the War on Drugs, the Annual United States Conference of Mayors passed a resolution in 2007 that said, in part, "The U.S. Conference of Mayors believes that the War on Drugs has failed and calls for a New Bottom Line in U.S. drug policy, a public health approach ..."[29] On June 13, 2013, it further recommended that the federal government let states decide marijuana laws for themselves.

Many have looked to President Obama, who has famously admitted to using illegal drugs in the past, to take the lead and allow individual states to proceed with legal regimes. In an interview with Barbara Walters, he had said, "It does not make sense, from a prioritization point of view, for [the] U.S. to focus on recreational drug users in a state that has already said that under state law, that's legal."[30] This was far, however, from a promise not to prosecute. And it was a very timid offering from someone who once said, "The War on Drugs has been an utter failure."[31]

In Colorado, Denver businessperson Kristi Kelly already operates three stores and two indoor grow-ops under the laws allowing for medical marijuana.[32] There are five hundred such businesses in the state. In fact, there are more medical marijuana outlets than liquor stores in Denver.[33] These businesses sold $186 million worth of marijuana in 2012 and provided $5.4 million in sales tax to the state. This is expected to rise to $920 million annually under new legalization laws.[34]

In Kelly's operation, each marijuana plant must be placed under video surveillance and tracked from seed to sale, sometimes by carrying a bar code. She has complied with all regulations, and goes to great lengths to ensure the security of her business.

However, the hurdles presented to people in the medical marijuana business have been many and substantial. Banks would deny Kelly loans, and often they will not even allow operators involved in the business to open an account.[35] Kelly lost four bank accounts in 2012 because the institutions said they could not risk handling her business. She also must pay high rent on her properties because landlords believe her clientele are undesirables and she is not allowed to accept credit cards, forcing it to be a cash-only industry.[36] Kelly spends thousands of dollars on security, with a two-ton safe bolted to the floor in her store containing the marijuana and cash. Because selling medical marijuana is not a legitimate business expense under the tax code, she cannot deduct most expenses. She can't run ads because no outdoor ads are allowed, and the media refuse to get involved.

It also appears that the Internal Revenue Service (IRS) "has been functioning as an arm of justice," using the tax code as a weapon in the War on Drugs.[37] The IRS is using a rule that was aimed at illegal trafficking, resulting in audits and heavy tax bills. It is taxing legal businesses at a rate that drives them out of business by disallowing deductions like rent, payroll, product, and advertising. This may be less glamorous than a DEA raid, but it can be as effective.

Kristi Kelly would like to expand under the new legalization laws to grow and sell marijuana for recreational purposes, but she fears the federal authorities might intervene to seize the substantial sums she has invested in the business and put her in prison. As of January 2014, by state law, outlets have been able to sell marijuana to anyone over the age of twenty-one. Businesses have geared up for this new industry. Everything from equipment suppliers to training facilities are getting ready. In five years, it is expected that the industry will grow by a factor of five. With an expected tax rate of about 15 percent, the state has already earmarked forty million dollars to build new public schools — a number that should rise now that the tax revenues are expected to amount to double the original estimate. Neighbouring states, meanwhile, are worried about the spill-over effect, a concern that has yet to materialize.

The remaining critical question was whether the federal government would decline to prosecute. President Obama says the issue of illegal drugs is not a priority for him, and he has ordered his administration to stop using the phrase "War on Drugs." He says the conversation is legitimate, but that he personally thinks that legalization is not the answer.[38] He believes the capacity of a large-scale drug trade to dominate if allowed to operate legally without any constraint would be a problem.[39]

Most advocates of legalization agree that a no-holds-barred, without-constraint approach would create problems. In fact, only a few libertarians and strict Chicago-school neo-liberals endorse such a free-market model. Those who advocate a public health approach (including Washington and Colorado) are busy designing regimes with multiple constraints, largely to ensure that no single commercial entity can develop a monopoly.

Despite the uncertainty, brave entrepreneurs are beginning to line up to take advantage of the new legal market.[40] More than forty potential investors met near Wall Street with eighteen startup companies in June 2013, to look into investing in legal marijuana companies — everything from providing security and lighting to storage. Profits will be made by service providers, and the potential for more profits increases as more states begin to legalize the drug. *Bloomberg News* reports that penny stocks related to legalized marijuana have soared since January 1, 2014.[41] Hemp Inc., for example, went up 205 percent to eight cents in three days. The company focuses on industrial hemp for making clothing and camping gear.

On August 12, 2013, a sizable chink in the War-on-Drugs armour appeared when U.S. Attorney General Eric Holder addressed the American Bar Association and announced his plan to reduce the number of drug offenders going to prison.[42] Responding to the alarm created by out-of-control incarceration (and out-of-control prison budgets), he instructed his federal prosecutors to make sure defendants in low-level drug cases would no longer receive the mandatory minimum sentences that are now on the books.

New charging policies will mandate that "low-level, nonviolent drug offenders who have no ties to large-scale organizations, gangs or cartels will no longer be charged with offenses that impose draconian mandatory minimum sentences," Holder said.[43] Specifically, prosecutors are being told not to specify the amount of drugs when drafting indictments (meaning mandatory minimum sentences will not apply) as long as the defendants meet four criteria: they did not use violence or weapons and did not sell to minors; they are not leaders of a criminal organization; they have no significant ties to large-scale gangs or cartels; and they have no significant criminal history.[44]

There is ample room under these criteria for prosecutors to ignore the instructions and continue to prosecute to the full extent of the law as before. How, for example, will they define "significant" ties or a "significant" criminal history? Further, it is unclear how the plan will be enforced and whether the Justice Department will track implementation by the ninety-three U.S. attorneys to hold them accountable.[45] The overall impact of the changes will also be limited on a national scale because federal inmates account for only 14 percent of the nation's 1.6 million prisoners. Nonetheless, Holder's statement represents a sea change in attitude, and is accompanied by language that signals an understanding of the underlying causes of drug use, as well as of the discriminatory ways in which the laws are being applied.

More recently, the Attorney General promised to deal with the banking issue. As noted, banks are currently barred from handling proceeds from marijuana sales (under money-laundering rules) and from issuing credit for marijuana businesses. Sheer pragmatism requires that this be dealt with, since there are public safety issues associated with a regime where marijuana businesses have no choice but to carry huge amounts of cash and have nowhere to deposit the money.

In response to these concerns, guidelines were issued for banks in February 2014.[46] Unfortunately, banks say the guidelines are insufficient as long as marijuana continues to be illegal under federal law. The new rules do not provide immunity from prosecution; rather, they direct prosecutors and regulators "to give priority to cases only where financial institutions have failed to adhere to the guidance." As a sign that not much has really changed, banks will still be expected to file regular "suspicious activity" reports on marijuana businesses.

The U.S. Attorney General is moving forward on drug reforms on a number of fronts. For example, in a major shift of approach, he is proposing to increase the use of drug treatment programs as alternatives to incarceration. In this, he is taking a page from conservative states like Texas and Arkansas. These states acted in response to runaway prison expenses by implementing alternatives to incarceration, expanding job training and re-entry programs, and offering drug treatment. By implementing such social programs while reducing the amount of incarceration, these states are mirroring the highly successful Portuguese model. It appears that by pursuing both objectives at the same time, positive results can be obtained.

A bipartisan approach, which has been sorely lacking in U.S. politics of late, has also begun to move this file forward. The conservative Right on Crime group (including Jeb Bush, Ed Meese, and Newt Gingrich) is now working together with the progressive American Civil Liberties Union in an effort to achieve significant change.[47] This is a very positive development that deserves to be supported.

INTERNATIONAL MOMENTUM FOR CHANGE

A study by the Latin American Commission on Drugs and Democracy in 2009 identified major problems with the status quo of drug prohibition.[48] These were: the development of parallel powers in susceptible nations, the criminalization of political conflicts, the corruption of public life (especially police, justice, and penitentiary systems), the alienation of youth (especially the poor), and the dislocation of farmers and stigmatization of traditional cultures.

In 2013, the Organization of American States (OAS) gave serious consideration to drug policy and produced a study that proposes several possible scenarios, none of which recommends the status quo of prohibition.[49] José Miguel Insulza, secretary-general of the OAS, has called for a shift from repression to an emphasis on citizen security. He would like to see an experiment with regulations designed to strengthen community resilience and reduce the possibility of creating narco-states. Insulza says we should be treating drug users for their medical problems, and not putting them in prison, which "can aggravate their condition even beyond the point of no return."[50] And unlike many such studies, the report carefully distinguishes between decriminalization and legalization. The OAS study notes that the experiments with decriminalization now underway in various countries around the world, "rather than causing problems as predicted by their critics..., are generating positive and measurable results."

Experts say that this new report "puts Europe and North America on notice that the current situation will change, with or without them."[51] The report is "seen in some quarters as the beginning of the end for blanket prohibition," and it has been called an "historic moment." Whether it is or not will depend upon whether the OAS is prepared to act upon these recommendations in the face of expected fierce opposition by the United States and the U.N.

In a letter approving of the OAS approach, several members of the Global Commission on Drug Policy say that "leaders across the Americas need to take this study seriously and consider how their own policies can be improved. In doing so, they will be breaking the vicious cycle of violence, corruption, and overcrowded prisons and will put people's health and security first."[52] The Global Commission recommended in a 2012 report that leaders need to replace the criminalization of drug use with a public health approach while experimenting with models of legal regulation designed to undermine the power of organized crime.[53] The list of commissioners of the Global Commission reads like a who's who of expertise in drug policy, human rights, economics, and HIV/AIDS issues. They include former U.N. High Commissioner for Human Rights and Supreme Court of Canada Justice Louise Arbour, former U.S. Secretary of State George P. Shultz, former Chair of the U.S. Federal Reserve Paul Volcker, and several former heads of state.

This commission is a force to be reckoned with, and it has come down firmly and unequivocally on the side of replacing criminalization with a public health model. Together with the OAS, the Global Commission has gone further in the direction of a consideration of legalization than any previous international organization.

Up to now, states that have tried to end the War on Drugs have not done more than decriminalize. They have tended to balk at the idea of legalization (with the remarkable exceptions of Washington, Colorado, and Uruguay). The tension between these two approaches — decriminalization and legalization — is palpable. Arguments both against and in favour are discussed in the next chapter.

Chapter Ten

Prohibition, "Prohibition Lite," or Legalization?

There are two main responses to the War on Drugs in the twenty-first century. One is to remain with the status quo, which is full prohibition and criminalization. This will perpetuate the situation we find ourselves in today, with no end to the War on Drugs in sight, and no achievements to show for the continued costs, both human and financial. The second is to repeal prohibition and adopt a model that allows governments to control and regulate the trade in those drugs that are currently illegal. The latter accepts that the goal of a drug-free world is unattainable, and argues that legalization will remove control from organized crime, with the many benefits this entails. The word *legalization*, though, excites such a visceral reaction that many advocates avoid it, preferring instead to refer to a "controlled and regulated" regime.

The option people think of as a third possibility — decriminalization — is in fact a variation on prohibition. Decriminalization leaves criminal sanctions in place for traffickers and producers, and also for many users.[1] This necessarily perpetuates all of the negative consequences of full prohibition: dangerous products, criminal records for many, easy access by everyone (including children), and the continued violence and corruption of organized crime. This is nonetheless the option chosen by many states, and it does achieve some positive results, with fewer people imprisoned and more users seeking treatment. It will not, however, end the War on Drugs.

Let's take a closer look at all three options.

THE STATUS QUO: FULL PROHIBITION

Continuing with the status quo of prohibition, while increasing law enforcement and providing more education, prevention, and treatment is the first option I will explore. In a recent book setting out the arguments for and against marijuana legalization, Jonathan P. Caulkins et al. cover the issues.[2] *Marijuana Legalization: What Everyone Needs to Know* is mostly dismissive of the idea of legalization, yet at the end, each of the authors states his or her own conclusions, and none of them is in support of full, unqualified prohibition. Ironically, two of the four authors are now working as advisers to Washington State as it designs a new legal marijuana regime.

The authors claim marijuana might be a gateway drug and it might or might not have therapeutic value. They say prohibition drives drug use down, and legalization would result in a doubling or tripling in numbers of marijuana users. They provide no evidence for these assertions, while ignoring reliable research that clearly refutes these claims.

The authors engage in fearmongering — a common tactic of those opposed to legalization — implying, for example, that parenting is negatively affected by marijuana use (even though they admit it might mean parents use less alcohol and tobacco).[3] They imply that legalization means no regulation, which is certainly not the case, and they choose mostly to ignore the debilitating and violent influence of organized crime in a prohibition regime.

The book dismisses evidence from the 1920s that alcohol prohibition was a violent and dismal failure, when organized crime was rampant, people died from drinking homemade alcohol, and none of the expected benefits emerged (like gains in productivity or reduced absenteeism). Many experts have recorded the extraordinary negative effects of alcohol prohibition, and many contemporaries agreed. Albert Einstein, for example, said, "The prestige of government has undoubtedly been lowered considerably by the Prohibition Law. For nothing is more destructive of respect for the government and the law of the land than passing laws which cannot be enforced. It is an open secret that the dangerous increase of crime in this country is closely connected with this."[4]

The authors of *Marijuana Legalization* are also not swayed by the fact that thousands of Americans would no longer be incarcerated if marijuana were legalized. They say legalization would not reduce the 860,000 arrests per year to zero, which is true but hardly the point. Thousands of people would avoid criminal records, millions of dollars would be saved, and public safety would not have been jeopardized.

Perhaps worst of all, the authors fall back upon moralizing, saying things like, "I think the majority who would use [marijuana] responsibly ought to be willing to give up their fun to protect the minority who would not," and "In a free society there are plenty of other ways to have fun without insisting on a right to use something that becomes a stumbling block for others."

The four authors of this book are recognized experts in their fields. The text itself belies the conclusions that are reached by each of the authors at the very end of the book. One of them would vote for legalization in the name of "rational, consistent and fair" laws. One would decriminalize and allow home growing and sharing. One would permit production and use through small not-for-profit co-operatives, with a ban on commerce. And the fourth prefers an incremental approach to some version of decriminalization that would stop short of full commercialization. And as noted, two of the authors — Caulkins and Kleiman — are now working as advisers to Washington State as it forges a new regime to legalize marijuana.

How to explain, then, the unaccountable skewing of the more general argument about legalization? The book presents a good example of the contortions involved in bolstering a broken, unworkable model like prohibition. Billed as a non-partisan discussion, it mostly trivializes arguments for legalization while adopting a tone of disrespect and even contempt for such a model.

This dismissive tone and lack of serious analysis characterizes the position of many opponents of legalization. David Brooks, a highly respected commentator, wrote of his experience with marijuana as a youth.[5] Saying Colorado and Washington will produce more users because the price will drop, and completely ignoring the element of organized crime, he adopts a moral tone: "I'd say that in healthy societies government wants to subtly tip the scale to favor temperate, prudent, self-governing citizenship. In those societies, government subtly encourages the highest pleasures, like enjoying the arts or being in nature, and discourages lesser pleasures, like being stoned."

He goes further, saying that these two states are "nurturing a moral ecology in which it is a bit harder to be the sort of person most of us want to be."

This is all very high-minded, but what is missing is any sense that the extreme coercion implicit in any system of prohibition is harmful in itself. As well, there is no recognition that an individual's right to his or her own type of recreation should not be criminalized when it does no harm to others. Raising the discussion to a higher level will necessarily require that we consider all of these factors.

"Prohibition Lite" (Decriminalization)

At the risk of repetition: decriminalization means that everything continues to be prohibited, but individual users may no longer suffer prosecution and become saddled with a criminal record. They are still, though, compelled to buy their drugs from criminals (traffickers), and to carefully monitor the amount of drugs they possess at any one time lest they be arrested for the criminal offence of possessing too much. Significantly, the default position in the event of failure to comply with any ticket or fine is still criminal prosecution. Users continue to be exposed to the health risks posed by an uncontrolled market and to the violence of black marketeers. Organized crime is in control of the industry and billions are spent by law enforcement fighting gangsters. Under decriminalization models, billions in profits are the gift that keeps giving to cartels, gangs, and mafias. Prohibition permeates the model. Decriminalization is Prohibition Lite.

Having pointed out the negatives involved in decriminalization, in the opinions of many observers, such regimes have produced certain welcome improvements (for example, fewer incarcerations and fewer criminal records). Despite the generally positive perception of experiments like that of Portugal, though, many remain unconvinced of the usefulness of decriminalization either in and of itself, or as a step on the way to legalization.

A trio of respected experts has taken this position, saying that decriminalization as an interim measure is not sensible. Senator Pierre Claude Nolin, who chaired the Canadian Senate Committee recommending legalization, says decriminalization is not the route to go because "We're kidding ourselves with decriminalization, because we're keeping [marijuana] illegal."[6] Canadian activist David Malmo-Levine says that "decriminalization is worse than nothing at all." Directly addressing the perceived positive results of fewer incarcerations and criminal records, he says, "Harmless people don't need to be harmed less, they need to stop being harmed."[7] The only way to achieve this is to legalize. Mark Kleiman, drug guru in Washington State, agrees.

Nonetheless, decriminalization appears to be the preferred route internationally. The United Nations Office on Drugs and Crime (UNODC) in 2009 effectively endorsed the decriminalization of all drugs in its document *From Coercion to Cohesion: Treating Drug Dependence Through Health Care, Not Punishment.*[8] For the first time since 1961, the U.N. said that "treatment, rehabilitation, social reintegration and aftercare should be considered" as an alternative to criminal sanctions. It suggested ways in which this could be achieved without impinging on human rights and without contravening international conventions. Once again, the emphasis was upon decriminalizing drug use and possession as opposed to tackling the larger issues surrounding the black market in illegal drugs.

The UNODC document is very specific about how to decriminalize the use of drugs. It recommends that drug users be diverted from the criminal justice system if they consent to treatment, but if they withdraw at any time, it suggests they may be returned to face criminal sanctions. The report sets out in detail the clinical requirements for such treatment, and recommends that other forms of social support for basic needs should be provided. However, the hammer of the criminal justice system still hangs over this system. Thus, the UNODC approach represents the least possible deviation from the current model of prohibition. Also, there are serious human rights issues surrounding a system that coerces drug users into treatment rather than encouraging them to take this step voluntarily. Some of the rights commonly forfeited by those in treatment include the right to plead not guilty, the right to be secure from unreasonable search and seizure, and the right to confidentiality.[9]

Human rights abuses in the War on Drugs are becoming a focus of attention. Former president of Brazil Fernando Henrique Cardoso and former president of Switzerland Ruth Dreifuss write that by dehumanizing drug users, we make these abuses possible.[10] In a statement that pulls no punches, they say that human rights abuses are "an inevitable result of what governments do when they set repressive and unrealistic goals to eliminate supply and demand for widely available commodities and exhibit zero tolerance for human behaviour." They cite imprisonment, violent punishments, hanging, shooting, and beheading, as well as beatings and abuse to obtain information. They also draw attention to abuses in so-called treatment centres and denial of life-saving medicines as some of the currently practised abuses of human rights.

Cardoso and Dreifuss specifically indict the United Nations for its complicity in these abuses. They say that the International Narcotics Control Board (INCB) has refused to condemn torture or "any atrocity" carried out in the name of drug control. The U.N. Committee against Torture has also failed to condemn widespread abuse of drug users in the Russian Federation, one of the prime offenders: "In Russia, drug users are routinely cramped in large numbers in one room in woeful conditions, with inadequate food, often tied to beds for periods of up to 24 hours. Those singled out as troublemakers are injected with haloperidol, which causes muscular spasms and spinal pain, and often are tortured and beaten to force confessions. Requests for medical assistance often result in more beatings."

While tolerating such abuses, the Russian government continues, inexcusably, to prohibit the prescription of oral methadone to people who are injecting heroin or other opioids, fueling the HIV epidemic and risks of overdose.

It is encouraging that the United Nations General Assembly is planning a Special Session on Drugs to be held in 2016. No doubt the human rights record of participating nations and of the U.N. itself will come under scrutiny at that meeting.

One of the nations most dedicated to fighting the War on Drugs is the United Kingdom. All recent advice to the government to consider alternatives has been summarily rejected. A 2012 report from the UKDPC (the *Runciman Report*) reviewed the socio-economic underpinnings for drug use in great detail, and then offered modest recommendations for change.[11] It suggested that possession of small amounts of all illegal drugs should be dealt with by means of civil penalties rather than criminal sanctions. Trafficking and major production of drugs should continue to be the subject of criminal charges, with the possible exception of marijuana. It suggested lesser sanctions for those who were growing marijuana for their own use, but these would still be criminal sanctions. It recommended a review of criminal penalties for all drugs with an idea to lowering sentences. The report said that the focus of any reforms should be on marijuana as a "first step," with careful evaluation and monitoring.

The *Runciman Report* was very disappointing to those who were anxiously awaiting its recommendations. It goes almost no distance toward changing the criminal justice approach to illegal drugs or offering alternative suggestions. Its model of decriminalization is much less than the half-measure adopted by most regimes. Yet despite the timidity of the report, Home Secretary Theresa May rejected its recommendations and ruled out any moves at all toward decriminalization, claiming that marijuana is a gateway drug.[12]

Later in 2012, an extensive report on illegal drugs was tabled by the Home Affairs Committee of the United Kingdom.[13] Its recommendations were equally timorous. Among other things, the report recommended that the government should give "significantly closer consideration" to the Portuguese model, and should also monitor the changes occurring in Washington and Colorado states. In its *Government Response to Drug Report U.K.*, the Home Office was again unequivocal.[14] "This government does not believe there is a case for fundamentally rethinking the U.K.'s approach to drugs," and "the coalition government has no intention of decriminalising drugs."

Celebrities in the United Kingdom are teaming up with experts to encourage the government to decriminalize drug possession.[15] Respected actor Judi Dench, colourful entrepreneur Richard Branson, and pop star Sting have joined with three former police chiefs to promote a petition. It calls for those caught in possession of illegal substances to be fined rather than jailed, and for addicts to be referred for treatment rather than given a criminal record.

Other countries, particularly those with the most to lose from the War on Drugs, have been far more proactive in proposing alternatives. In Mexico, the state of Jalisco has a particular interest in the War on Drugs because its capital city, Guadalajara, is widely believed to be the financial centre of the industry in Mexico. An extraordinary amount of violence has been perpetrated in the area. In response, an important new study from Jalisco's government has just been published.[16]

The book is entitled *Beyond the War on Drugs*, and it contemplates changes within what it calls the "prohibition consensus." It calls for a national effort to deal with the drug problem, including opening the debate about legalization. It recommends bringing to Mexico best practices from other parts of the world, including the Portuguese model. It suggests removing penalties from the consumption of drugs, and preventing and treating problem consumption. It would like to see the government fulfill the letter and spirit of existing public health laws, educate the public about drugs, and, importantly, raise Mexico's voice internationally to revise the prohibitionist consensus.

This detailed strategy represents a giant step in the evolution of a plan to extricate Mexico from the extreme violence and disruption caused by the War on Drugs. It represents a form of decriminalization that the authors recommend should be adopted nationwide. Unfortunately, the Attorney General of Jalisco has asserted his total opposition to any notion of legalizing drugs.[17]

Many proponents describe decriminalization as a "first step" to a gradual opening up of the illegal drugs industry. They understand that allowing organized crime to control the market is not the optimal outcome. Yet, canvassing the many countries that have some form of decriminalization, it is immediately apparent that this "first step" has not yet led to any further liberalization of the laws. This is as true for countries that legislated decriminalization thirty years ago as for those that are just beginning to experiment with it now. It is as though, having taken that "first step," legislators feel that they have satisfied the immediate concerns and have no need to do more. It is easy for apathy to set in when the public is not clamouring for further reforms. It is also easier, if not cheaper, for governments to continue supporting a well-entrenched law enforcement regime than to instruct it to step down altogether.

Legalization — Why and How?

The main benefits of legalization that are not available under prohibition or decriminalization include: the ability to provide safe products; the reduction in incarcerations; and the wresting of control from organized crime. Any number of prominent advocates have recently stepped forward on the subject of full legalization of all drugs.

The United Kingdom, despite its tough prohibitionist stance, has produced its fair share of such advocates. To the dismay of the Labour Party, one of these is Bob Ainsworth, former drugs minister in the Home Office.[18] He has called for the exploration of all policy options, including decriminalizing possession of all drugs and legally regulating their production and supply — in other words, legalization. He was backed in his request for an independent, evidence-based review by a former Conservative Party deputy leader.

Ainsworth stressed that legal regulation would make the world a safer, healthier place, and would "take the trade away from organized criminals and hand it to the control of doctors and pharmacists." He said his time as defence minister with responsibilities in Afghanistan showed him that "the war on drugs creates the very conditions that perpetuate the illegal trade, while undermining international development and security."[19] He said that the War on Drugs had been "nothing short of a disaster," and admitted that he was only now able to express his views because he was no longer on the front bench of government.

In another statement that took the U.K. government by surprise, the former president of the Royal College of Physicians proposed that heroin and cocaine use should be decriminalized.[20] Sir Ian Gilmore said he would like to see "a regulatory framework set up to allow these drugs to be controlled by law.... [The demand for drugs] will be met one way or another, and we have a choice — we can either leave that supply in the hands of the worst possible people — the illegal market controlled by violent criminal profiteers — or we can control it by appropriate authorities in ways that will reduce the harm it causes."[21] It seems clear that the regime he envisioned was in fact legalization.

Some police officers in the U.K. are also calling for the legalization of all drugs. There is the organized advocacy of LEAP, as mentioned, but individual members are also stepping forward. Edward Ellison, former head of Scotland Yard's Anti-Drug Squad says, "I'm determined my children don't get hooked — which is why I want all drugs legalized.... I say legalize drugs because I want to see less drug abuse, not more. And I say legalize drugs because I want to see the criminals put out of business."[22] Mike Barton, Chief Constable of the Durham Constabulary, and thirty-four years a police officer, says that legalization will not turn into a feared "free-for-all,"[23] as many opponents seem to think. He says the War on Drugs is not reducing supply and that Britain could cut off gang incomes by providing access to drugs through, say, the National Health Service.

More detailed is the response of the Police Foundation of the United Kingdom, which sets out the rationale for changing the law on marijuana:[24]

> Our conclusion is that the present law on cannabis produces more harm than it prevents. It is very expensive of the time and resources of the criminal justice system and especially of the police. It inevitably bears more heavily on young people in the streets of inner cities, who are also more likely to be from minority ethnic communities, and as such is inimical to police-community relations. It criminalizes large numbers of otherwise law-abiding, mainly young, people to the detriment of their futures. It has become a proxy for the control of public order; and it inhibits accurate education about the relative risks of different drugs including the risks of cannabis itself.

This eloquent statement provides an insightful and fundamental understanding of the problems presented by prohibition. Unlike many others, the Police Foundation fingers racism and social control as central drivers of current policy. It also recognizes the danger of misleading the public by pursuing efforts at education that lump all drugs together as "bad."

Even the Prison Governors Association of the U.K. has recently called for a "fundamental review of the prohibition-based policy."[25]

Dr. David Nutt points out that there are lots of alternatives to a "free-for-all" of completely unregulated sales. This is what governments profess to be concerned about, whether in the U.K. or the United States or here in Canada. But virtually no one arguing for legalization is recommending anything like an unregulated marketplace. Dr. Nutt lists a number of possible alternatives: making drugs available on prescription; selling drug from pharmacies; licensed sales; licensed premises for consumption on site; and membership-based licensed premises.[26]

The Transform Drug Policy Foundation (TDPF) of the U.K. has provided a detailed blueprint for regulation.[27] The TDPF points out that legalization and regulation do not represent the leap into the dark that many politicians and others fear. Its recommendations for change are based upon existing science, and resemble closely those set out by Dr. Nutt. However, the TDPF goes on to describe in practical terms the mechanics of putting regulations in place. These pragmatic details are what governments will need if they are ever to legalize drugs. They are also the kinds of information that might finally sway skeptics and encourage them to see the advantages of legalization.[28]

Controls on production are an important starting point. The TDPF points out that opiates, cocaine, and marijuana are already in production for purposes of supplying pharmaceutical companies, and for other medical uses, flavourings for drinks, and so on. Thus, industry already has the ability to prepare such pharmaceutical drugs under carefully controlled, strictly regulated production rules. Little or no change to these regimes would be required in order to produce safe supplies of these drugs for a legalized market.

Controls over availability will also be essential. Completely restricting availability, as we do now under prohibition, results in a black market and few if any such controls. Under a legal drug regime, we can control availability in order to achieve particular goals or react to changing circumstances. This allows for flexibility, ensures the market is no longer controlled by criminals, and allows qualified people and institutions to provide the controls under public scrutiny.

To control the drugs themselves, the TDPF recommends making drugs available in standard units. These would vary depending upon the type of drug — risky drugs would be more restricted as to the size of unit. Microtaggants (microscopic traceable identification particles) would ensure that all drugs could be traced, thus making it harder to move drugs into an illegal market.

Prices would have to be carefully managed through taxation or direct price-fixing or both. The main objectives of pricing would be to prevent diversion of the drugs to an illegal market, and to discourage people from abusing drugs.

Drug packaging would follow the same rules as pharmaceutical plain packaging. Packages should be tamper- and child-proof. Full information including effects, risks, and so on should appear on the package, as should the name of the user. On-pack branding or marketing communications should be avoided.

Controlling suppliers and outlets would be essential. There would be a total ban on advertising, promotion, and marketing.[29] The location and density of legal outlets would be strictly controlled, and vendors could be held partly responsible for any incidents resulting from drug use at their premises. Sales to individual users could be limited in volume, and a time delay could be established between the drug order and pickup, to avoid bingeing.

There would be controls over purchasers and end-users. For example, no drugs could be sold to minors. Governments would invest more in education, prevention, and harm reduction efforts, as well as in alternative activities like youth clubs. With respect to adult users, drugs would not be sold to those who are already intoxicated. Vendors might have to witness consumption of some drugs, as they do now for methadone. Users could be required to have a licence to purchase, which they would obtain after passing a test and taking a related training program. Or users could be required to show that they are members of a relevant club or group that provides education and ensures standards of behaviour. Use could be confined to certain locations, as with alcohol consumption.

In implementing this detailed but achievable regime, the TDPF recommends a cautious, phased approach. It is expected that the least risky drugs would be the first in line for a legal framework. A realistic assessment of harms associated with each drug must be undertaken. Importantly, this must ensure a separation of primary harms (those caused by taking the drug) from secondary harms (those caused by the fact that the drug is illegal).

Different levels of government would have responsibility for different aspects of the new regulatory regime. The TDPF suggests that the United

Nations might deal with human rights and trade issues, and be responsible for research and data collection. Individual nations would determine their own policies and frameworks. And local and municipal governments would take care of the details of regulation, licensing, and enforcement.

The TDPF goes on to detail proposed models for the regulation of different drugs, with supporting rationale.[30] Briefly, it suggests that cannabis and opium sale and consumption should be conducted in membership-based, coffee-shop-style licensed premises. Cocaine powder should be sold in licensed pharmacies to licensed/named purchasers. The riskiest drugs (including injectable drugs) that are most associated with problematic use or addiction should be sold by prescription and used in supervised conditions. Lower risk drugs would be sold in a range of licensed sales models.

The TDPF tackles head on the issue of making all drugs legal. It agrees that all drugs have risks, even marijuana. But it argues that the marijuana debate "dominates the wider drugs debate in a way that grossly overstates its importance, and it has become a distraction from more important issues." In fact, it is because drugs are dangerous that they need to be properly regulated. The more dangerous a drug is, "the more imperative it becomes to legally regulate it, and take it out of the hands of criminals." As the organization points out, "We should regulate drugs not because drugs are safe but because they are potentially dangerous. And no drug is made safer when it's sold by gangsters and unregulated dealers."[31]

"But what about crack cocaine?" is the usual rejoinder. As the TDPF points out, it is crucial to move beyond the fantasy that crack cocaine or any other drug problem can be eradicated by criminal justice efforts.[32] People will use crack. We need to consider what we know about interventions that are effective at reducing the harm crack causes.

The TDPF considers crack to be even harder than heroin to deal with, partly because there is no equivalent of methadone for treatment. It says that the simplest option would be for powder cocaine to be sold or prescribed under strict conditions (as it already is in the U.K.). Determined crack users would still be able to create smokable crack from the powder form, but at least they would have a supply of known strength and purity.

It also suggests that legalization could reduce the use of crack cocaine. If crack and powder cocaine were priced similarly, an abuser of crack might stop using the higher intensity drug in favour of a slower high from powder cocaine. Indeed, crack would probably never have been developed in 1984 if it were not for the clampdown on powder cocaine, which sent people looking for a cheap alternative.[33]

In the search for new solutions, another influential science-based organization has weighed in on the types of specific regulations that would be required to operate a legal marijuana regime. The International Centre for Science in Drug Policy (ICSDP) was formed to "conduct and disseminate original scientific research, including systematic reviews and evidence-based drug policy guidelines."[34] Its founders include prominent Canadian advocates Dr. Evan Wood, Dan Werb, Dr. Benedikt Fischer, Dr. Julio Montaner, and Dr. Thomas Kerr.

The ICSDP's *Tools for Debate* document examines marijuana prohibition in the United States, and sets out a prescription for an improved and legal regime. The details are not dissimilar from those of the TDPF. The ICSDP uses as its template the familiar regimes that govern legal substances like alcohol and tobacco. It is careful to acknowledge the shortcomings of these regimes, saying that regulatory controls vary from place to place and often "do not implement optimally health focussed systems." It notes that, in the United States, the interests of the alcohol and tobacco industries "have commonly trumped the public health interests of maintaining high prices, reducing advertising and promotion, and fully incorporating [other effective regulatory controls]."

The controls for legalized marijuana recommended by the ICSDP include issuing permits for marijuana users and establishing age restrictions. They suggest conditional licensing systems for marijuana dispensaries based on adherence to regulatory guidelines. There would be restrictions on driving or operating machinery while intoxicated. Hours of sale and outlet density would be under restrictions. Regulations would restrict bulk sales and limit potency, and would control the location or circumstances of use. There would be a strict prohibition of marketing and product branding to avoid promotion of marijuana use. With respect to packaging, there would be standard labelling on content containing factual health warnings and the packages would be tamper-proof. Prices would be kept high enough to limit use, but low enough to avoid creating a new illegal market.

Many other thoughtful observers have weighed in on how best to implement new legal systems. Pulitzer Prize–winning journalist Bill Keller is one of these.[35] He notes that states with legal medical marijuana programs have not seen an increase in use by teenagers, and that in order to maintain this level of control, it will be necessary to prevent the takeover of the industry by a few big corporations. Corporations like tobacco companies are obliged to produce profits for their shareholders, and thus they will be pushing for people to use more, rather than less, of the product on offer if they are given a free pass to take over the marijuana industry.

Keller thus recommends a model similar to that of the wine industry, with many producers, none of them dominant. This will require limiting the size of licensed purveyors, which will excite howls of protestations from Big Tobacco, but will be essential. In addition to allowing individuals to grow a few marijuana plants at home, Keller recommends a number of regulations with respect to the commercial industry: certifying laboratories to test for potency and contamination (to detect pesticides, moulds, salmonella); establishing rules on labelling; providing inspectors; limiting advertising; having the same regulations for all aspects of the industry, including pot pastries, candies, beverages, lozenges, ice cream, and vapour inhalers.

Keller acknowledges that it will be difficult to determine a tax rate that will discourage the black market, and perhaps difficult to determine how the tax revenues should be shared. He also says there needs to be more research on the subject of drugged driving.

Many of these suggestions have been adopted by the two new legal marijuana jurisdictions in the United States. The one significant difference in Colorado from the Washington regime is that adults will be allowed to grow up to six plants for personal use. (Washington voters did not approve of home production.) Comprehensive regulations deal with every aspect of production, distribution, and use.[36] Colorado adults over the age of twenty-one may purchase up to one ounce of recreational marijuana from specialty licensed retail shops. In an effort to reduce interstate trafficking, visitors to Colorado are limited to buying a quarter-ounce in a single transaction. (Adults can still legally possess a full ounce, whether residents or not.) Coloradans may also grow up to six plants for their own personal use. Only three of these can be flowering at one time.

Seed-to-sale tracking has been established for the commercial industry. Only Colorado residents can own or invest in retail stores and licensees will need to have been Colorado residents for two years. (This is in response to fears that Colorado might become a production destination for criminal drug cartels.) The first such stores opened on January 1, 2014, with much fanfare and few problems.

For the first nine months, only existing medical marijuana dispensaries may apply for the recreational sales licence in Colorado. Retailers must label all products with warning labels, serving size, and THC potency. Cities may not open marijuana shops, and local and county governments may ban retail pot sales if they wish. Marijuana collectives that might sell the product tax-free and cheaper to members are banned. Private marijuana clubs that allow communal pot smoking will not be exempt from clean air laws.

Marijuana magazines must be displayed behind counters, and children will be protected from the trade. There will be a new crime of sharing marijuana with persons under the age of twenty-one. There will be child-proof packaging, and a ban on certain types of marketing designed to appeal to children.

Taxes are proposed, but these must still be voted on in 2014. A 15 percent excise tax and a 10 percent sales tax are being recommended. The first $40 million raised from the 15 percent excise tax will go to school construction, and some of the taxes will go to education campaigns to convince young people not to use marijuana. State officials have said that the cost to the state of enforcing recreational marijuana regulations will not be greater than thirty million dollars annually, so that a proposed combined tax of 25 percent will yield more than sixty million dollars to the state. As noted earlier, these figures will be revised (upward) now that the tax revenues are expected to approach $150 million in the first year.

In an effort to deal with concerns about impaired driving, Colorado passed a controversial measure that sets the THC-blood limit for drivers at five nanograms. Drivers will be ticketed as they would for alcohol impairment, but will have the option to prove they are not in fact impaired. Many argue that the five-nanogram limit is too low for frequent pot smokers (such as marijuana patients), who would effectively lose their driving privileges for good. Meanwhile, Dr. Nutt of the U.K. says that the U.S. states with legal medical marijuana actually have fewer deaths on the road.[37] His data show that drivers with alcohol in their blood cause ten times more fatal crashes than those with marijuana in their blood. As for nanogram limits, it is known that the active ingredient in marijuana (THC) remains in the body long after use. Thus, people who have not been using marijuana recently enough to be impaired will still be prosecuted.[38]

A recent study of U.S. federal crash data shows that after adjusting for demographics and the presence of alcohol, marijuana use did not statistically increase the risk of a car crash. While drunk drivers tend to drive faster than normal and to overestimate their skills, stoned drivers drive more slowly and underestimate their skills. Also, while most marijuana users light up at home, most drinkers go out to drink, driving cars to and from the venue.

In Washington State, the Liquor Control Board (LCB) was charged with setting up the new marijuana industry rules.[39] The LCB envisages three different licences — grower, processor, and retailer. Legal marijuana should be available in shops by the spring of 2014.

To arrive at the first draft rules, the LCB conducted hundreds of hours of research, held consultations with industry experts, and received input from more than three thousand individuals who attended state-wide forums. Some of the key elements included regulations about licence requirements for vendors. Applicants and financiers would provide background checks, including criminal history and fingerprints. An applicant could be disqualified according to a point system similar to that employed for (sale of) liquor infractions. (Two misdemeanor convictions for possession within three years would not disqualify an applicant.) Licences would cost one thousand dollars plus the application fee of $250. The number of retail outlets would be limited, but growers and producers would not be limited as to either number or size.[40]

With respect to public safety issues, Washington said that producers may grow marijuana indoors or in greenhouses. Strong traceability software would be employed from start to sale. There would be a strict tiered system of violation penalties, similar to that for liquor infractions. On-site surveillance systems would be required. Advertising within a thousand feet of schools, public parks, transit centres, arcades, and other areas where children are present would be banned. There are additional restrictions on advertising directed at children.

As to consumer safety, packages would be held behind the counter, and there would be no open containers. There would be package and label requirements (so consumers would know the contents and potency of the product). There would be defined serving sizes equal to ten milligrams of THC and products would be limited to one hundred milligrams. Independent accredited laboratories would ensure uniform testing standards.

A critique of the proposed Washington regulations was provided by a law firm with some experience in marijuana reform. The lawyers noted that hashish would not be allowed for sale at retail stores unless it was infused in another product. Thus, sales of hash would still be illegal, and the black market would not have been eliminated. They were also concerned that fingerprints of anyone with an interest in the industry, including financiers, would be sent to the FBI. Since the federal government still regards marijuana as illegal, this regulation would require potential interested parties to incriminate themselves and expose themselves to prosecution. And finally, the regulations did not allow for outdoor grow operations. But growing outdoors, they said, is less expensive, while forcing everyone indoors increases energy consumption.

Other interested parties also weighed in on the proposed regulations. For example, organizations concerned primarily with prevention, treatment, and public health argued for tighter restrictions on packaging, labelling, and advertising. They also urged shorter hours for retail outlets. Meanwhile, minority groups urged the LCB to take steps to ensure that their communities do not become dumping grounds for marijuana retail outlets.

The National Organization for the Reform of Marijuana Laws (NORML) requested that, when it comes to growing marijuana, priority be given to individuals who are willing to grow ninety-nine or fewer plants, since federal mandatory minimum sentences apply to grow-ops of one hundred plants or more. Also, federal enforcement authorities are not as likely to target smaller growers.

Diversion — having the industry spread illegally beyond the borders of the state — is a large concern for both Washington and Colorado. Washington proposes to allow people to buy an ounce of marijuana at a time, whether they are residents or visitors. Thus, visitors could go from shop to shop buying an ounce at a time, but this would not necessarily result in diversion. As lawyer Rachel Kurtz points out, "Economically, it just doesn't make sense. If someone from North Dakota wants to sell pot there, they could come here, but they would be paying full retail and having to go to a bunch of stores, and they wouldn't have much of a profit margin paying retail. Or they could just grow some in their basement in North Dakota."

Diversion from cultivation sites is more of a concern, Kurtz agrees, but she says that security measures combined with grower self-interest should limit this problem. The regulations will require record-keeping, security cameras, and product quarantines, for example. More importantly, though, people will be investing a lot of money in marijuana as a legitimate business. They will hardly be tempted to jeopardize their licences in order to sell to the black market.

Importantly for those embroiled in the debate about marijuana use by youngsters, Children Alliance's Jon Gould is supportive of legalization. He says prohibition "has had damaging effects on children and families." The disproportionate enforcement of marijuana laws on African-Americans and communities of culture are of particular concern to his organization. He stresses the importance of creating a competitive industry, where profits can be made, but where public health and children's concerns will be placed first and profiteering will be discouraged.

In July 2013, the new version of Washington's proposed regulations in response to the expressed concerns was released.[41] Outdoor grow-ops will be allowed as long as they are fenced and have security cameras and alarm systems. Outlets can sell highly potent marijuana extracts like hash as long as they are adulterated with some inert substance such as vegetable oil. Finally, baked goods can now be purchased up to a weight of one pound, and beverages up to four and a half pounds.

In this careful, evolutionary process of creating a safe and sensible regime for legal marijuana, lawmakers have worked hard to accommodate the concerns of the citizenry, and have listened to the experts in designing the rules. Mark Kleiman has been a central player in the Washington process. A drug policy expert at UCLA (and one of the authors of *Marijuana Legalization*), he was opposed to marijuana legalization in 2002 because he felt it would result in much more consumption. His concern was mainly for youth and heavy users, who could be harmed by the drug. While he was prepared to agree that possession by adults for personal use was sensible, he did not agree with the idea of full legalization.

Today, though, Kleiman is referred to by some as the "pot czar" and he promotes minimizing harm by creating a well-regulated market for marijuana. As leader of the team producing the Washington regulations, he says "At some point you have to say, a law that people don't obey is a bad law." Kleiman saw the challenge in creating an industry like this from scratch. He and his colleagues did not want to repeat the experience of other markets like alcohol, tobacco, and gambling. A large part of the job was to keep industries like Big Tobacco from taking over the marijuana trade. Big Tobacco, says Bill Keller, is "a powerful oligopoly with every incentive to turn us into a nation of stoners." This is something none of the legislators or citizens of Washington State wanted to see. As Kleiman says, they need to "design a system that gets us to 'orderly' without getting us 'way too stoned.'"

The only nation so far to legalize marijuana, Uruguay, has created a similar set of rules.[42] It allows a household to grow up to six marijuana plants and up to 480 grams per year.[43] Co-operatives may grow up to ninety-nine plants, as long as they are not for sale. Private companies can grow the drug, but must sell it to the government, which will then market the marijuana in licensed pharmacies. The state-run Institute for the Regulation and Control of Cannabis will oversee planting, harvesting, and sales. The seeds will be imported by the government, and potency will be controlled. In order to buy the drug, Uruguayans must be registered in a confidential federal registry, must be over eighteen years old, and will be limited to purchases of forty grams per month at a cost of one dollar per gram. By limiting purchases to Uruguayans, the government hopes to stave off a flood of foreigners. The government also believes that if it prices the marijuana correctly, it will be able to keep users from experimenting with harder drugs.

One other nation has passed a law which effectively legalizes and regulates certain drugs. This is New Zealand, which has a problem unique to its geography.[44] Apparently, traffickers are not interested in delivering conventional hard drugs to a population of four million people thousands of miles from the nearest contact point. Thus, people are manufacturing alternatives. The government tried to ban each new designer drug as it emerged, but swiftly realized this was a losing battle.

In the summer of 2013, New Zealand passed a law offering drug designers the chance of getting official approval for their products. They have to prove to the authorities that their products are low risk by subjecting them to clinical trials of about eighteen months (much less than for medicines, because the drugs will be tested only for toxicity, not for efficacy). Drugs that are already banned internationally, like cocaine and marijuana, are not eligible for the program. A new drug may be licensed whether or not it gets people "high." Once licensed, the product may be sold only at authorized shops, without advertising, and not to children.

Clearly, it will be important for New Zealand, like other jurisdictions, to get the details right. It must define "low risk" in a way that does not comprise prohibition by another name. It must determine levels of taxation that do not encourage a black market. These are not weaknesses of the program, though, but are rather its greatest strength. While New Zealand and Uruguay are discussing levels of toxicity and dosage, every other country in the world is leaving these matters to criminals who do not care, and who sell to children.

If anything can be learned from the foregoing, it is that legalizing drugs does not involve a reinvention of the wheel. Experts in Britain, the United States, Uruguay, and elsewhere have worked out the finest details and appear to have thought of every eventuality. These models will be available for observation and emulation by other interested states and nations. It remains to be seen whether there is the political will elsewhere to continue this trend.

Chapter Eleven

The Outlier: Canada

CANADA'S ILLEGAL DRUG TRADE

The international reach of the Canadian illegal drug trade is well illustrated by the following recent account.[1] A billion-dollar empire centred in Montreal involved members of four different branches of organized crime in three countries. According to reports, Alessandro Taloni, a member of Vito Rizzuto's Montreal Mafia, pleaded guilty to being involved in a scheme whereby Canadian high-potency marijuana was smuggled from British Columbia to Quebec, then across the border via the Akwesasne and Kanesatake Mohawk reserves to New York. There it was sold and the money moved to California, where it was used to purchase cocaine from the Sinaloa Cartel of Mexico. The cocaine was then moved on to Canada where it was distributed by Rizzo and Associates, including the Hell's Angels.

The size of the operation was staggering: $5.5 million was seized from one private jet; $2.6 million and eighty-three kilograms of cocaine were seized from Taloni's Mercedes Benz and from various stash houses in Beverly Hills. The Canadian kingpin in charge of the operation, Jimmy Cournoyer, accepted a plea bargain in New York that carries with it a twenty-year mandatory minimum sentence. He also forfeited ten million dollars in seized cash and an additional one billion dollars.

Canadian mobsters are involved in the movement of illegal drugs all over the continent. The RCMP reports that some Canadian gangsters are dealing directly with Mexican cartels, eliminating the middleman in the United States and increasing profits. Between 2008 and 2012, the RCMP say that nine Canadians with extensive criminal records were shot or killed in Mexico, and that there have been more killings in British Columbia related to Mexican cartels.[2]

At the other end of the spectrum of drug criminalization is the recent arrest of a Canadian medical doctor who signed forms permitting his patients to use medical marijuana. Dr. Rob Kamermans came to the attention of the authorities because of the sheer volume of licences that were granted as a result.[3] He has been charged with everything from fraud to forgery to money laundering and attempted trafficking. He was taken from his Coe Hill, Ontario, clinic in handcuffs, leaving the clinic without its only emergency physician on that day. His wife, a nurse, was also charged. Dr. Kamermans could hardly be described as a desperado, but in not-unheard-of overkill, twenty police officers showed up at his clinic to make the arrest.

Dr. Kamermans freely admits that he has been signing the forms that allow his patients access to medical marijuana. He believes marijuana to be safe and effective. He says it has allowed his patients to get off their dependencies on oxycontin, oxycocet, and other painkillers, and has also helped them to treat their pain. Most of his patients are between the ages of forty-five and sixty-five — not stereotypical stoners trying to scam the system.

Dr. Kamermans may not be facing a minimum of twenty years in prison, but he is facing serious consequences. This is true even though he was participating in a legitimate federal program designed to help patients deal with their pain and other symptoms. The consequences to the doctor could very well include prison (attempted trafficking carries a mandatory minimum prison sentence). He may also face discipline from his professional association.

Thus, we have two polar opposites in terms of what activities, and who, come to the attention of Canadian law enforcement in the War on Drugs. On the one hand, there are dangerous and violent members of organized crime; on the other, a physician who is apparently trying to provide good care for his patients. In between these extremes are all those hapless users and sellers of drugs who languish in our prisons. Something is wrong with this picture, and only a serious adjustment to our approach to illegal drugs will rectify the clear disparities and injustices created by our drug laws.

CANADIAN DRUG USE AND PUBLIC OPINION

The Canadian public has been weighing in on this issue and their opinion seems to be seriously at odds with the current federal government's policies. While the Conservatives are taking a very hard line, the Canadian public is adopting a more tolerant attitude. A Forum Research poll from August 2013 showed that 70 percent of Canadians want marijuana to be decriminalized or legalized.[4] About half of these (36 percent) preferred legalization as compared to 34 percent who would choose decriminalization.

A poll by Angus Reid asked a broader question and found that 68 percent of Canadians believe that the War on Drugs is a "failure."[5] Legalization of marijuana was favoured by 57 percent of those polled. In British Columbia, home to a thriving marijuana industry, 75 percent of those polled supported the regulation and taxation of marijuana — in other words, legalization. Only 14 percent now think possession of a joint should lead to a criminal record. With respect to harder drugs, though (cocaine and heroin, for example), support for legalization hovers around only 10 percent.

Canadians are also voting with their feet on marijuana laws. Forty percent of Canadians fifteen years of age and older told a 2011 Health Canada survey that they had smoked marijuana at least once in their lifetime. Canadian children and youth are the heaviest users of marijuana in the developed world. UNICEF, referring to a 2013 WHO survey, found that 28 percent of Canadian children aged eleven, thirteen, and fifteen had tried marijuana in the past twelve months, the highest rate among twenty-nine nations. Health Canada, on the other hand, estimated the number of youth (ages fifteen to twenty-four) who have tried marijuana at only 22 percent, a number confirmed by a survey conducted in Ontario by the Centre for Addiction and Mental Health. Either way, the number is not insignificant.

Liberal leader Justin Trudeau was castigated mercilessly by the governing Conservatives and by the media when he suggested legalization would ensure better control over access by children. It will clearly be impossible to reduce to zero the ability of children to obtain marijuana even under a legal regime with stringent controls. However, if we take tobacco as a comparison, controls like public information campaigns and other aggressive measures have reduced the number of children who smoke. Canadian children have the third-lowest rate of tobacco smokers among twenty-nine developed nations. We did not have to send our children to prison in order to achieve this.

According to UNICEF, in 2006, 4,700 Canadian children between the ages of twelve and seventeen were charged with marijuana offences. About a million and a half Canadians have criminal records for possessing small amounts of marijuana, and we add about fifty thousand more to those numbers every year.[6] UNICEF says that "legal sanctions against young people generally lead to even worse outcomes, not improvements in their lives."[7]

Statistics Canada reports that in 2012, 109,000 drug-related incidents were reported by police.[8] Two-thirds of all drug-related incidents were for marijuana. The number of Canadians arrested for marijuana possession has increased by 41 percent since the Conservatives came into power in 2006.[9] There were more than 405,000 marijuana-related arrests in the first six years of their tenure, about the same number as the combined populations of Regina and Saskatoon. In British Columbia alone, it costs about $10.5 million per year to enforce marijuana possession laws, and this number is expected to increase over the next five years to $18.8 million. These figures do not include the cost of imprisoning more people for longer periods of time under the new mandatory minimum sentences.

The Canadian Centre on Substance Abuse, using Health Canada data, estimates that 94 percent of the cost to society of marijuana comes from the fact that it is illegal.[10] For the year 2002, marijuana-related health costs were twenty dollars per user, but enforcement costs were $325 per user. (Comparable figures for alcohol use were $165 per drinker for health costs and an additional $153 for enforcement. Health-related costs for tobacco users are over eight hundred dollars per user.)

We know that increased suppression does not reduce the supply of illegal drugs or the number of users. It often produces the opposite effect to the one desired, and exacerbates ills from a public health point of view. Despite, or perhaps because of, the crackdown on drugs by the Harper government, there is a growing public interest in finding alternatives to the War on Drugs. This interest in pursuing change began more than forty years ago.

From Le Dain to the Senate Report

In Canada, arguments for legalizing or decriminalizing marijuana have been made at the highest level for decades. In 1972, forty years before Washington and Colorado became the first jurisdictions to vote for legalization, the Le Dain Commission recommended decriminalization for simple possession, for sharing small amounts, and for cultivation of marijuana for personal use. Everything else would attract criminal sanctions.[11]

The publication of the Le Dain Commission report caused a furor.[12] Health Minister John Munro was prepared to implement the recommendations immediately by removing marijuana from the *Criminal Code* and placing it in the *Food and Drug Act*. Unfortunately, he did not consult with the justice minister, John Turner, who was adamantly opposed to any reduction in the use of criminal sanctions to control the drug. The CBC reported that Mr. Turner could "barely contain his wrath."

The report's recommendations also unfortunately coincided in time with the announcement of the War on Drugs by Richard Nixon. Since no Canadian politician wanted to appear "soft on drugs," or do anything to incur the wrath of the United States, the recommendations of the Le Dain Commission were shelved.

There followed thirty years in which no progress was made. Trudeau's government declared in a 1980 speech from the throne, "It is time to eliminate imprisonment for simple possession of marijuana."[13] However, in the wake of tougher laws and enforcement south of the border, and a hardening of opinions at home, Canadian justice officials increased enforcement efforts, sending more drug offenders to prison.

In 1987, under Mulroney's Conservative government, the first drug strategy was launched under the purview of Health Canada.[14] Successive Liberal governments, though, gradually reduced its budget until in 1993 there was no budget at all. By 2001, the government was still claiming a "balanced approach" to illegal drugs, but the Auditor General reported that only 5 percent of the available budget was going to treatment, education, and prevention. The other 95 percent went to law enforcement.[15] Since the Conservatives took power in 2006, and projecting to 2017, most of the available drug strategy funding will continue to be spent on law enforcement.

Parliamentary reports on illegal drugs were produced in 2002. The House of Commons Special Committee on the Non-Medical Use of Drugs presented a number of liberal recommendations.[16] The committee was in favour of substitution treatments (like methadone), needle exchange programs, safe injection sites, drug treatment courts, and more research. It also recommended a form of decriminalization. Possession and cultivation of up to thirty grams of marijuana for personal use should no longer attract a prison sentence. This created division among committee members, with the NDP and Bloc Québécois members saying the recommendations did not go far enough, while the Conservatives rejected all of the recommendations, saying abstinence was the only appropriate goal.

In 2002, the Senate Special Committee on Illegal Drugs also reported its findings on marijuana. This committee was determined to produce a report that relied upon scientific evidence and not what Le Dain had referred to as polemics.

Eugene Oscapella was one of the witnesses before the Senate committee. A founding member of the Canadian Foundation for Drug Policy, he referred scathingly to those who "live off the avails of prohibition."[17] He listed those who profit from the War on Drugs, aside from organized crime: the legal profession, police, politicians, the military, and the prison industry. Oscapella described the reach of organized crime into the political sphere in Canada, and cited the case of a sitting Member of Parliament who had to be put under RCMP protection because drug gangs were threatening him. The MP was refusing to co-operate with their scheme to have farmers in his riding grow marijuana for them.

Oscapella regaled the committee with an extraordinary example of how Canadian tax money is being spent in the War on Drugs. On one occasion, it was discovered in Victoria that heroin was being smuggled into the country inside duck eggs. The inspectors had to crack all 174,000 eggs in order to find the 1,700 that contained the heroin. At this point, police warned merchants that there was about to be an increase in crime because the price of heroin just went up.

Neil Boyd, another well-known expert in drug law, also testified before the committee. He talked about "selective criminalization," and tried to dispel some of the myths about heroin addiction. For example, he said, most people believe that heroin is the hardest drug from which to withdraw. Yet, according to Boyd, prison inmates find it much easier to quit heroin than tobacco, even though both are readily available to them in prison.

After listening to much testimony in the same vein, the Senate Special Committee threw down the gauntlet. Unlike Le Dain, it concluded that there were "basically only two systems: a prohibition system and a legalization system."[18] The senators had come to recognize that any version of decriminalization necessarily included prohibition. This nullified any attempt to remove the element of organized crime and its attendant harms. Thus the Special Committee could see no purpose in recommending anything less than legalization of marijuana and no downside in doing so.

As a first step, the Senate Special Committee recommended that Canada notify the United Nations of its intention to declassify marijuana (making it legal), thus placing Canada at odds with international conventions. The committee was skeptical about public health being central to the conventions' intent, since alcohol and tobacco were never targets of the international community's policy of criminalization.

The committee found that current policies of repression had failed to reduce consumption and supply, and that "police activity has no dissuasive effect on cannabis experimentation by young students." In fact, prohibiting marijuana had "little, if any, influence on levels of use." The committee found no evidence that marijuana use led to the use of other drugs. And when it came to the costs to society, the committee concluded that "we can safely state that criminalization is the principle source of social and economic costs."

The authors said that criminal law was not an appropriate tool to deal with matters of personal choice where others are not harmed: "Even if cannabis were to have serious harmful effects, one would have to question the relevance of using the criminal law to limit these effects."

In keeping with these findings, the committee recommended the outright legalization of marijuana with a regulatory system that would honour five basic principles. It wanted to see law enforcement more effectively target illegal trafficking (for example, selling to children), and to continue working to reduce the role played by organized crime. It wanted to see new programs of prevention, better monitoring of products (for quality and properties), and better information and education for users. It wanted Parliament to respect individual collective freedoms, bringing in legislation more in tune with Canadian behaviour. Behaviour causing harm to others should be strictly prohibited. This would include illegal trafficking (which it emphasized did *not* include sharing an amount of marijuana that could be consumed on a single occasion), selling to minors, and driving while impaired by the drug.

The committee wrote: "It has been maintained that drugs, including cannabis, are not dangerous because they are illegal but rather illegal because they are dangerous." It emphatically rejected this proposition as it relates to marijuana. The members stressed that "current approaches are ineffective and inefficient — it is throwing taxpayers' money down the drain on a crusade that is not warranted by the danger posed by the substance." Yet only a few years later, Prime Minister Harper eerily echoed the Senate when he said that drugs are not "bad" because they are illegal but illegal because they are "bad."[19]

Finally, the Canadian Senate Special Committee boldly rejected the idea of decriminalizing marijuana, calling it the "worst possible scenario." It said:

> In the opinion of some authors, decriminalization is in fact simply less severe prohibition. In other words, in the guise of a socially responsible and rational measure, decriminalization in fact furthers a prohibitionist logic. Same grounds, different form. This model has no greater capacity for prevention or education than a strict prohibition model. Even worse, the prohibition model is based on clear and consistent theory, whereas the same cannot be said of decriminalization as an approach. Some will say that decriminalization is a step in the right direction, one that gives society time to become accustomed to cannabis, to convince opponents that chaos will not result, to adopt effective preventive measures. We believe however that **this approach is in fact the worst-case scenario, depriving the State of a regulatory tool needed in dealing with the entire production, distribution, and consumption network, and delivering a rather hypocritical message at the same time.**
> [Emphasis in the original.]

The Liberal Government's Approach

In the face of an international community and a powerful neighbour dedicated to the harshest treatment of certain drugs, the Senate report was courageous. Its recommendations were taken under consideration by Paul Martin's Liberal government, but its crucial rejection of decriminalization was ignored.

The government proceeded to craft legislation that was designed to please everybody but ended up pleasing no one. Bill C-17 was supposed to offer decriminalization of small amounts of marijuana, while continuing to criminalize trafficking and production, increasing maximum prison sentences. A user would be allowed to possess up to one gram of hash or up to fifteen grams of marijuana. Anything more would result in a prison sentence.

It was swiftly pointed out by advocates of legalization that under this law simple possession of marijuana would continue to be a criminal offence. The promised avoidance of prosecution would only occur if and when the government made it possible for police to issue tickets to users. Once that happened, there would be a net-widening effect (as in Australia). People who in the past were sent home with a warning would now be caught up in the judicial system. Thus, the ultimate and alarming effect of the new legislation would be to create three *new* offences for possession of small amounts of marijuana, as well as to *raise* the maximum sentences for many others.

Critics also said increased enforcement with respect to production would be likely to increase organized crime's hold on the industry rather than reduce it. Drug kingpins do not tend to worry about the likely consequences of getting caught, so they would continue in the trade while others might drop out. It was suggested that the legislation was a response to public perceptions that drug sentences were lenient. Thus, Parliament had chosen to legislate higher maximum sentences while failing to remove simple possession from the ambit of criminal law — the exact opposite of what the Senate had recommended.

Similar legislation produced very negative results in another country — Brazil.[20] In 2006, its new law decriminalized possession of drugs for personal use, but toughened up penalties for trafficking. The distinction between the two was left to the arresting officer. Human rights advocates swiftly condemned the way in which light-skinned yuppies were left in peace while dark-skinned slum dwellers were thrown in jail. Under this law, the number of people held for trafficking increased from 33,000 in 2005 to 138,000 in 2012.

There is another aspect of the Canadian legislation's history that should be noted before moving on. In an unusual move, Canada actually briefed the United States government before tabling Bill C-17. Quite possibly, Canada's relationship with its neighbour explains why this legislation was so strangely at odds with the recommendations of the Senate Special Committee.

American drug czar John Walters pronounced that even Bill C-17 would create problems at the border and would affect trade between the two countries.[21] Ambassador Paul Celucci warned of massive border delays, to which the prime minister retorted, "Canada will make its own laws, pure and simple."[22] Ethan Nadelman, executive director of an American organization, the Drug Policy Alliance, thought there was something else going on. He believed that the United States was opposed because Canada's new law would have shown stricter American laws to be out of touch compared with much of the Western world.[23] In the event, Bill C-17 died on the order paper, so we will never know what effect it would have had upon Canada-U.S. relations.

The Conservative Government's Approach

The Harper government swiftly put paid to any notion of rethinking drug prohibition. It instituted a National Anti-Drug Strategy in 2007, taking leadership for the file away from Health Canada and giving it to Justice, thus signalling its intent to continue pursuing a law enforcement approach. Tony Clement, minister of health at the time, announced these changes by saying, "The party's over." Twelve government departments were to be involved in the strategy. About 70 percent of its considerable budget goes to enforcement.

Budgets for drug treatment, community work, and crime prevention have all been reduced significantly over the years since 2007, even though these programs were proven successes. Harm reduction was specifically removed from the anti-drug strategy (for the first time in twenty years), although it has also been highly successful and has gained acceptance internationally as a well-established health practice. UNODC, UNAIDS, and WHO have all endorsed the importance of harm reduction.[24] As with the international conventions to which Canada is a party, tobacco and alcohol are not part of the mandate of Canada's National Anti-Drug Strategy. Yet the harms caused by these drugs must surely be of concern.

When the Conservatives were elected in 2006, the ministers of public safety (Vic Toews) and justice (Rob Nicholson) moved swiftly to crack down on drug offences. Although in 1988, Mr. Nicholson had been vice-chair of a parliamentary committee that recommended mandatory minimum sentences *not* be used except in the case of repeat violent sexual offenders, as justice minister he immediately moved to implement them for drug offences.[25] The new sentences — which are in effect today — included six months minimum imprisonment for growing a modest six marijuana plants and a one-year minimum for producing any amount of hash oil or resin. Sentences increase considerably under new "aggravating circumstances" and "health and safety" laws, so illegal drug offences now attract much longer sentences across the board.

Many of the sentences are so ill-defined and vague that offenders will clearly be consigned to longer incarceration than is justified. For example, the six months minimum for growing six plants expands to nine months if "the accused used real property that belongs to a third party to commit the offence." This would include a college student growing six plants in her rented apartment or university dormitory. Trafficking or possession-for-the-purpose-of-trafficking marijuana attracts a minimum sentence of two years if the offence occurs "in or near a school, on or near school grounds, or in or near any other public place usually frequented by persons under the age of eighteen years." The definition of "in or near any other public place usually frequented by persons under the age of eighteen years" will be interpreted very widely in some jurisdictions, not so widely in others. In some cities, practically every location will be "near school grounds." Criminal consequences are supposed to be predictable and easily defined. That is the point of the theory of deterrence upon which the Conservative government is relying. Yet predictability and clarity are not features of the new illegal drug regime.

Mandatory minimum sentences also have a distorting effect on the criminal justice system, as police, prosecutors, and judges push the limits of their authority to save some offenders from unjust prison sentences. For example, until the 1980s there was a minimum seven-year sentence for importing drugs. The Prison for Women in Kingston housed a number of young, naïve women who had believed the drug dealer who told them they could have a free vacation in the Caribbean and a bonus to take home — all they had to do was bring in a small amount of soft drugs.

Amber was picked out of the line at the airport coming home from Jamaica, and was found to be wearing a body pack filled with hash. When she made her first appearance in court, she was facing seven years minimum. The Crown immediately made an offer of three years if she would plead guilty to the lesser charge of possession for the purpose of trafficking. There was no haggling involved, the deal was done in a matter of minutes, and Amber went off to prison to learn her lesson.

This deal could probably only have been made because word had come down from the Attorney General's office that the seven-year minimum was to be avoided wherever possible. Crown attorneys were routinely making the same offer to first-timers like Amber. Cutting this kind of deal meant the Crown had to read facts into the record, which were short on details. For example, the fact that Amber was picked up in the international airport was not mentioned. Yet everyone in the courtroom, including the judge, could read between the lines. This is not the way justice is supposed to be done, but it is what happens when bad laws dictate bad results.

In 1987, the seven-year minimum for importing drugs was ruled to be contrary to the Charter of Rights and Freedoms by the Supreme Court of Canada.[26] It said that the arbitrary minimum would "inevitably result, in some cases, in a legislatively ordained grossly disproportionate sentence." It also said that relying upon Crown counsel to deal with the issue was not an appropriate solution.

In response to the blizzard of mandatory minimums legislated by the Harper government, there have been a number of lower court judges ruling them to be unconstitutional. These are currently working their way to the Supreme Court of Canada for adjudication.

In the United States, meanwhile, instructions have just been issued to federal prosecutors by Attorney General Eric Holder. Canada's tough-on-crime neighbour, whom our politicians have been imitating in matters of criminal justice for decades, has just recognized the harm and expense that mandatory minimum sentences have been causing, and has acted upon this knowledge. Prosecutors are no longer to send low-level drug offenders to prison. Mr. Holder expressed a very low opinion of the mandatory minimum sentences that had caused a colossal expansion of the federal prison population and, in his words, "breed disrespect for the system."[27] He went on: "When applied indiscriminately, they do not serve public safety. They have had a disabling effect on communities. And they are ultimately counterproductive." This is a rare condemnation of a system that has been in effect for decades. And it comes from the highest legal authority in the land.

In an astonishing about-face, Mr. Holder talked about being "smarter on crime" as well as "tough on crime." He expressed specific approval of the seventeen states that had directed money away from prison construction and toward programs and services, including treatment and supervision designed to lower the number of re-offenders. Saying that "we cannot simply prosecute or incarcerate our way to becoming a safer nation," he described "a vicious cycle of poverty, criminality and incarceration [that] entraps too many Americans and weakens too many communities. However, many aspects of our criminal justice system may actually exacerbate this problem, rather than alleviate it."

Redefining the purpose of the criminal system in terms that were unheard-of at that level of government, he said, "We need to ensure that incarceration is used to punish, deter and rehabilitate — not merely to convict, warehouse and forget." He pointed to the discriminatory aspect of enforcement priorities, saying "[they] have had a destabilizing effect on particular communities, largely poor and of color."[28] He noted that black male offenders receive sentences nearly 20 percent longer than white offenders convicted of similar crimes. And in a reference to the "root causes" of crime, he said, "We must never stop being tough on crime. But we must also be smart and efficient when battling crime and the conditions and the individual choices that breed it."

This is very strong language, and represents a complete rethinking of the purposes and methods of the American justice system, particularly as it applies to illegal drugs. Couched in this kind of language, the Attorney General seems to be signaling further significant changes to the system in the near future.

What was Canada's response to the Americans' new approach, so different from our own government's tough-on-crime stance? The newly minted justice minister, Peter MacKay, claimed that Canada was actually leading the way and the United States was following. "I'm glad to see that he, to some degree, is moving in the direction that we've already moved," said MacKay,

claiming Canada has moved away from harsher sentences for simple possession of drugs while maintaining very severe penalties for trafficking.

In fact, the Conservative government has never legislated lighter sentences for any criminal offence in their eight years in power. And their new
mandatory minimum sentences for drug offences are very draconian. Mr.
MacKay did not address himself to Mr. Holder's other reforms, including the
early release of some non-violent prisoners, the provision of alternatives to
incarceration, and the drafting of new guidelines to determine when federal
charges should be laid and when they should not, tailored to local conditions.

It is odd that Canada should be so out of step with, of all people, the top
criminal justice authorities in the United States. Mandatory minimum sentences there are being repealed in state after state. The current U.S. drug czar
says they should be reserved for big drug financiers or traffickers.[29] The head
of the U.S. Drug Enforcement Agency met with the House of Commons
public safety committee and urged Canada not to institute mandatory minimum sentences.[30] Rick Perry, governor of the conservative state of Texas,
surprised everyone at the World Economic Forum in Davos, Switzerland, in
January 2014 by supporting a proposal to discuss decriminalization.[31] And
President Obama opined to the *New Yorker* that marijuana was no more
harmful than alcohol. He said, in fact, that marijuana was safer than alcohol
with respect to its impact on the individual user.[32]

Using criminal law and long prison sentences to deal with drug use is not
only counterproductive and inhumane, it is antithetical to stated Canadian
values as they have evolved over the years. In 1969, the *Ouimet Report* said
that "no act should be criminally proscribed where its incidence may be ade-
quately controlled by social forces other than the criminal process."[33] In the
victimless, non-violent world of drug use, whether alcohol or heroin, public
health and other non-criminal-justice models should be recommended.

In a further reiteration of this basic value, the Law Reform Commission
of Canada in 1982 said, "Since many acts may be 'harmful,' and since
society has many other means for controlling or responding to conduct,
criminal law should be used only when the harm caused or threatened
is serious, and when the other, less coercive or less intrusive means do
not work or are inappropriate."[34]

Yet what the Senate Special Committee referred to as a crusade against
drug users, including mass incarceration, continues apace in Canada.

Chapter Twelve

A Popular Groundswell for Change

MARIJUANA

It is clear from the public opinion polls cited that Canadians are ahead of
their government on the subject of reforming marijuana laws. And there
are a number of organizations and individuals in Canada who champion
its legalization and regulation. Marijuana is the least worrisome and most
popular of illegal drugs, and so it is expected to be the first to be dealt with.
As Washington and Colorado and Uruguay break ground, a Canadian
chorus in favour of legalization is growing in numbers and strength.

The Canadian branch of NORML has long been among those arguing
for the change. As a non-profit, public interest, member-operated and
member-funded organization, it was created by a federal charter in 1978.
It argues for the legalization, regulation, and taxation of marijuana. Like
many others, it suggests that an acceptable interim step would be the
decriminalization of possession or production of small amounts.[1]

Much of the activity around reforming the marijuana laws is taking place in British Columbia, where record amounts of the drug are
grown, sold, used, and exported. Sensible B.C. is a group headed by
Dana Larsen that recently failed in its attempt to have a referendum on

decriminalization held at the next provincial election.[2] This referendum would have required the B.C. government to pass a *Sensible Policing Act* ordering police to stop searching and arresting people for simple possession of marijuana. It would also have required the B.C. government to demand a federal repeal of prohibition.

There are those who would argue that this would comprise provincial intrusion into exclusive federal jurisdiction under the constitution (criminal law being a federal matter). Sensible B.C. argues that it is within the province's jurisdiction to take these steps — that it would, in fact, be nothing new for the province to put its own stamp on a federal law.

British Columbia has effectively decriminalized other offences in the past. It was among eight provinces refusing to enforce the federal *Firearms Act*, saying the money would be better spent prosecuting substantive criminal offences.[3] It also replaced the federal impaired driving regime in 2011 with a provincial regulatory scheme. As well, the Vancouver Police Department (VPD) has had a long-standing policy of not laying charges for marijuana possession unless there is a complaint. Since the province has authority over the RCMP in B.C., Larsen argues that its Attorney General could simply instruct the force to adopt the same approach as the VPD. Finally, the province successfully opposed federal efforts to close down InSite. Since health care is in provincial jurisdiction, B.C. could also stand up for the health and safety of the thousands of marijuana users in the province by ordering no further prosecutions.

Another new organization is called Stop the Violence BC. This coalition published a report in 2011 called *Breaking the Silence: Cannabis Prohibition, Organized Crime and Gang Violence in B.C.*[4] It was accompanied by an Angus Reid poll that found 85 percent of those surveyed in B.C. attributed gang violence to drug trafficking, in which groups fight over the profits.[5] The report points out that the profit margins for marijuana are actually higher than for heroin or cocaine. This is because it is grown locally, while the others must be imported. Also, more than 430,000 people in B.C. use marijuana, far more than either of the other drugs. The report concludes that the marijuana industry accounts for a high proportion of drug trade violence. Homicides, drive-by shootings, kidnappings, vicious ordered assaults, extortion, and arson are all part of the drug scene.[6]

Some have argued that regulating marijuana will mean that organized crime will simply move into other more dangerous criminal activities. Stop the Violence BC replies that since marijuana is a "key revenue stream" for gangsters, regulating it will remove their ability to finance other activities. It will "[force] them into activities that are less profitable and more visible to police."

The coalition also addresses concerns about Canada's relationship with the United States. It points out what is by now obvious — that the United States is ahead of Canada on all fronts in the move to regulate marijuana. One state after the other has legalized medical marijuana. One after the other has decriminalized its use. And, since the publication of the coalition's report, two states have fully legalized and regulated the drug.

Stop the Violence BC recommends "a legal market for adult recreational cannabis use, with strict regulatory controls placed upon it." Taking the glamour out of the market is a "key objective" of the organization. Treating all drugs as equivalent by equally prohibiting them has contributed to the failure of the War on Drugs, so treating them all as equivalent when it comes to legalization would also fail. Thus the coalition says there need to be "unique strategies ... individually tailored" to other drugs such as heroin and cocaine. In this respect, the coalition is on the same page with the U.K.'s TDPF, and with experts like Dr. Nutt and Neil Boyd.

This B.C. coalition provides a coherent, evidence-based argument for the regulation of marijuana. Negative repercussions of such a program would be highly unlikely. What then have been the reactions of the governments to whom these ideas are addressed? Perhaps not surprisingly, their responses have been curt and dismissive. The federal ministry of justice has "no intention" of decriminalizing or legalizing marijuana, claiming to focus on "prevention and access to treatment for those with drug dependencies, while at the same time getting tough on drug dealers and producers who threaten the safety of our youth and communities."[7] It is worth repeating that this is the government that has seriously reduced funding for such programs.

The B.C. government responded in similar fashion. Attorney General Shirley Bond said proposals by the coalition were not being considered by the province. That was in 2011. A year later, four former Attorneys General of British Columbia (including a former premier of B.C., Ujjal Dosanjh) signed a letter endorsing the recommendations of Stop the Violence BC.

They said, "As former B.C. Attorneys General, we are fully aware that British Columbia lost its war against the marijuana industry many years ago. The case demonstrating the failure and harms of marijuana prohibition is airtight. The evidence? Massive profits for organized crime, widespread gang violence, easy access to illegal cannabis for our youth, reduced community safety, and significant — and escalating — costs to taxpayers."[8]

So many British Columbians flout the law by using marijuana that the legal system is being brought into disrepute. Former Attorney General Geoff Plant commented, "We like to think that in Canada we live in a society governed by the rule of law, but if one in 10 British Columbians exist outside that … it's almost kind of a joke." He lamented the amount of violence occasioned by the fact that marijuana is illegal: "You would be hard pressed to find a better example of a law whose unintended consequences are more perniciously contrary to its intended effect than this one…. [Marijuana prohibition has provided] the economic incentive for an enormous underground economy and routinely kills people on our streets."[9]

The four former politicians also expressed their opposition to mandatory minimum sentences for marijuana offences. Premier Christy Clark responded by saying criminal sentencing was up to the federal government.

Former mayors have also come out in support of the Stop the Violence BC report.[10] Sam Sullivan, Michael Harcourt, (now Senator) Larry Campbell, and Philip Owen, all highly respected Vancouver mayors, wrote to their provincial MPs, MLAs, mayors, and councillors saying that the status quo must change. Repeating the arguments made in the report, they forcefully argued for an "urgent and novel response" in order to reduce the availability of marijuana to young people, carefully recognizing that the drug is "not without health-related harms." They claim that a strictly regulated market would directly address "organized crime concerns by starving them of this cash cow." Pointing to the single most intransigent barrier to reform — that "elected officials are out of step with the public on marijuana prohibition" — they called for all politicians to step up and join the discussion "before further damage is done to our B.C. communities."

A powerful submission was also made in 2013 by Larry Campbell, Geoff Plant, Ujjal Dosanjh, and Kash Heed (former chief of the West Vancouver Police Department and former B.C. Solicitor General) against opting for decriminalization in the case of marijuana. Now Senator Larry Campbell put it this way:

> Decriminalization to me doesn't make any sense. As an ex-police officer, as a coroner, as mayor and as a senator, it doesn't make any sense whatsoever.... I'd rather have it exactly the way it is than decriminalize. [Decriminalization] says to [the gangs], this isn't that big a deal. It is a big deal. I think we should legalize it, we should control it, we should tax the hell out of it, and all the money should go into health care, and I've been saying that for over 20 years.

Despite these convincing arguments against decriminalization and in favour of legalization, the idea of ticketing users for possessing small amounts of marijuana is gaining traction with the current Conservative government. The Canadian Association of Chiefs of Police recently asked the government to allow this.[11] They say that their only choices at the moment are to charge a person and start the wheels of the justice system grinding or, alternatively, to warn the offender and send him on home. They would like the option to issue tickets as well, and the prime minister is taking this under consideration.

This is, of course, a net-widening proposal.[12] Tickets would now be used for all those who formerly would have been released. Anyone failing to pay the fine will no doubt be subject to additional (criminal) sanctions. These people will be caught up in the criminal justice system, and some kind of record will inevitably be kept. This will represent an increase in the criminalization of the drug — the exact opposite of decriminalization.

Concentrating the discussion on marijuana, though, has a way of skewing the argument about illegal drugs. While many Canadians approve of legalizing marijuana, we know most do not feel the same way about heroin and cocaine. Hysterical government and media reports make it hard to discuss the possibility of similar regulatory regimes for controlling harder drugs. Yet as a way of eliminating the influence of organized crime, providing for the health and safety of users, and offering prevention, education, and treatment, nothing else will work.

ALL ILLEGAL DRUGS

The *World Drug Report 2013* says that Canadians were using opioids at about half the rate in 2010 as in 2009,[13] with the annual prevalence of use at about one-third of 1 percent. Cocaine use was up slightly, to just over 1 percent.

These are not alarming figures on their face, but a February 2014 report said heroin use has been on the rise in both the United States and Canada over the past seven years.[14] The report explained that this was because prescription drugs like oxycodone were becoming scarce and expensive. Addicts were moving to heroin. The report also claimed that organized crime had begun producing heroin on an industrial scale to meet the new demand. These are not positive developments, and a means must be found to deal with them.

One suggestion gaining popularity is to create a careful and phased-in regime of legalization for these drugs, tailoring programs to reflect the difference in each drug. The lobby for just such a solution is growing in Canada, and it has some formidable backers. Among the foremost advocates for legalizing all drugs is a group of law enforcement officers. The organization, based in the United States, has been in operation since 2002. It calls itself LEAP — Law Enforcement Against Prohibition. Today, it boasts one hundred thousand supporters worldwide, 75 percent of these in the United States. Chapters of LEAP exist in about 190 countries.

David Bratzer, president of the Canadian branch, is a serving police officer. John Anderson, the vice-president, is a former correctional officer and professor of criminology at Vancouver Island University. Ross Lander, former justice of the B.C. Supreme Court, is a member. This organization was quick to support the Liberal Party of Canada's resolution to legalize marijuana.[15] At the same time, it wishes to be clear that marijuana legalization is not its ultimate goal. LEAP wants all drugs to be fully legalized and regulated. The organization does not offer proposals about the details of the regulations, believing that policy-makers are best placed to design the programs.

A powerful statement of LEAP's objectives, together with the rationale, appears on the American website:[16]

> For four decades the U.S. has fueled its policy of a "War on Drugs" with over a trillion tax dollars and increasingly

punitive policies. More than 39 million arrests for nonviolent drug offenses have been made. The incarcerated population quadrupled over a 20-year period, making building
prisons the nation's fastest growing industry. More than 2.3
million U.S. citizens are currently in prison or jail, far more
per capita than any country in the world. The U.S. has 4.6%
of the population of the world but 22.5% of the world's prisoners. Each year this war costs the U.S. another 70 billion
dollars. Despite all the lives destroyed and all the money so
ill spent, today illicit drugs are cheaper, more potent, and
much easier to access than they were at the beginning of
the War on Drugs, 40 years ago. Meanwhile, people continue dying on the streets while drug barons and terrorists
continue to grow richer, more powerful, better armed.

Not one of the stated U.S. drug policy goals of lowering the incidence of crime, addiction, drug availability, or juvenile drug use, has been achieved. Instead, our
approach has magnified these problems by creating a
self-perpetuating, ever-expanding policy of destruction, yet the U.S. still insists on continuing the war and
pressuring other governments to perpetuate these same
unworkable policies. The drug war wreaks havoc, funds
terrorism, and causes major corruption around the globe.
This is the very definition of a failed public policy.

Aside from law enforcement officers, other Canadian organizations
are dedicated to liberalizing the laws banning illegal drugs. The Canadian
Drug Policy Coalition (CDPC) was formed in 2011. It is a broad coalition
of NGOs and individuals committed to a new approach that puts protection of public health and safety, social justice, and equity at the forefront
of the debate about illegal drugs. In a recent report, it provides an excellent synthesis of the arguments for changing the status quo and moving
the focus away from criminalization and toward public health models.[17]

The authors of the report say supply and demand are at their lowest
when drugs are controlled by public health regulation. They describe this
type of regime as "the point where the substance is available in a regulated

market with appropriate age and other controls and appropriate programs that address the harms and benefits of substance use." This description sounds very much like legalization, and includes the kind of social supports that were central to Portugal's successful program.

The CDPC argues that "legalization with many restrictions" would not provide an equivalent low level of supply and demand to that of the public health model. The authors appear to regard the two models as somehow mutually exclusive. This is a curious conclusion. I would argue that the two intersect perfectly, and together would provide all of the protections needed.

The CDPC does go on to describe what could properly be called a legalization regime. It states that "one of the key priorities of the CDPC is to eliminate the criminalization of drug use," and that

> This paper recognizes that careful thought must be put into all aspects of a regulatory model for drugs. It also recognizes that changing how we control substances requires a robust governmental response to provide adequate health care and other supports. In particular, a public health approach proposes that the supply chain for drugs would be under comprehensive societal control in order to maximize control over availability and accessibility and reduce consumer demand.

This would seem to be a reference to controlling production and distribution — the supply chain — and it constitutes a necessary element of legalization if we are to remove organized crime from the trade. The CDPC would apply this model to all illegal drugs.

This coalition recognizes the challenges of arguing for such a change under the current government. "The Federal government," it says, "remains openly hostile to evidence-based measures like key harm reduction services and has clearly taken a punitive approach to addressing drug problems."

The organization is also conscious of the many backward steps taken in past years. It describes the many programs that would be helpful but are unlikely to be funded under the current government. Victoria, British Columbia, for example, had a stand-alone fixed needle distribution site until 2008, when public pressure forced it to close. The NAOMI project was another successful program that provided heroin-assisted therapy (HAT). Canada is the only country that has not continued to provide HAT to its patients. The research is now clear that permanent HAT programs should be set up.

Other effective and affordable programs should be adopted, says the CDPC. For example, harm reduction kits for crack smokers help users avoid contracting Hepatitis C. The kits cost only fifty-nine cents.

And there are ways to reduce the number of deaths by overdose that Canada could pursue. Eighty-five percent of users who overdose on opioids do so in the presence of others.[18] "Take Home Naloxone" programs provide the drug needed to reverse opioid overdoses, and friends and families of users should be able to buy it. This remedy is not fully available in Canada because naloxone may not be covered by provincial drug plans, the cost is high, and in most provinces it is only available on prescription. One emergency physician suggests that, since it would save lives, naloxone should be available over the counter, as it is in Italy. He says that, for those who insist this would encourage more drug use, it is like saying air bags and seat belts encourage dangerous driving.

Another simple and inexpensive program called 911 Good Samaritan would also save lives. This would enable people who have overdosed, or who suspect someone else is overdosing, to call 911 without having to worry about being arrested. Many users die rather than make the call, and many friends of users are similarly deterred from calling for help. Several states in the U.S. have this service, and it is easy and inexpensive to set up. Again, this simple program would save lives.

The CDPC report is one of the most thorough in assessing Canada's role in the drug war. It reviews the history as well as our current government's puzzling determination to accelerate the War on Drugs, pushing back against the tide that is swelling on both sides of the Atlantic. The report makes a compelling argument for the adoption of a public health model, and for retreating from the law enforcement approach. But the Justice Department has responded to the report by reiterating that the government has "no intention" of considering alternatives.[19]

There are other organizations pushing back against Ottawa, and some of these are not afraid to use the word *legalization* with respect to illegal drugs. The Health Officers Council of British Columbia has been urging the government since 1998 to legalize and regulate heroin and cocaine as well as marijuana.[20] Citing the extraordinary amount of gang violence in Vancouver, they, too, take the position that violence could be alleviated or stopped by taking away the drug trade from organized crime. As Donald MacPherson, Vancouver's drug policy coordinator, said, "Why should we leave it to organized crime to regulate these drugs?" This is a question that remains unanswered by advocates of continued prohibition.

The number of Canadian voices in support of a change to the status quo — and regulated legalization at that — is growing. The Conservative government, though, has shown its hostility to scientific, evidence-based policy-making in many areas. It has muzzled scientists, cut the budget for Statistics Canada, closed research institutions, and castigated those who rely upon facts and statistics.

The government prefers to spend its resources bolstering the RCMP's drug enforcement efforts, providing them, for example, with $16 million more over 2012–2017 specifically to fight marijuana grow-ops and drug laboratories. Fully 54 percent of all drug crimes reported by police in 2011 (113,100 of them) were for simple marijuana possession.[21] Is this the way Canadians want their government to spend scarce resources?

The Politics

The Canadian government's stubborn approach to illegal drugs is well illustrated by its most recent response to the Supreme Court of Canada's decision ordering it to grant an exemption to InSite, the supervised injection site in Vancouver, allowing it to continue its work. Having lost its battle to close the facility, the government has responded by creating complex requirements designed to defeat both InSite and any new efforts to establish supervised injection sites in Canada. Introducing the legislation in June 2013, Health Minister Leona Agglukaq stated, "Our government believes that creating a location for sanctioned use of drugs obtained from illicit sources has the potential for great harm in the community."[22]

If there were any doubt that the Conservative government's new complex legislation is designed to defeat applications for new safe injection sites, a letter sent by the Conservative Party to its supporters is crystal clear.[23] Under the subject line "Keep heroin out of our backyards," the letter says in part, "Do you want a supervised drug consumption site in your community? These are facilities where drug addicts get to shoot up heroin and other illicit drugs. I don't want one anywhere near my home. Yet, as I write this, special interests are trying to open up these supervised drug consumption sites in cities and towns across Canada — over the objections of local residents and law enforcement."

In fact, law enforcement in Vancouver is in favour of InSite, and so are the Canadian Medical Association and the Canadian Public Health Association, which have also come out in opposition to the new regulations.[24] Doctors Julio Montaner and Evan Wood of the British Columbia Centre for Excellence in HIV/AIDS deplore the new legislation. They point out that supervised injection sites are preferable to needle exchanges (which the government has approved) because they impose more rigorous controls, ensuring the safety of clients and the public. Europe has recognized this advantage and has established more than ninety safe injection sites in over sixty cities.

Toronto is the latest Canadian city to weigh in on the issue. Its medical health officer has just recommended the city push the province to fund a trial program for a safe injection site.[25] The provincial government was swift to respond: "Supervised injection sites aren't something that we're moving forward with right now," said the health minister, Deb Matthews. Mayor Rob Ford and Police Chief Bill Blair also oppose the plan. On the other hand, the Registered Nurses' Association of Ontario, St. Michael's Hospital, and the Canadian HIV/AIDS Legal Network support it.

This response appears to reflect a growing trend. Politicians are the ones opposing all such public health approaches, while public health officials are strongly in favour. Questions arise: Whose interests are at stake in this struggle? Why does political expediency appear to trump the public interest and well-being in these cases? Who stands to gain from these programs? Are there any losers if we adopt a harm reduction approach? Why are we unable to reconcile the positions?

The Conservative government is also changing the medical marijuana system in ways that will guarantee increased problems with the regime and potential suffering to patients. As of July 2013, more than thirty thousand Canadians had licences to use marijuana for medical purposes.[26] Health Canada says 72 percent of them suffer from arthritis, spinal cord injury, spinal cord disease, multiple sclerosis (MS), cancer, AIDS/HIV, or epilepsy.[27] Sixty-one percent of users of medical marijuana have annual incomes below thirty thousand dollars, and 20 percent have less than twenty-thousand dollars per year in income. Thus, it matters a great deal that under the new regime the price of marijuana is expected to rise from $1.80–$5 per gram to $8.80 per gram.[28] Many patients will probably have to continue growing their own, often resorting to "guerrilla growing" — that is, growing on land that they do not own. Patients will also purchase more on the black market, where the price is lower. The potential for prosecution of such users is high. A recent court case argued that taking away patients' rights to grow their own medicine is unconstitutional. The federal court judge granted an interim injunction allowing licenced patients to continue growing their own marijuana until the matter could be set down for a full hearing

The RCMP had been quick to oppose the existing medical marijuana program.[29] They said that organized crime was using the program to get around the law. Criminals were using family members and people with clean police records to abuse the program and sell the drugs on the street. The RCMP said the tactics included producing quantities of marijuana in excess of the quantity allowed under the Health Canada permit and selling the surplus.

The RCMP pronounced that in 2010, seventy licence-holders were violating the terms of their agreements. Forty of those were trafficking in marijuana. Yet with over thirty thousand licence-holders in Canada, clearly only a tiny proportion is abusing the system. This must be seen as a testament to the success of the system, and to the law-abiding nature of the vast majority of medical marijuana users.

The government says it is proposing new medical marijuana legislation because there is a risk of fire and break-ins when people grow their own marijuana. Yet growers like "Jim" have invested substantial amounts to ensure that there will not be problems.[30] For four thousand dollars, Jim is able to pay for the electricity required, grow his marijuana in a locked room with a fan system that removes odour and moisture buildup, and provide noise baffles so that the fans cannot be heard beyond his yard. Eliminating the odour and noise are the main ways of providing security, plus the most important rule: "Tell no one."

Department insiders at Health Canada have a long list of reasons why they say the existing system needed to be changed.[31] They say that their department (The Medical Marihuana Access Division of Health Canada) never knew if applicants actually existed or not. While applicants' addresses were verified, no one ever determined whether the applicants in fact lived there. Health Canada never called a doctor to verify information unless the dose was above fifty grams/day, while applicants could simply choose a doctor from the list on the available websites. The doctor's address was not verified by anyone, and sometimes licences were sent to a post office box of the applicant/grower. Finally, most growers were never checked as to the amount they were growing, or whether they were near a day care or school, or whether they presented a fire risk.

None of these reasons would appear to warrant a complete overhaul of the system. Each concern could have been easily and inexpensively rectified by more rigorous follow-up and inspections. It is possible the government did not pursue this seemingly obvious solution because removing government control from the program coincides with a fundamental Conservative philosophy of smaller government. It also encourages the type of free market capitalism approved by the government, in that it hands over production and distribution to large corporations. Thus, the new rules give responsibility to doctors (who don't want it) and to commercial enterprises, which will have to produce profits and will have no particular interest in providing controls or policing.

By prohibiting people from growing their own marijuana, the government is also paradoxically ensuring that local authorities will not know either the location or the safety of the inevitable new clandestine operations until there is a problem. By simply providing safety and health guidelines for growers, requiring local governments to issue permits to those who meet the standards, and allowing for inspections, governments could have ensured the ongoing safety of existing growing operations.

The Conservative government's extraordinary efforts to compromise programs like InSite and the original medical marijuana program can only be described as mean-minded, moralistic, and ideologically driven. Let's review some of the programs that would actually save Canadian lives, and note that the overwhelming response of the federal government has been to refuse access. We know InSite saves lives. We know naloxone, the antidote for heroin overdoses, saves lives. Clean crack pipes and syringes save lives. Cannabidiol for Dravet syndrome saves lives, including the lives of small children. None of these is likely to be made available to Canadians under this government. These decisions to deny access to life-saving therapies can only be described as cynical, since they appear to represent a clear-eyed decision to pursue the War on Drugs as a vote-getter.

In addition, the war, like all wars, is a profitable industry for some. Eugene Oscapella believes that the dogged opposition to legalization that exists in the United States federal government is largely a result of the entrenched industry that depends upon prohibition — particularly private prisons and private and public police forces.[32] The largest prison operator in the United States, Corrections Corporation of America (CCA), recently told forty-eight states that it would buy their existing prisons and run them if the states could guarantee 90 percent occupancy.[33]

But this is just one way in which some interested parties are able to gain a financial advantage. Relatively new legislation in Canada is providing another reason to continue the War on Drugs. Civil forfeiture laws were intended to fight organized crime. Instead, they often penalize ordinary citizens who may or may not have broken the law.[34]

Eight Canadian provinces have these laws allowing authorities to seize and dispose of private property, even where illegal activities have not been proven or charges laid. Judges can order cash and property taken when they are convinced on the balance of probabilities (a relative low burden of proof) that they are proceeds or instruments of an illegal activity. Items most commonly taken are cash, cars, jewellery, cellphones, and computers. Since there is no need to prove that the primary use of the property was unlawful, many say this is a substitute for the criminal process and a "cash grab."

One member of LEAP says these laws provide an opportunity for drug enforcement departments to boost their budgets: "There's a certain amount of asset forfeiture that plays right into the development of their drug enforcement squad and equipment and what not, because they get money back quite often. That's right across the country and in the U.S. as well. It's kind of like telling a traffic officer he's going to get a dollar for every traffic ticket he hands out."[35]

When asked if he meant that police departments benefit financially from the War on Drugs, the officer answered, "Absolutely.... There's asset forfeiture laws that they pushed dramatically in these major drug conspiracy situations where there's homes or cars or whatever. The other thing is, it gives the perception to the public that they are actually effective and doing something. [Arresting a drug user is] like shooting fish in a barrel for police, and many of them like to have that power."

Here is one example of how civil forfeiture laws work in Canada:[36]

> Regina resident David Mihalyko was broke and his 13-year-old Chevy Blazer truck was out of gas. It was September 2010, and all he had in his pocket were some oxycontin tablets, "legally prescribed for him as a result of an injury he suffered to his foot," according to court documents. Mr. Mihalyko decided to raise some cash by selling two tablets to a woman he thought was a prostitute, working the Regina stroll. She paid $60 for the tablets. Mr. Mihalyko spent all of the cash on fuel for his truck.
>
> The woman was an undercover police officer. Mr. Mihalyko was arrested and charged with trafficking in a controlled substance. He pleaded guilty to the offence, and received a conditional sentence of nine months. But the Crown in Saskatchewan wasn't satisfied. It turned to relatively new civil forfeiture laws to extract more from the hapless defendant. The state went after his truck, claiming it was an instrument of crime.
>
> Unlike most targets of civil forfeiture in Canada, Mr. Mihalyko fought back. His case went to Saskatchewan Court of Queen's Bench, where a judge decided he really wasn't much of a drug dealer. The oxycontin sale was an "isolated incident," the judge found, and the truck seizure was "disproportionate to the offence." The judge said Mr. Mihalyko should have his truck returned to him.
>
> But the Crown appealed. In April 2012, a panel of three judges found Mr. Mihalyko's offence to be considerably more serious than the trial judge had indicated. The appeal was allowed, and Mr. Mihalyko's truck was lost for good.

Eugene Oscapella thinks the federal government understands perfectly the financial and political implications of the War on Drugs: "You see it in the current administration in Ottawa, who profit from being tough on drugs. They know it doesn't work. Harper's not stupid — he's an economist, he can understand the economics of prohibition, as can many of his MPs. But as long as they figure they can gull the public into believing that getting tough on drugs is the right thing to do, they get elected on those things.[37]

This crass domestic agenda still does not explain some of Canada's activities on the international stage. Its unaccountable opposition to the Vienna Declaration of 2012[38] and to Bolivia's efforts to exempt chewed coca leaf from the U.N. Conventions are two cases in point. As well, when ninety-five countries, including the United States, recently passed a U.N. resolution to hold a Special Session on drug policy internationally in 2016, Canada inexplicably opposed this as well. The Conservative government apparently rejects even the idea of a discussion about illegal drugs.

Canada has recently become more involved in the War on Drugs internationally than ever. Canadian Forces are operating in Latin America. They are running counter-narcotics missions in the Caribbean and East Pacific. Canadian warships and aircraft are acting as eyes and ears for United States interdiction efforts.

Meanwhile, the cat has definitely landed amongst the pigeons with Liberal Leader Justin Trudeau's recent endorsement of marijuana legalization and personal admission of marijuana use, even while an elected Member of Parliament. His party's draft policy paper suggests that legalization will create thousands of jobs and produce sizable revenues for government in the form of taxes.[39] The report emphasizes the party's position that mere decriminalization will leave organized crime in charge of the industry.

The report provides details. It says Canada would need about 2,700 retail outlets in order to serve the three million Canadians who use marijuana. It recommends using provincial liquor stores, similar to the Washington model, or specialty private stores. It proposes a four ounce limit for possession, estimating that a "regular" user would use about one ounce per month. In contrast to the current Conservative proposal for medical marijuana, which will raise the price of marijuana, the Liberal Party maintains that it is critical to lower the price of the drug in order to make the industry unattractive to organized crime.

Critics conveniently ignore the details of the plan. *Globe and Mail* columnist Margaret Wente remarks that "simple logic says [Trudeau is] wrong, when people want something and you make it easier to get, demand generally goes up. Especially if the price goes down.... That's because marijuana is ridiculously easy to produce."[40] But Wente is wrong when she says legalization will make marijuana "easier to get." The contrary is the case. The whole point of legalization would be to make it harder to obtain than is currently the case.[41] We know that users, including children, can obtain any amount of marijuana any time with a simple telephone call or stroll down the street. This would no longer be the case under legalization. Ms. Wente also ignores the plan's emphasis on controlling the price of the drug so that organized crime can be eliminated from the trade.

Wente quotes from Caulkins et al. in *Marijuana Legalization*, claiming that marijuana use will double or triple under a legal regime. We know that this is not the case under decriminalization regimes. In fact Canadian children now use more pot than young people in regimes that have liberalized their laws. Germany, Poland, Belgium, Italy and the Netherlands all have lower rates of marijuana use than Canada among the very young.[42] No one in the legalization camp believes that it is possible to stop all use by children, but the critics appear to feel that zero use is the only sensible goal.[43] None of the critics recognize the urgent need to remove organized crime from the picture, ending the violence and ensuring that the products are safe. These essential goals can only be addressed by a regime of legalization.

How are the politics of legalization playing out across the Canadian political spectrum? The Liberal Party is now the only party aside from the Greens to endorse legalization of marijuana. The New Democrats have called the Liberal position "political pandering," implying that it is nothing more than a bid for the youth vote. At the same time, its own official policy is puzzling. It says the party supports "decriminalizing marijuana possession with the goal of removing its production and distribution from the control of organized crime."[44] Yet clearly it is not possible to eliminate organized crime without a system of legalization. The Conservative Party is opposed to anything but full prohibition. And nobody ventures to talk about what to do with harder drugs.

Will the new approach to marijuana be an advantage to the Liberals on election day? Commentator John Ibbitson calls Trudeau's stance "an honest and principled stand on a contentious issue," but does not venture an opinion as to whether the votes he will gain will outweigh those he will lose.[45] The evidence, however, seems to be in Trudeau's favour. In Washington State in 2012, with legal marijuana on the ballot, the percentage of young people voting more than doubled to 22 percent, helping to push the ballot over the top.[46] Colorado and Oregon showed a similar increase. It is widely accepted that most of these voters were in favour of legalization. There is every reason to expect that the same will hold true here in Canada. And with polls showing support for legal marijuana growing, it is unlikely that the number of lost votes (those who support the status quo) will balance the surge in favour of legalization.

Long-time observer Lawrence Martin says that Trudeau's stance "puts [him] brightly on the progressive stage, it contrasts him with the fogey class of leaders and it will increase voter turnout among youth." As to the approach of the Conservatives, he says, "The weed is treated as being truly evil by our governing authorities. It's time-warp politics, stuff that appeals to the Conservatives' hard-core base."

The commentator who expresses best and most concisely the paradox of the Conservative position is columnist Chris Selley:[47]

> I refuse to believe that Mr. Harper doesn't realize, at some level, the insanity of this approach [prohibition]. Anyone with a rudimentary understanding of economics can see its negative effects: It restricts production, distribution and profit to criminals willing to take the risk, thereby inviting (successfully) all the ills that accompany organized crime, while filling the market — and oh lord, 29% of our children's lungs! — with an untested and largely unknown product.

The marijuana legalization issue will assume larger proportions in the next Canadian election than many think. It sets up a liberal-conservative smack-down with a well-defined issue that distinguishes yesterday's prejudices from today's clear-eyed assessment — that it is not so much the drugs that are evil, but the fact of their criminalization. Coming up the middle of this brawl should be a grounded, sensible discussion of a public health approach to all drugs, with controls that meet the needs of all Canadians.

Conclusion

You would think that someone who has defended legions of drug offenders in criminal court would have formed a substantial and sophisticated opinion on the War on Drugs, but you would be wrong. Toiling in the trenches did not lend itself to developing a reasoned and nuanced approach to the system that incarcerated so many of my clients. On the contrary, I was busy trying to keep these people from getting criminal records and going to prison. Larger questions about the appropriateness of the criminal justice system for handling illegal drugs did not really penetrate in any meaningful way. I knew it was a cruel and wasteful system, but the question of what to do about it never surfaced long enough to produce an informed opinion.

When I embarked on the research for this book, therefore, I was only prepared to go as far as suggesting we begin with the less serious drug, marijuana, and start reducing penalties with an eye to legalization down the road. Questions about harder drugs remained unexplored. What today seem like sensible solutions were not then obvious to me. But as I unearthed reams of research about the War on Drugs and discovered that many jurisdictions have already taken substantial steps away from the war, it became clear that Canada is in a time warp.

If we are to design a workable response to drug use, we will have to first clear our minds of the propaganda that has permeated the debate for the past century. Myths about cocaine and overblown fears about heroin permeate popular culture and have infiltrated much of the discourse. Like most others, I bought the whole package. But it turns out drugs are just drugs, although some are more harmful than others. And the biggest problem today actually relates to the abuse of legal prescription drugs — not heroin and cocaine. Our objective should be to reduce the harm caused by all of them.

I believe that the most fundamental questions are not being asked. How, for example, did we ever think that the solution to curbing the use of certain drugs was to be found solely in the implementation of the criminal justice system? Why did we think it appropriate to criminalize people for ingesting substances that we disapprove of, even when there was no victim and no violence involved? We don't incarcerate people who ingest excessive amounts of tobacco or alcohol, even though the potential harms are serious and quantifiable.

Well, you say, people use psychoactive drugs to get "high," and somehow that is supposed to justify it. (People don't use alcohol to get "high"?) Using this reasoning, we make a conscious choice every day to treat people who abuse certain substances as criminals, rather than as what they are, which is ill. How different would the scene be today if we had started a hundred years ago employing our public health system to deal with drug addiction instead?

Much is explained by the bigotry of the past, but by 2014 we should have advanced beyond these attitudes. It is clear to me that we have to begin by rejecting the rationale behind criminalization. It is essential that we stop considering drug users as "the other." When we set up this kind of dichotomy, it becomes easy to justify harsh treatment of people whom we consider to be "lesser." Yet far from being the demented, dangerous individuals that we seem to fear, drug users are our friends, neighbours, and family members. It behooves us to treat them as we would want to be treated — with care, respect, and compassion.

Root causes of drug use and addiction must be a part of this discussion. Our current prime minister thinks a consideration of root causes is an offence in itself — "committing sociology," as he puts it. But we as a society need to put resources into identifying and alleviating these root causes. Virtually every drug addict is dealing with some other issue — mental illness, dysfunction or violence in the home, the effects of colonialism, or just the pressure of a job. Instead of demonizing users, we could start by trying to deal with these issues, which I believe would have long-lasting positive effects.

We must also consider the negative effects that are directly caused by the criminalization of drugs. These have been enumerated: violence, disease, damage from incarceration, disruption of communities and families, the inability to ensure quality control of substances. Criminalization allows organized crime to control the illegal drug industry. Gangsters and bikers are not concerned with the common good or morals. They are concerned with only one thing: profits. In this, they are perfect models of corporatism.

How then do we justify the perpetuation of a system that enables organized crime to amass billions of dollars in profits, leaving dead bodies in its wake? Why would we support a system (and we *are* supporting it) that gives full responsibility over the sale and production of illegal drugs to criminal elements that are quite prepared to sell anything to anybody, including our children? Why do we tolerate the presence of gangsters who use drug money to influence and corrupt our judicial and political systems?

No one appears to be arguing that legalization would fail to remove organized crime from the illegal drug industry. Most opponents of legalization simply ignore the issue. Yet the pursuit of this outcome must be central to any discussion of the drug war. Of course, it is probable that a certain amount of black market activity would continue even after legalization — much like the smuggling of cigarettes that still occurs across the Canada-U.S. border. I would argue that if we can price the product right, gangsters will decide it is not worth their while to pursue the trade. Even if a residual amount of underground activity takes place, we will have broken the back of the illegal industry.

The evidence is overwhelming that drugs should be controlled and regulated by governments; that is, by the people. Governments already preside over the regulation of many addictive and potentially harmful drugs. After all, governments are elected to look after the common good, and they are supposed to have our best interests at heart. We entrust them with helping us care for our health and safety. When they fail in this, we have the opportunity to replace them.

Some feel legalization of drugs would lead to a "free-for-all." Yet it should be clear by now that the current system *is* the free-for-all. When young people are asked how hard it is to obtain illegal drugs, they say it takes about ten minutes to buy just about anything they want. This cannot be what Canadians want, especially given the millions of dollars we spend on law enforcement and incarceration. The failure of fifty years of suppression demands a thoughtful and sensible search for alternative solutions.

It is disheartening in the extreme to watch Canada regressing in its approach to illegal drugs while the rest of the world moves on. Not only has our prison population increased by 16.5 percent over the past decade, but the number of black inmates has increased by 75 percent and the number of Native people by 45 percent.[1] Much of this increase is due to drug offences. What does this say about who we are as a people? We have been wholly unwilling or unable to prevent the entrenchment of a discredited and biased approach to controlling illegal drugs.

And this despite the fact that even the United States is showing signs of retreating from the tough-on-crime model by beginning the process of pardoning non-violent offenders who were unjustly sentenced to long prison terms for using drugs and ensuring no imprisonment for small-time users. The U.S. Attorney-General has even recognized the shocking disparity in the way drug laws have been applied to incarcerate disproportionate numbers of African-Americans and Latinos: "This over-reliance on incarceration is not just financially unsustainable. It comes with human and moral costs that are impossible to calculate."[2]

Not only is Canada quickly falling behind the United States in this regard, but other countries we regard as "undeveloped" are also leaving us in the dust. We have much to learn from Evo Morales's staunch defence of culture and tradition as he convinced the United Nations to allow his people to continue using coca. Unlikely jurisdictions like Kyrgyzstan and the Chinese province of Guizhou put us to shame by adopting more compassionate approaches. And José Mujica's Uruguay is blazing a trail by legalizing marijuana, the first nation in the world to do so.

It is not expected that the sky will fall in Uruguay any more than it has in Colorado and Washington after legalization. Colorado has been dealing with a legal marijuana regime since January 1, 2014. Even though it's early days, the state has reported no increase in crime or traffic accidents since the new regulations came into effect.[3] In fact, there has been a spill-over tourist boom. Bakeries are reporting that business is up more than 1,000 percent. One medical marijuana dispensary that used to make a thousand dollars a day is expecting to make one hundred times that much by autumn. And the state expects to reap double the estimated amount in taxes — something in the region of $150 million, the funds largely earmarked for building schools.

These are encouraging figures for those who have been advocating for marijuana legalization. However, we still face the obstacle of convincing the public that harder drugs deserve similar treatment. Indeed, I am convinced that those are the very drugs that most require control and regulation by responsible governments. The production and distribution of heroin and cocaine should not be left in the hands of criminals. For the sake of our own health and that of our neighbours, we need to take charge.

There remains a stubborn belief that harm reduction efforts such as safe injection sites somehow encourage more drug use. Yet the evidence shows the opposite: drug use tends to remain the same or decrease while health and mortality statistics improve. Switzerland's heroin maintenance program is a good example. In twelve years (1990–2002), the number of new heroin users fell by 82 percent, while the overall population of users was down 4 percent. The number of injection drug users also dropped.

In Canada, our current government has made its choice. Harm reduction is out. Punishment for drug users is in. Offenders convicted of victimless, non-violent drug offences face mandatory minimum prison terms. The idea of providing prescribed maintenance doses of heroin to addicts is anathema. Needle exchanges are frowned upon. Small children are denied the medicine they need. Medical marijuana users in general are targeted in the push to punish drug users, as Health Canada says failure to comply with new rules will result in a visit from police.[4, 5] These patients — who say they have a right to their medicine — have launched a constitutional challenge. In a landmark ruling, Federal Court Judge Michael Manson has granted a temporary injunction allowing patients currently licensed to grow their own pot to continue doing so until such time as this challenge can be heard by a court.[6]

The federal government's hard-line attitude is spreading to provincial governments as well. New provincial laws permit civil forfeitures of property in outrageous proportion to the related offences. Other laws permit informers to complain about perceived nuisance neighbours, enabling law enforcement to shut down everything from drug dens to the corner drug store that might have sold mouthwash to a homeless person.[7] Human rights advocates say such laws provide police with a huge amount of authority but little accountability. There is a serious cost to our privacy and security, and a very low burden of proof.

New laws like these are proliferating in today's Canada in the face of evidence that more suppression is futile. None of the objectives of the War on Drugs has been met by the determined and stubborn efforts of law enforcement. Endlessly repeating this behaviour while expecting a different result is the very definition of insanity.

Having come to the conclusion that a public health regime makes more sense than resorting to the criminal justice system, what are the next steps for climbing down from the War on Drugs? As it turns out, some steps are already being taken.

At least one province is offering resistance to the new medical marijuana proposals. The Vancouver Police Department and a number of mayors have said that those who have home grow-ops or medical marijuana dispensaries will not be arrested after the April 1 deadline.[8] As Mission mayor Ted Adlem says, "I'm not really interested in going after a little guy that's growing for his own personal use. That makes no sense, it is absolutely ludicrous."

This appears to represent the opinion of the majority of Canadians, who do not think people should go to jail for using marijuana. It would seem that the time is ripe to legalize the drug. I am not convinced that decriminalization is "the worst case scenario" (even if I do call it Prohibition Lite), since under decriminalization fewer people actually go to jail and end up with criminal records. Also, where hard drugs are decriminalized, there is a tendency for more users to seek treatment.

However, jurisdictions that have adopted decriminalization never do go on to liberalize the laws further, so it is important that we not get hung up on decriminalization. Since we also need to eliminate the influence of organized crime, it makes sense to skip the interim measure and go straight to legalization, with control and regulations residing in governments.

As to the question of harder drugs, I agree with those who argue that these require our intervention and regulation even more than soft drugs like marijuana. We need to get in front of the problem by taking control of these drugs. Currently, we are mitigating damage by providing safe injection sites and needle exchanges, but we need to continue pushing for more of such harm reduction programs across the country. At the same time, we should urge governments to permit researchers to do the clinical trials necessary to establish any valuable therapeutic uses for these drugs.

A committed government, with the assistance of knowledgeable public health workers and scientific advice, will be more than capable of designing a legal and regulated regime that works both for the users and for the community at large. There are ample templates available from those with deep knowledge about the drugs in question. There is a wealth of information out there that we should exploit. We simply need the will to act.

The violence and corruption represented by organized crime in the current scenario cannot be over-emphasized. It may be true that most people purchasing substances for their own use do not experience the murder and mayhem firsthand, but they *are* on the receiving end of a lack of quality control that can lead to sickness and death, and the crime statistics related to the trade are very real. We need to put the gangsters out of business, stop entrusting the futures of our children to bikers and crime bosses, assume our responsibilities as protectors of the public good, and elect governments that will pursue these ends.

Notes

INTRODUCTION

1. Dan Baum, *Smoke and Mirrors: The War on Drugs and the Politics of Failure* (New York: Little, Brown and Company, 1996), 5, 7, 72.
2. Andrew B. Whitfield and Jeffrey Yates, *Presidential Rhetoric and the Public Agenda* (Baltimore: Johns Hopkins University, 2009), 58, 253.
3. Jimmy Carter, "Call Off the Global Drug War," *New York Times*, June 16, 2011.
4. J. Rehm, D. Baliunas, S. Brochu, B. Fischer, W. Gnam, J. Patra, S. Popova, A. Sarnocinska-Hart, B. Taylor, et al., *The Costs of Substance Abuse in Canada 2002 Highlights* (Ottawa: Canadian Centre on Substance Abuse, March 2006), 1.

CHAPTER 1: HOW WE GOT INTO THIS PREDICAMENT

1. *CBC News*, April 18, 2012.
2. Margaret Atwood, "Through the One-Way Mirror," *Comparison and Contrast* (1.1: 1984), 10.
3. From this point on, for the purpose of simplicity, I will say that twenty-one states allow medical marijuana.
4. Adam Cohen, "Will States Lead the Way to Legalizing Marijuana Nationwide?" *Time Magazine*, January 28, 2013.
5. Judge James P. Gray, *Why Our Drug Laws Have Failed and What We Can Do About It* (Philadelphia: Temple University Press, 2001), 11.
6. Ibid., 182.
7. David Nutt, *Drugs Without the Hot Air: Minimising the Harms of Legal and*

Illegal Drugs (Cambridge: UIT Cambridge Ltd., 2012), 5, 7, 21.

8. Fernando Henrique Cardoso, César Gaviria, Ernesto Zedillo, "The War on Drugs Is a Failure," *The Wall Street Journal*, February 23, 2009.

9. Roque Planas, "Vicente Fox Sits Down with *High Times Magazine* to Blast Drug War," *Huffington Post*, July 16, 2013.

10. Vicente Fox, "For Mexico, Legalization Is Freedom," *Globe and Mail*, February 17, 2014.

11. Otto Pérez Molina, "We Have to Find New Solutions to Latin America's Drugs Nightmare," *The Observer*, April 7, 2012.

12. John Mulholland, "Juan Manuel Santos: It Is Time to Think Again about the War on Drugs," *The Observer*, November 12, 2011.

13. Jaime Sánchez Susarrey, "La Victoria de Evo," *Mural*, January 19, 2013.

14. Staff, "Uruguay Won't Be Pot-Smokers' Haven, President Vows," *Globe and Mail*, August 1, 2013.

15. Mulholland, "Juan Manuel Santos."

16. Uki Goni, "Excitement, but Anxiety Too, As Uruguay Sets Liberal Path with a New Cannabis Law," *The Observer*, August 3, 2013.

17. Gray, *Why Our Drug Laws Have Failed*, 19ff.

18. Nutt, *Drugs Without the Hot Air*, 74, 182, 64.

19. Mark Easton, "Can We Imagine a Britain Where All Drugs Are Legal?" *BBC News*, December 16, 2010.

20. Eugene Jarecki, *The House I Live In*, a film produced by Danny Glover, John Legend, Brad Pitt, and Russell Simmons (Virgil Films and Entertainment: 2013).

21. Gray, *Why Our Drug Laws Have Failed*, 21, 25.

22. Dave Philipps, "Now Popular in Colorado, Marijuana Oil Has Long Success History That's Often Been Ignored," *Colorado Springs Gazette*, January 27, 2014.

23. THC (tetrahydrocannabinol) is the ingredient that provides the "high" sought by marijuana users. Catherine Carstairs, *Jailed for Possession: Illegal Drug Use, Regulation and Power in Canada, 1920–1961* (Toronto: University of Toronto Press), 44.

24. Neil Boyd, *High Society: Legal and Illegal Drugs in Canada* (Toronto: Key Porter Books, 1991), 8.

25. Catherine Carstairs, *Jailed for Possession*, 44.

26. Senate Special Committee on Illegal Drugs, *Cannabis: Our Position for a Canadian Public Policy* (Ottawa: Senate of Canada, 2002), 256.

27. Ibid., Summary Report, 22.

28. Paula Mallea, *Fearmonger* (Toronto: James Lorimer Publishing, 2011), 113.

29. American Civil Liberties Union, *The War on Marijuana in Black and White: Report*, June 3, 2013.

30. Editorial, "Racially Biased Arrests for Pot," *New York Times*, June 15, 2013.

31. Dr. Carl Hart, *High Price: Drugs, Neuroscience and Discovering Myself* (London: Penguin Books Ltd., 2013).

32. Michelle Alexander, *The New Jim Crow: Mass Incarceration in the Age of Colorblindness* (New York: The New Press, 2012).
33. Scott Kaufman, "Noam Chomsky: The Drug War Is the Latest Manifestation of a Centuries-Old 'Race War,'" *The Raw Story*, January 6, 2014.
34. Alan Travis, "Theresa May Bans Qat 'To Protect Vulnerable Members of Communities,'" *The Guardian*, July 3, 2013.
35. Axel Klein, Pien Metaal, and Martin Jelsma, "Chewing Over Khat Prohibition: The Globalisation of Control and Regulation of an Ancient Stimulant," Transnational Institute Series on Legislative Reform of Drug Policies, Nr. 17, January 2012.
36. Global Commission on Drug Policy, *War on Drugs* (June 2011), 16.
37. Mallea, *Fearmonger*, 141, 153. Eighty percent of federal inmates in Canada have a drug abuse problem.
38. Jim Farber, "The Stones' Keith Richards Does Time — Onstage — As His Heroin Sentence, but He May Face Worse," *People*, vol. 11, no. 18, May 7, 1979.
39. Transform Drug Policy Foundation, *www.tdpf.org.uk/Policy_Timeline.htm*.
40. Global Commission on Drug Policy, *War on Drugs*, 17.
41. Ibid., 10.
42. United Nations Office on Drugs and Crime (UNODC), *World Drug Report 2012* (United Nations Publication, Sales no. E.12.XI.1), 14–98.
43. See *www.viennadeclaration.com/2010/06/the-vienna-declaration-a-global-call-to-action-for-science-based-drug-policy*. Accessed March 5, 2014.
44. Global Commission on Drug Policy, *War on Drugs*, 10.
45. Greece is the only European country to have advocated "unsuccessfully" for the outright legalization of marijuana under the presidency of George Papandreou. "In Narco Veritas," *The Economist*, January 21, 2012: 66.
46. Report of the Global Commission, *War on Drugs*, 17.
47. United Nations Office on Drugs and Crime (UNODC) *2013 World Drug Report: Stability in Use of Traditional Drugs, Alarming Rise in New Psychoactive Substances* (United Nations: UNODC, 2013).

Chapter 2: A Declaration of War Leads to a Shambles

1. Interview with Eric Sterling, *Day 6*, CBC Radio One, August 17, 2013.
2. Hart, *High Price*, 18. Dr. Hart points out that white people actually use crack more than blacks, according to national statistics, but that blacks are prosecuted disproportionately. He says that in Los Angeles (population four million) at the height of the crack epidemic, not a single white person was arrested on federal crack cocaine charges, even though whites were using and selling crack. *See also* Transform Drug Policy Foundation.
3. Editorial, "Sentencing Reform Starts to Pay Off," *New York Times*, August 1, 2013.
4. Matt Apuzzo, "Justice Department Starts Quest for Inmates to Be Freed," *New York Times*, January 30, 2014.

5. Abby Rapaport, "Why Obama Should Take a Cue from Gerald Ford on Crack Pardons," *The American Prospect*, February 6, 2014.

6. Thomas Mann, "Rosie Rowbotham: Canada's Longest Serving Marijuana Prisoner," *Cannabis Culture*, April 30, 1998.

7. Auditor General of Canada, *Illicit Drugs: The Federal Government's Role* (Office of the Auditor General of Canada, 2001), 6.

8. Ibid.

9. Liberal Party of Canada (B.C.), Standing Policy Committee, *Legalization of Marijuana: Answering Questions and Developing a Framework* (Draft, January 2013), 6 and 21.

10. See *www.cbc.ca/news/health/story/2009/08/14/f-medical-marijuana.html*. Accessed March 5, 2014.

11. Boyd, *High Society*, 12, 37.

12. Rod Mickleburgh, "Harper Tories Endorse Heroin Research Project," *Globe and Mail*, October 12, 2011.

13. Andrea Woo, "Report Says B.C. a Model for Treating Opioid Addiction," *Globe and Mail*, August 6, 2013.

14. Glenn Greenwald, *Drug Decriminalization in Portugal: Lessons for Creating Fair and Successful Drug Policies* (Washington, DC: The Cato Institute, 2009.)

15. James Ball, "Silk Road: The Online Drug Marketplace That Officials Seem Powerless to Stop," *The Guardian*, March 22, 2013.

16. Noel Randewich, "New Silk Road Internet Drug Bazaar Opens a Month after FBI Bust," *Reuters*, November 6, 2013.

17. Adam Miller, "Silk Road Drug Website: Canada Among Top Buyers at the New eBay for Illegal Drugs," Canadian Press, *Huffington Post*, August 15, 2012.

18. Olivia Solon, "Police Crack Down on Silk Road Following First Drug Dealer Conviction," February 1, 2013, *www.wired.co.uk/news/archive/2013-02/01/silk-road/crackdown*. Accessed March 5, 2014.

19. James Ball, *Silk Road*.

20. Jeb Boone, "Silk Road: Can an eBay for Meth, Smack and Pot Prevail?" *Global Post*, February 27, 2013, *www.globalpost.com/dispatch/news/business/technology/130220/Silk-Road-eBay-drug-trafficking-emerging-markets-technology-innovation*. Accessed March 5, 2014.

21. UNODC, *2013 World Drug Report*.

22. Mary O'Hara, "Drug Policymakers of the 1980s Knew the Score," *The Guardian*, June 18, 2013.

23. Katherine Pettus, Institutional Association for Hospice and Palliative Care, International Drug Policy Consortium, 2013, *http://idpc.net/blog/2013/06/launch-of-the-unodc-world-drug-report-2013-between-holy-war-and-holistic-policy*. Accessed March 5, 2014.

24. Mike Power, "Rise in Legal Highs Is Fuelled by Drug Prohibition," *The*

Guardian, May 29, 2013.

25. Alan Travis, "More Than 280 'Legal Highs' Now on European Drug Experts' Radar," *The Guardian*, May 28, 2013.

26. Canadian Council on Substance Abuse, *First Do No Harm: Responding to Canada's Prescription Drug Crisis*, March 2013.

27. Valerie Hauch, "Canada Second Highest in World for Prescribed Opiate Drug Use," *Toronto Star*, March 26, 2013.

28. Jillian Berman, "How a Big Drug Company Inadvertently Got Americans Hooked on Heroin," *Huffington Post*, February 24, 2014.

29. Gloria Galloway, "U.S. Senators Urge Canada to Stop 'Hillbilly Heroin,'" *Globe and Mail*, April 3, 2014.

30. Jacques Gallant, "Fentanyl Use by Opioid Addicts on the Rise," *Toronto Star*, August 1, 2013.

31. Maria Cheng, Associated Press, "Marijuana Most Popular Illegal Drug, but Painkiller Addiction Causes Most Death: Study," *Huffington Post*, August 28, 2013.

32. Global Commission on Drug Policy listed seventeen drugs, including seven legal ones, and graphically displayed the assessment of risk as estimated by independent experts. Marijuana occupies a position at No. 10. That is, nine other drugs are assessed as riskier (including alcohol and tobacco), while six are assessed as less risky (including LDS, ecstasy, and qat). *War on Drugs*, 12.

33. Michelle Alexander, *The New Jim Crow*, 143.

34. *CBC News*, "Super Bowl Contest Winner Denied Entry to U.S.," February 3, 2013.

35. James Keller, "Legal Pot in U.S. Could Cause Problems for Canadian Travellers, Experts Warn," Canadian Press, *Huffington Post*, November 24, 2013.

CHAPTER 3: HEROIN: FEAR AND LOATHING

1. Licia Corbella, "Vancouver's Easy Drug Access May Have Helped Kill Monteith," *Calgary Herald*, July 26, 2013.

2. "Licia Corbella Cory Monteith Death: Internet Erupts As Calgary Editor Blames Vancouver for Death," *Huffington Post*, July 19, 2013.

3. "Cory Monteith's Death: Police Issue Toxic Heroin Alert," *Hollywood Reporter*, July 17, 2013.

4. Benedict Carey, "Prescription Painkillers Seen as a Gateway to Heroin," *New York Times*, February 10, 2014.

5. Simon Jenkins, "Philip Seymour Hoffman and a Double Standard Over Drugs," *The Guardian*, February 3, 2014.

6. See *http://heroininfo.org/heroin_facts.html*. Accessed March 5, 2014.

7. See *http://methoide.fcm.arizona.edu/infocenter/index.cfm?stid=176*. Accessed March 5, 2014.

8. Hart, *High Price*, 331.

9. Ibid.

10. Bruce K. Alexander, *The Myth of Drug-Induced Addiction*, submission to the Senate of Canada, *www.parl.gc.ca/content/sen/committee/371/ille/presentation/alexander-e.htm*. Accessed March 5, 2014.

11. Nutt, *Drugs Without the Hot Air*, 265.

12. Ibid., 67–68, 142.

13. "Understanding Heroin Addiction," *Globe and Mail*, video, February 3, 2014.

14. Kirk Makin, Sunny Dhillon, and Ingrid Peritz, "Supreme Court Ruling Opens Doors to Drug Injection Clinics Across Canada," *Globe and Mail*, September 30, 2011.

15. Lewis Lapham, "Why the War on Drugs Is a War on Human Nature," *The Guardian*, December 10, 2012.

16. Global Commission on Drug Policy, *The War on Drugs and HIV/AIDS: How the Criminalization of Drug Use Fuels the Global Pandemic* (June 2012), 5.

17. The following Health Canada website sets out the health concerns associated with heroin use: *www.hc-sc.gc.ca/hc-ps/drugs-drogues/learn-renseigne/heroin-eng.ph*. Accessed March 5, 2014.

18. Makin, et al., "Supreme Court Ruling Opens Doors."

19. Ken MacQueen and Martin Patriquin, "Are We Ready to Subsidize Heroin?" *Maclean's*, October 7, 2011.

20. The British medical journal *The Lancet* said that since InSite opened the number of overdose deaths in the immediate area of the clinic had declined by 35 percent. See also "Supervised Injection for the Sake of Public Health," Editorial, *Globe and Mail*, May 10, 2011.

21. André Picard, "Vancouver's Safe Injection Site Cuts Overdose Deaths," *Globe and Mail*, August 23, 2012.

22. Kathryn Marshall, "Addicts Don't Need InSite, They Need Support," *Huffington Post*, September 27, 2013.

23. Mark Hasiuk, "Is InSite Really All It's Cracked Up to Be?" *Huffington Post*, September 18, 2013.

24. Ian Bailey, "Vancouver Police Urge Addicts to Use InSite Following Deaths," *Globe and Mail*, September 16, 2013.

25. Urban Health Research Initiative of the B.C. Centre for Excellence in HIV/AIDS, *Drug Situation in Vancouver*, 2nd ed., June 2013: 2. See *http://uhri.cfenet.ubc.ca/content/view/98*. Accessed March 5, 2014.

26. Editorial, *Globe and Mail*, May 10, 2011.

27. Gloria Galloway, "Proposed Law Would Jeopardize New Supervised Injection Sites," *Globe and Mail*, June 6, 2013.

28 "Montreal to Get Four Supervised Injection Sites," *CBC Radio News*, December 11, 2013.

29. André Picard, "The Lack of Needles and the Damage Done," *Globe and Mail*, February 18, 2010: L4.

30. The Correctional Investigator Canada, *Annual Report of the Office of the Correctional Investigator 2009–2010* (Ottawa: Her Majesty the Queen in Right of Canada, 2010), 5–6; Picard, ibid.

31. "Prison Policies: Gilding the Cage," *The Economist*, August 17, 2013: 52.

32. *Hansard* (Ottawa: House of Commons) April 23, 2010.

33. MacQueen and Patriquin, "Are We Ready to Subsidize Heroin?" The results of the trial were reported by the *New England Journal of Medicine* in August 2009.

34. Rod Mickleburgh, "Harper Tories Endorse Heroin Research Project," *Globe and Mail*, October 12, 2011.

35. Andrea Woo, "Showing Promise in B.C., Prescription Heroin Now in Peril," *Globe and Mail*, October 5, 2013.

36. Frances Bula, "Heroin Substitute Offers Hope to Addicts," *Globe and Mail*, August 30, 2013.

37. See *www.providencehealthcare.org/salome/faqs.html*. Accessed March 18, 2014.

38. Peter Dawson, "Why the Methadone Doesn't Work," *The Guardian*, January 10, 2012. Dr. David Nutt confirms that withdrawal from methadone is more painful and takes longer than withdrawal from heroin. Nutt, *Drugs Without the Hot Air*, 166.

39. Rod Mickleburgh, "Harper Tories Endorse Heroin Research Project."

40. Andrea Woo, "Showing Promise in B.C."

41. Independent expert assessments of risks show ecstasy to be second-last of seventeen psychoactive drugs in terms of actual and potential harms they could cause to society. LSD is twelfth on the list. Heroin and cocaine place first and second respectively. Global Commission on Drug Policy, *War on Drugs*, June 2011: 12.

42. Adrian Morrow, "Health Minister Closes 'Loophole' on Doctors Prescribing Heroin to Addicts," *Globe and Mail*, October 3, 2013.

43. Canadian Press, "B.C. Health Provider and Patients File Lawsuit Over Prescription Heroin Access," *Times Colonist*, November 13, 2013.

44. Gray, *Why Our Drug Laws Have Failed*, 199.

45. Ibid., 204–05.

46. Global Commission on Drug Policy, *The War on Drugs and HIV/AIDS*, 17.

47. Ed Davey, "Drug Addicts in London Get Heroin Prescribed by NHS," *BBC News*, July 4, 2011.

48. Sophie M. Colleau, PhD, and David E. Joransen, MSSW, "Fear of Addiction: Confronting a Barrier to Cancer Pain Relief," *WHO Pain and Palliative Care Communications Program* 11, no. 3 (1998).

49. Dr. W. Gifford-Jones, November 6, 2011. Accessed at *http://docgiff.com*.

50. In 1956, under pressure from the United States, heroin was banned for medical use, but British doctors objected so strenuously that the decision was later overturned, and today it is used without problems.

51. Alexander, *The Myth of Drug Induced Addiction*.

52. Tom Carnwath and Ian Smith, *Heroin Century* (London: Routledge, 2002), 147–51. Tom Carnwath, MA, FRCPsych, FRCGP, is a consultant psychiatrist with a specialty in addiction psychiatry who worked with drug misuse services in Manchester, England. Ian Smith trained in sociology and was service development manager for drug services in Manchester.

53. Peter Dawson, "Why the Methadone Doesn't Work."

CHAPTER 4: COCAINE: WHITE LINES

1. See *www.narconon.org/drug-information/cocaine-history.html*. Accessed March 5, 2014.

2. See *www.protecthealthbenefits.org/health-news/cocaine-was-once-a-wonder-drug*. Accessed March 5, 2014.

3. Hart, *High Price*, 242.

4. See *www.cqld.ca/livre/en/en/10-cocaine.htm* and *www.thegooddrugsguide.com/cocaine/index.htm*. Accessed March 5, 2014.

5. Hart, *High Price*. The ONDCP is the American drug czar's office, the Office of National Drug Control Policy, 160, 190, 243, 343.

6. Nutt, *Drugs Without the Hot Air*, 186.

7. Hart, *High Price*, 189, 264.

8. Colleau and Joransen, "Fear of Addiction."

9. Hart, xi.

10. Baum, *Smoke and Mirrors*, 219. Emphasis in the original. Also 187 and 189.

11. Gray, 173.

12. Hart, *High Price*, 92–94.

13. A briefing kit for the cocaine study was leaked and can be found at *www.tni.org/sites/www.tni.org/archives/docs/200703081409275046.pdf*. Accessed March 5, 2014.

14. Ben Goldacre, "Cocaine Study That Got Up the Nose of the United States," *The Guardian*, June 13, 2009.

15. *www.undrugcontrol.info/en/component/flexicontent/items/item/269-who-six-horsemen-ride-out?pop=1&tmpl=component&print-1*.

16. See *www.tni.org/sites/www.tni.org/archives/docs/200703081409275046.pdf*. Accessed April 3, 2014.

17. Lisa C.B. Matthews, Gary A. Davies, B.G. Nadeau, Linda S. Wong, and B.K. Alexander, *The British Columbia Key Informant Study* (Simon Fraser University), *http://globalizationofaddiction.ca/articles-speeches/cocaine/182-who-site-report.html*. Accessed March 5, 2014.

18. Dr. Alexander's team of four researchers each contributed at least thirteen usable interviews from sixty consultants, the group being composed of cocaine users, dealers, drug counsellors, addicts, professionals working in the area of addiction, a therapist, and a judge. The interviewees were diverse by gender, age, type of cocaine use, location in the province, and socioeconomic class.

19. This information is contained in the briefing kit, which does not provide sources. Much of the original research was "burned" when the WHO decided not to release the study.

20. Jean Long, "Adulterants, Bulking Agents and Contaminants in Illicit Drugs," *Drugnet Ireland*, Issue 35, Autumn 2010: 18–20.

21. See *www.guardian.co.uk/society/video/2013/apr/19/whats-in-my-cocaine-video*. Accessed March 5, 2014.

22. *Daily Mail Reporter*, "Party-Goer Died After Swallowing Two Spoonfuls of Pure Caffeine Powder — Equal to 70 Cans of Red Bull," *Daily Mail*, October 29, 2010.

23. See *http://alcoholrehab.com/alcohol-rehab/adulterant-substances*. Accessed March 5, 2014.

24. Anna Lacey and Arturo Wallace, "A Safer High? A Night with the Illegal Drug Checkers," *BBC News*, June 28, 2013, *www.bbc.co.uk/news/health-23069825*. Accessed March 5, 2014.

25. Nutt, *Drugs without the Hot Air*, 30–31.

26. The Canadian Press, "Program to Distribute Free Crack Pipes to Vancouver Drug Users," *Huffington Post Canada*, September 31, 2011.

27. Toward the Heart is a project of the British Columbia harm reduction program, *http://towardtheheart.com/product/crack-pipe-mouthpiece*. Accessed March 5, 2014.

28. "Crack Pipe Vending Machines Aim to Curb Spread of Diseases in Vancouver," *Huffington Post*, February 8, 2014.

29. Kevin Drews, "Canadian AIDS Doctors Urge Obama, Romney to End War on Drugs," *Globe and Mail*, July 23, 2012.

30. The *2010 Vienna Declaration* was penned by a group of international experts on HIV/AIDS and drug policy. It calls for an end to the War on Drugs, and the incorporation of scientific evidence into illegal drug policies. Its aim is to improve community health and safety, *www.viennadeclaration.com/about*. Accessed March 5, 2014.

31. See *www.tni.org/sites/www.tni.org/archives/docs/200703081409275046.pdf*. Accessed April 3, 2014.

32. Lester Grinspoon and James B. Bakalar, "Medical Uses of Illicit Drugs," Schaffer Library of Drug Policy, *http://druglibrary.org/schaffer/hemp/medical/meduse.htm*. Accessed March 5, 2014.

33. See *www.encod.org/info/ON-THE-THERAPEUTIC-USE-OF-COCA.html*. Accessed March 5, 2014.

34. See *www.tni.org/sites/www.tni.org/archives/docs/200703081409275046.pdf*. Accessed April 3, 2014.

35. See *www.entnet.org/Practice/policyMedicalUseCocaine.cfm*. Accessed March 5, 2014.

36. P.F. Brain and G.A. Coward, "A Review of the History, Actions, and Legitimate Uses of Cocaine," *Journal of Substance Abuse*, 1989; 1(4): 431–51, from the abstract. Note that the more recent WHO report says cocaine is rarely physically addictive.

37. See *www.medicinenet.com/cocaine_hydrochloride-topical/article.htm*. Accessed March 5, 2014.

CHAPTER 5: MARIJUANA: SPARKING THE DEBATE

1. See *www.thegooddrugsguide.com/cannabis/index.htm*. Accessed March 5, 2014.
2. Liberal Party of Canada (B.C.), *Legalization of Marijuana*.
3. *Cannabis indica* relaxes muscles and works as a general analgesic, also helping with sleep. Cancer chemotherapy pain benefits from *Cannabis indica*, while people with depression benefit from *Cannabis sativa*: *www.thegooddrugsguide. com/cannabis/index.htm* and *www.medicalmarijuana.procon.org/view.answers. php?questionID=000638*. Accessed March 5, 2014.
4. Baum, *Smoke and Mirrors*, 265.
5. The *Good Drugs Guide* says physical addiction is possible, but virtually all sources say otherwise.
6. Jason Rehel, "Marijuana Use by Teens Linked to Permanent Brain Abnormalities Later in Life, Increased Schizophrenia Risk," *The National Post*, July 25, 2013.
7. T.H. Moore, S. Zammit, A. Lingford-Hughes, T.R. Barnes, P.B. Jones, M. Burke, G. Lewis, "Cannabis Use and Risk of Psychotic or Affective Mental Health Outcomes: A Systematic Review," *The Lancet*, July 28, 2007: 370 (9584): 319–28.
8. According to the *Merriam-Webster Dictionary*: Anandamide is a derivative of arachidonic acid that occurs naturally in the brain and in some foods (like chocolate) and that binds to the same brain receptors as the cannabinoids.
9. F.M. Leweke, D. Piomelli, F. Pahlisch, D. Muhl, C.W. Gerth, C. Hoyer, J. Klosterkötter, M. Hellmich, D. Koethe, "Cannabidiol Enhances Anandamide Signaling and Alleviates Psychotic Symptoms of Schizophrenia," *Translation Psychiatry*, March 20, 2012: 2:e94.doi: 10:1038/tp.2012.15.
10. See *www.truthonpot.com/2013/04/06/does-marijuana-cause-schizophrenia*. April 6, 2013.
11. Nutt, *Drugs Without the Hot Air*, 87.
12. This is according to the ACMD in the U.K., *www.ukcia.org/research/ SmokingGun/critique.php*. Accessed March 5, 2014.
13. Marc Kaufman, "Study Finds No Cancer-Marijuana Connection," *The Washington Post*, May 6, 2006.
14. NORML, "The List Goes On: Research Reveals Additional Benefits of Medical Marijuana," *July 2013 Newsletter*, *www.norml.ca/newsletters/newsletter2013-05. php*. Accessed March 5, 2014.
15. See *www.blf.org.uk/Page/Special-Reports*. Accessed March 5, 2014.
16. See *www.ukcia.org/research/SmokingGun/critique.php*. Accessed March 5, 2014.
17. Tom Blackwell, "Heavy Marijuana Smoking May Double Risk of Lung Cancer, Canadian Study Finds," *The National Post*, August 1, 2013.
18. El Jefe, "Too Much Marijuana," *Cannabis Culture Marijuana Magazine*,

September 7, 2008. Sinsemilla is a highly potent type of marijuana derived from female plants that are specially tended and kept seedless by preventing pollination in order to induce a high resin content.

19. Jason Rehel, "Pot Smoking Linked to Doubled Stroke Risk for Younger Adults: New Zealand Study," *The National Post*, February 8, 2013; see also "Marijuana Linked to Strokes in Young Adults: Study," *Huffington Post*, February 6, 2013.

20. Reuters, "Smoking Pot May Not Cause Drop in Teen IQ, New Study Suggests," *Toronto Star*, January 23, 2013.

21. Sharon Kirkey, "Doctors Refuse to Authorize Pot Use, Leaving Patients in Pain," *The National Post*, October 30, 2011.

22. *The Current*, CBC Radio One, September 28, 2012.

23. Quarterly Report #76, November 9, 2001–February 8, 2002, Table 3 (page 8), University of Mississippi Potency Monitoring Project (Oxford, MS: National Center for the Development of Natural Products, Research Institute of Pharmaceutical Sciences, 2002), Mahmoud A. ElSohly, PhD, Director, NIDA Marijuana Project (NIDA Contract #N01DA-0-7707), *www.cannabisconsumers.org/reports/drugwarfacts.php*.

24. Senate Special Committee on Illegal Drugs, *Cannabis*, 13.

25. Website for the U.S. Office of National Drug Control Policy, *www.ncjrs.gov/ondcppubs/publications*.

26. Leslie L. Iversen, PhD, FRS, *The Science of Marijuana* (London: Oxford University Press, 2000), 178, citing House of Lords, Select Committee on Science and Technology, "Cannabis — The Scientific and Medical Evidence" (London: The Stationery Office, Parliament, 1998).

27. U.S. Department of Justice, Drug Enforcement Agency, "In the Matter of Marijuana Rescheduling Petition" [Docket #86-22] (September 6, 1988), 57.

28. "B.C. Medical Health Officers Join Call to Legalize Pot," *CBC News*, December 22, 2011.

29. Samuel Perreault, "Police-Reported Crime Statistics in Canada, 2012," *Juristat*, July 25, 2013, *www.statcan.gc.ca/pub/85-002-x/85-002-x2013001-eng.htm*.

30. The new regulations were put on hold by a federal court judge on March 21, 2014, when he granted a temporary injunction in a case that argues the rights of patients are being contravened by the new system.

31. Kirkey, "Doctors Refuse to Authorize Pot Use." Interestingly, in 1991 Harvard University surveyed U.S. oncologists and found that of the thousand who responded, half said they would prescribe marijuana if it were legal. Of those, about half had already done so anyway. Dan Baum, *Smoke and Mirrors*, 314.

32. Anna Reid and Rocco Gerace, "Marijuana Is an Untested Drug. Doctors Shouldn't Be Told to Prescribe It," *Globe and Mail*, June 20, 2013.

33. Tom Blackwell, "Doctors Planning Clinic Devoted Solely to Medical Marijuana Hoping to Avoid Legal Quagmire over Cannabis Prescriptions," *The National Post*, August 13, 2013.

34. Jenna Valleriani, "How the New Medical Marijuana Rules Will Punish Patients," *Globe and Mail*, January 7, 2014.

35. Dana Larsen, head of Sensible BC, which lobbies for decriminalization of marijuana, interviewed on *The Current*, CBC Radio One, October 1, 2013.

36. *The News at Six*, CBC Radio One, January 29, 2014.

37. Sunny Freeman, "Court Ruling Won't Sway Health Canada on 'Narcotic' Marijuana," *Huffington Post*, March 21, 2014.

38. This journal is a publication of the American College of Rheumatology, *www.ccic.net/index/php?id=7,0,0,1,0,0*.

39. *CBC News*, "Toronto Parents Petition Health Canada over Pot for Kids," *Huffington Post*, July 19, 2013.

40. *The Current*, CBC Radio One, November 19, 2013, Interview with Kaitlyn's father.

41. See *www.cnn.com/2013/08/07/health/charlotte-child-medical-marijuana*.

42. *The Current*, November 19, 2013.

43. Dave Phillips, "Now Popular in Colorado, Marijuana Oil Has Long Success History That's Often Been Ignored," *The Colorado Springs Gazette*, January 27, 2014.

44. Drs. Grinspoon and Bakalar, "Medical Uses of Illicit Drugs."

45. Tom Blackwell, "Doctors Planning Clinic."

46. See *www.ccic.net/index/php?id=7,0,0,1,0,0*.

47. *The Current*, CBC Radio One, December 23, 2010.

48. "A Judge's Plea for Pot," *New York Times*, May 16, 2012.

49. Jim Wyss, "Colombia's Controversial Cure for Coke Addicts: Give Them Marijuana," *The Miami Herald*, June 3, 2013.

50. *CBC News*, "Smoking Pot May Help Relieve MS Pain," May 14, 2012.

51. Paul Taylor, "Marijuana May Cut Risk of Developing Diabetes: Study," *Globe and Mail*, May 15, 2013. Taylor is referring to a National Health and Nutrition Survey carried out by the United States Centre for Disease Control 2005-2010, and reported in *The American Journal of Medicine*.

52. R.T. Jones, "Cardiovascular System Effects of Marijuana," *Journal of Clinical Pharmacology*, November 2000: 42(11 Suppl): 58S–63S.

53. Thandi Fletcher, "B.C. Seniors Are Using Medical Marijuana to Get a Good Night's Sleep," *The Province*, May 27, 2013.

54. Carly Schwartz, "Marijuana May Stop the Spread of HIV," *Huffington Post*, February 11, 2014.

55. Kirk Johnson, "Providers of Medical Marijuana Face New Fears," *New York Times*, March 6, 2014.

56. Adam Nagourney, "California: Marijuana Seller Takes Plea Deal," *New York Times*, May 31, 2013.

57. NORML, "DEA Busts in Washington State Despite State Laws to the Contrary," *July 2013 Newsletter*, *http://norml.ca/newsletter2013-07.php*.

Chapter 6: The Economics of Illegal Drugs: Our Gift to Organized Crime

1. UNODC, *World Drug Report 2012*, 70–71.
2. J. Rehm, et al., *The Costs of Substance Abuse in Canada*, 8.
3. Jonathan P. Caulkins and Peter Reuter, "How Drug Enforcement Affects Drug Prices" (2010). In Michael Tonry (ed.) *Crime and Justice: A Review of Research* 39 (Chicago: University of Chicago Press).
4. Dan Werb, Thomas Kerr, Bohdan Nosyk, Steffanie Strathdee, Julio Montaner, Evan Wood, "The Temporal Relationship Between Drug Supply Indicators: An Audit of International Government Surveillance Systems," *BMJ Open*, September 30, 2013. Accessed at *www.bmjopen.bmj.com/content/3/9/e003077.full.*
5. Caulkins and Reuter, "How Drug Enforcement Affects Drug Prices."
6. Evan Wood, MD, PhD; Dan Werb, MSc; Benedikt Fischer, PhD; Carl Hart, PhD; Alex Wodak, MD; Francisco Inacio Bastos, MD, PhD; Julio Montaner, MD; Thomas Kerr, PhD, *Tools for Debate: U.S. Federal Government Data on Cannabis Prohibition* (Vancouver: ICSDP, 2010), 5.
7. Stop the Violence BC, "B.C. Medical Health Officers Join Call to Legalize Pot," *CBC News*, December 22, 2011.
8. Dr. Francisco E. Thoumi, "The Numbers Game: Let's All Guess the Size of the Illegal Drug Industry!" *Journal of Drug Issues* 35, no. 1 (Winter 2005): 185–200. Dr. Thoumi is former research director of the Global Programme against Money Laundering at the United Nations Office for Drug Control and Crime Prevention (UNODCCP), Vienna, and the author of several books and articles on illegal drugs.
9. Wood, et al., *Tools for Debate*, 8 and 21.
10. Alex Dobuzinskis, "Eric Holder Urged To Oppose Marijuana Ballots by Ex-DEA Heads," *Huffington Post*, September 7, 2012.
11. Robert DuPont, "Rights, Wrongs, and the War on Drugs," *The Mark*, September 11, 2012.
12. Baum, *Smoke and Mirrors*, 264, 298.
13. David Binder, "Washington Talk: Briefing; Bennett's Habit," *New York Times*, February 24, 1989. And Katharine Q. Seelye, "Relentless Moral Crusader is Relentless Gambler," *New York Times*, May 3, 2003.
14. Thoumi, "The Numbers Game," 195.
15. Auditor General of Canada, *Illicit Drugs*.
16. Rajeev Syal, "Drug Money Saved Banks in Global Crisis, Claims U.N. Advisor," *The Guardian*, December 13, 2009.
17. Nutt, *Drugs Without the Hot Air*, 276–77.
18. Anabel Hernández, *Narcoland: The Mexican Drug Lords and Their Godfathers* (London/Brooklyn, NY: Verso, 2013).
19. Ed Vulliamy, "Mexico's War on Drugs Is One Big Lie," *The Observer*, September 1, 2013.

20. Global Commission on Drug Policy, *War on Drugs*, June 2011.

21. I am grateful to Mark Haden of Vancouver Coastal Health for his compilation of statistics on the drug war entitled *Economic Fact Sheet: Facts and Figures Relating to Illegal Drugs*, dated December 2008.

22. "Experiments in Legalisation Are Showing What a Post-War Approach to Drug Control Could Look Like," *Economist*, February 23, 2013.

23. Note that these are global figures.

24. Alan Travis, "More than 280 'Legal Highs.'"

25. Auditor General of Canada, *Illicit Drugs*, 3.

26. UNODC, *World Drug Report 2012*, 60.

27. Syal, "Drug Money Saved Banks."

28. Liana Sun Wyler, "International Drug Control Policy: Background and the U.S. Response," *CRS Report for Congress IDCP*, Order Code RL 34543 (June 23, 2008), 21. Accessed at *www.fas.org/sgp/crs/row/RL34543.pdf.*

29. Beau Kilmer and Rosalie Liccardo Pacula, "Estimating the Size of the Global Drug Market, Report 2," prepared for the RAND Corporation for the European Union (Santa Monica, CA, 2009), 22.

30. Peter Reuter is a professor in the School of Public Policy and Department of Criminology at the University of Maryland, and founded and directed RAND's Drug Policy Research Center from 1989 to 1993. He has written a number of books on the illegal drug market, and was Principal Investigator for the RAND Corporation document, prepared for the European Union, "Assessment of World Markets and Policies, 1998–2006."

31. Thoumi, "The Numbers Game," 191.

32. Jeremy Haken, "Transnational Crime in the Developing World" (Washington, DC: Global Financial Integrity, Centre for International Policy, February 2011), 3.

33. ONDCP, "What America's Users Spend on Illegal Drugs, 2000–2006" (Washington, DC: Executive Office of the President), 13. The ONDCP is an arm of the American government.

34. Sunny Freeman, "Court Ruling Won't Sway Health Canada on 'Narcotic' Marijuana," *Huffington Post*, March 21, 2014.

35. Gary Mason, "The Case for Legalizing Marijuana," *Globe and Mail*, October 7, 2010.

36. Alison Stateman, "Can Marijuana Help Rescue California's Economy?" *Time Magazine US*, March 13, 2009.

37. Guy Kovner, "State's Pot Crop Worth $14 billion, Dwarfs Wine Grapes," *The Press Democrat*, October 18, 2010.

38. Liberal Party of Canada (B.C.), *Legalization of Marijuana*, 11.

39. Auditor General of Canada, *Illicit Drugs*, 3.

40. Kilmer and Pacula, "Estimating the Size of the Global Drug Market," 21.

41. This fact sheet created by the CBC relies upon numbers provided by the United States Drug Enforcement Agency and by Canadian economist Stephen T. Easton,

"Marijuana Growth in British Columbia," *Public Policy Sources*, Number 74 (May 2004). See *www.cbc.ca/documentaries/doczone/2010/cannabiz/factsheet.html*.

42. Comparator industries were construction ($5.7 billion), logging and forest products ($5.6 billion), mining ($3.7 billion), manufacturing ($3.4 billion), and agriculture ($2.1 billion). C. Skelton, "B.C.'s Top Commodity: Marijuana," *The Vancouver Sun*, July 7, 2001, referring to estimates by the Organized Crime Agency of British Columbia and British Columbia provincial statistics.

43. Easton, "Marijuana Growth in British Columbia," 21.

44. Sunny Dhillon, "Demand, Price for B.C. Bud Dropping in Wake of U.S. Legalization," *Globe and Mail*, November 20, 2013.

45. See *www.cbc.ca/documentaries/doczone/2010/cannabiz/factsheet.html*.

46. Easton, "Marijuana Growth in British Columbia," 20.

47. The Canadian Press, "Crime Bill: Marijuana in Small Quantities Still Won't Attract Charges, Say B.C. Police," *Huffington Post*, November 11, 2011. As a matter of interest, a 2005 report from the Royal Canadian Mounted Police (RCMP) found that if the black market were factored into provincial finances, B.C.'s trade surplus would increase 230 percent to $8.6 billion. See *www.cbc. ca/documentaries/doczone/2010/cannabiz/factsheet.html*, quoting *Maclean's*.

48. Chris Brummitt, "Canada Marijuana Finds Asian Market in Asia, East-to-West Trade," *Huffington Post*, October 23, 2013.

49. J. Rehm, et al., *The Costs of Substance Abuse in Canada*: 1, 8. The Canadian Centre on Substance Abuse receives core funding in the order of five hundred thousand dollars per year from the federal government.

50. Auditor General of Canada, *Illicit Drugs*.

51. The report is referring to statistics produced by J. Rehm, et al., *The Costs of Substance Abuse in Canada*.

52. The costs are not insignificant. One U.S. study, for example, found that ex-offenders suffered employment losses that resulted in a lost output of goods and services in the order of fifty-seven to sixty-five billion dollars per year. John Schmitt, Kris Warner, and Sarika Gupta, "Ex-Offenders and the Labour Market," Center for Economics and Policy Research (Washington, DC, November 2010), 14.

53. Kirk Johnson, "Providers of Medical Marijuana face New Fears," *New York Times*, March 6, 2014.

54. Kora De Beck, Evan Wood, Julio Montaner, and Thomas Kerr, "Canada's 2003 Renewed Drug Strategy — An Evidence-Based Review," Canadian HIV/AIDS Legal Network, *HIV/AIDS Policy and Law Review* 11, nos. 2/3 (December 2006).

55. Kevin Drews, "Canadian AIDS Doctors Urge Obama, Romney to End War on Drugs."

56. Letter to Government Expressing Opposition to Bill S-10, signed by 563 health professionals and other experts from across Canada (Vancouver: Urban Health Research Initiative/B.C. Centre for Excellence in HIV/AIDS, February 6, 2011), *http://uhri.cfenet.ubc.ca/content/view/88*.

56. Katherine Dinner, Tracey Donaldson, Jeff Potts, Josie Sirna, and Tom Wong, "Hepatitis C: A Public Perspective and Related Implications for Physicians," *Public Health Agency of Canada*, in *Royal College Outlook* 2, no. 3 (Fall 2005): 22.

57. Thomas Kerr, *Safe Injection Facilities: Proposal for a Vancouver Pilot Project* (Vancouver: Harm Reduction Action Society, November, 2000).

58. Internal Audit Report, Portland Hotel Society Community Service Contracts, February 26, 2014 (page 14), *www.vch.ca/media/Portland-Hotel-Society-Audit-Report_VCH.pdf*.

59. Kirkey, "Doctors Refuse to Authorize Pot Use."

60. Susan Boyd and Connie Carter, *Killer Weed: Marijuana Grow Ops, Media, and Justice* (Toronto: University of Toronto Press, 2014). Report by James Keller, "Police, Media Misled British Columbians on Marijuana, New Book Claims," *Globe and Mail*, December 25, 2013.

61. The coalition comprises law enforcement officials, legal experts, public health officials and academic experts.

62. See *http://stoptheviolencebc.org/about-us*.

63. The Canadian Press, "Canada Gang Violence: Marijuana Legalization Would Curb Violence and Create New Revenue, Experts Say," *Huffington Post*, October 27, 2011.

64. ICSDP, "Effect of Drug Law Enforcement on Drug-Related Violence: Evidence from a Scientific Review," April 2010.

CHAPTER 7: PROHIBITION VS. THE ALTERNATIVE: THE BOTTOM LINE

1. Wood, et al., *Tools for Debate*, 17.

2. United Nations Office for Drug Control and Crime Prevention, *Global Illicit Drug Trends 1999* (New York: UNODCCP, 1999), 51.

3. Jennifer Yang, "Canadian Researchers Find Illegal Drugs More Plentiful Despite Police Seizures," *Toronto Star*, September 20, 2013, referring to a study by the ICSDP published in *BMJOpen* by Dr. Evan Wood, et al.

4. Peter Chalk, "The Latin American Drug Trade: Scope, Dimensions, Impact and Response," RAND Corporation for the U.S. Air Force (Santa Monica: 2011), 47.

5. Liana SunWyler, "International Drug Control Policy," 21.

6. National Center on Addiction and Substance Abuse, "Shovelling Up II: The Impact of Substance Abuse on State Budgets" (New York: CASA, May 2009), 58.

7. Global Commission on Drug Policy, *The War on Drugs and HIV/AIDS*.

8. Wood, et al., *Tools for Debate*. The last year that the United States Office of National Drug Control Policy reported these statistics was 2000.

9. "Prison Reform: An Unlikely Alliance of Left and Right," *The Economist*, August 17, 2013: 23.

10. Megan McLemore, "Canada Has Been a Regional Leader in Drug Policy, but Bill S-10 Would Waste Billions of Dollars on Ineffective Approaches That Only Appear

To Be Tough on Crime," *The Mark News*, February 16, 2011. Megan McLemore is senior researcher with Health and Human Rights, Human Rights Watch.

11. See *www.drugpolicy.org/drug-war-statistics*.

12. Liana SunWyler, "International Drug Control Policy," 29.

13. Editorial, *Globe and Mail*, April 16, 2012.

14. Eric Single, "The Economic Costs of Illicit Drugs and Drug Enforcement," *Policy Options* (October 1998), 5.

15. Rehm, et al., *The Costs of Substance Abuse in Canada*, 8. This CCSA report is dated 2006.

16. De Beck, et al., "Canada's 2003 Renewed Drug Strategy."

17. John Geddes, "Harper's Anti-Drug Strategy Gets a Little Less Compassionate," *Maclean's*, July 25, 2012.

18. Wood, et al., *Tools for Debate*.

19. Dana Larsen, Sensible BC, email dated February 11, 2014.

20. Jeff Davis, "Prison Costs Soar 86% in Past Five Years: Report," *The National Post*, August 5, 2011.

21. Boyd, *High Society*, 83ff.

22. A typical sentence at the time for manslaughter was six years, for violent sexual assault three years, for repeated armed robbery six years.

23. Interview with Steve Paikin, *The Agenda*, TVO, September 28, 2011. Accessed at *www.youtube.com/watch?v=J3Dnfg_5jtw*.

24. Tonda MacCharles, "Federal Prison Population in Canada Growing," *Toronto Star*, October 23, 2012.

25. See *www.hc-sc.gc.ca/hc-ps/drugs-drogues/stat/_2011/summary-sommaire-eng.php*.

26. See *www.unodc.org/wdr/en/maps-and-graphs.html*.

27. Mia Dauvergne, "Trends in Police-Reported Drug Offences in Canada," *Juristat* 29, no. 2 (May 2009); Shannon Brennan, "Police-Reported Crime Statistics in Canada, 2011," *Juristat*, July 24, 2012, cat. no. 85-002-X.

28. Ken MacQueen, "Why It's Time to Legalize Marijuana," *Maclean's*, June 10, 2013.

29. Jeffrey A. Miron and Katherine Waldock, "The Budgetary Impact of Ending Drug Prohibition," Cato Institute, 2010, Executive Summary.

30. Mason, "The Case for Legalizing Marijuana."

31. Chris Selley, "Marijuana Prohibition Isn't a Conservative Position," *The National Post*, June 14, 2011.

32. Opendoors, "The Criminal Justice Costs of Marijuana Prohibition in Rhode Island," (Providence, RI: March 2010), 1.

33 "The Law of the Weed," *The Economist*, July 17, 2010: 32.

34. Dan Werb, Bohdan Nosyk, Thomas Kerr, Benedikt Fischer, et al., "Estimating the Economic Value of British Columbia's Domestic Cannabis Market: Implications for Provincial Cannabis Policy," *International Journal of Drug Policy*, vol. 23, Issue 6, November 2012: 436–41.

35. Easton, "Marijuana Growth in British Columbia," 21.

36. Miron and Waldock, "The Budgetary Impact of Ending Drug Prohibition."

37. Selley, "Marijuana Prohibition Isn't a Conservative Position."

38. Robert Ali, et al., *The Social Impacts of the Cannabis Expiation Notice Scheme in South Australia: Summary Report* (Canberra, Australia: Department of Health and Aged Care, 1999), 44.

39. *The Economist*, "The Law of the Weed."

40. Jack Healy, "Up Early and In Line for a Marijuana Milestone in Colorado," *New York Times*, January 1, 2014.

41. Andrea Rael, "Colorado Marijuana Sales Surpass $1 million on First Day: Shop Owners," *Huffington Post*, January 3, 2014.

42. Adam Gabbatt, "Justice Department Won't Sue Colorado and Washington over Marijuana Laws," *The Guardian*, August 29, 2013.

43. Tobi Cohen, "Experts Disagree on Economic Impact of Legalizing Marijuana in Canada," *The National Post*, August 27, 2013.

44. Kirk Johnson, "In Montana, an Economic Boon Repeal Effort," *New York Times*, March 5, 2011.

45. Mike Moffatt, "Time to Legalize Marijuana? — 500+ Economists Endorse Marijuana Legalization," n.d., *www.economics.about.com/od/incometaxestax-cuts/a/legalize_pot.htm*.

46. Wood, et al., *Tools for Debate.*

47. UNODC, *From Coercion to Cohesion: Treating Drug Dependence Through Health Care, Not Punishment.* Discussion paper based on a scientific workshop. Vienna, October 28–30, 2009. (United Nations: New York, 2010), 7.

48. Specialist drug courts operate to divert offenders from a sentence of incarceration to supervised drug treatment. They provide an alternative to criminal justice sanctions, and have been found to significantly reduce drug use and crime and save money as well. They are not without controversy, though, as most models include a coercive element. For example, if an offender fails to complete treatment, he or she may be returned to the criminal court to be sentenced.

49. Justice Policy Institute, "Substance Abuse Treatment and Public Safety" (Washington, DC: January 2008), 2.

50. C.P. Rydell and S.S. Everingham, "Controlling Cocaine," prepared for the ONDCP and the U.S. Army (Santa Monica: Drug Policy Research Center, RAND Corporation, 1994), xvi.

51. C.P. Rydell, J.P. Caulkins, and S.S. Everingham, *Enforcement or Treatment? Modeling the Relative Efficacy of Alternatives for Controlling Cocaine.* Operations Research (RAND) 1996, 44(5): 687–95.

52. Gray, *Why Our Drug Laws Have Failed*, 207.

53. T. Turner, *Review of Methadone Services in Vancouver/Richmond Health Region* (Vancouver: Transformation Solutions, Ltd., June 2001).

54. Angela Hennessy, "The Canadian Prison System Is Keeping Prisoners Doped Up on Methadone," *Vice*, September 4, 2013. *www.vice.com/en-ca/read/the-canadian-prison-system-is-keeping-prisoners-doped-up-on-methadone.*

CHAPTER 8: A SHIFTING INTERNATIONAL CONSENSUS

1. Konrad Yakabuski, "Republicans Suddenly Get Smart on Crime," *Globe and Mail*, March 20, 2014.
2. These are: the *1961 Single Convention on Narcotic Drugs*, the *1971 Convention on Psychotropic Substances* and its *1972 Amending Protocol*, and the *1988 Convention Against Illicit Traffic in Narcotic Drugs and Psychotropic Substances*.
3. UNODC, *From Coercion to Cohesion.*
4. Connie I. Carter and Donald MacPherson, *Getting to Tomorrow: A Report on Canadian Drug Policy* (Vancouver: Canadian Drug Policy Coalition, 2013), *http://drugpolicy.ca/report/CDPC2013_en.pdf.*
5. UNODC, *World Drug Report 2012*, 17, 66. Marijuana is one drug whose rate of use has declined in some parts of the world. There is 50 percent less marijuana use in the United States than in 1979 (its peak year) (page 73). There has also been a decline in use in Europe (page 22). See also 85–86.
6. "Africa's Drug Trade: Blazing Saddles in the Sahara," *The Economist*, September 22, 2012.
7. Senior DEA officials say that the highest levels of the military are involved in drug trafficking. United Nations officials say the coup was itself perpetrated by people "totally embedded in the drugs business." Adam Nossiter, *New York Times*, November 1, 2012. Guinea-Bissau's military chief was recently arrested on cocaine and weapons-smuggling charges. Adam Nossiter, "U.S. Indicts Guinea-Bissau's Military Chief in Drug Case," *New York Times*, April 18, 2013.
8. Nutt, *Drugs Without the Hot Air*, 278.
9. "Boom Boom: Trafficking in North Africa," *The Economist*, August 17, 2013: 42–43.
10. Janet McFarland, "Trinidad Wants to Buy Canadian Aircraft to Watch Drug Activity," *Globe and Mail*, April 26, 2013.
11. See *www.countthecosts.org/seven-costs.*
12. UNODC, *World Drug Report 2012*, 39. Also, Editorial, "Summit of the Americas Agrees War on Drugs a Failure," *Globe and Mail*, April 16, 2012.
13. This figure is from the Transform Drug Policy Foundation in the U.K. Accessed at *www.tdpf.org.uk/case-for-reform#responsible-regulation.*
14. Editorial, "Summit of the Americas Agree War on Drugs a Failure," *Globe and Mail*, September 6, 2012.
15. Otto Pérez Molina, "We Have to Find New Solutions to Latin America's Drugs Nightmare," *The Observer*, April 7, 2012.
16. Ari Rosmarin and Niamh Eastwood, "A Quiet Revolution: Drug Decriminalisation Policies in Practice Across the Globe," *Drugs, The Law*

and Human Rights (2012), a publication of the organization Release. The details of the twenty-one countries which follow are drawn from the report accessed at *www.release.org.uk/downloads/publications/release-quiet-revolution-drug-decriminalisation-policies.pdf.* I would like to express my gratitude to the authors of this document, which I have found very useful.

17. The numbers that follow were current in 2012, the time of the publication of the Release report.

18. In 2002, 19 percent of Western Australians had used marijuana in the past year. This was reduced to 12 percent in 2007.

19. Portugal's current thresholds: heroin (one gram), cocaine (two grams), marijuana (twenty-five grams of herbal). Home Affairs Committee — Ninth Report, *Drugs: Breaking the Cycle*, December 3, 2012. Accessed at *www.publications.parliament.uk/pa/cm201213/cmselect/cmhaff/184/18401.htm.*

20. Associated Press, "Theses Countries Mull Over Marijuana Legalization after Uruguay Ruling," February 16, 2014.

21. "Kicking the Habit," *The Economist*, September 15, 2012: 41.

22. Hunter Stuart, "When It Comes to Marijuana, North Korea Appears to Have Liberal Policy of Tolerance," *Huffington Post*, October 10, 2013.

23. UKDPC, *A Fresh Approach to Drugs: The Final Report of the U.K. Drug Policy Commission* (October 2012), 120.

24. Rosmarin and Eastwood, *A Quiet Revolution*, 19, 33.

25. Paul Ames, "Haze Clears over Dutch Cannabis Law," *Global Post*, January 13, 2013.

26. United Nations Drug Control, Transnational Institute, "Councils Increase Pressure for Legal Cannabis Production," April 27, 2013. Accessed at *www.dutchnews.nl/news/archives/2013/04/councils_up_pressure_for_legal.php.*

27. Associated Press, "These Countries Mull Over Marijuana Legalization."

28. "Experiments in Legalisation Are Showing What a Post-War Approach to Drug Control Could Look Like," *The Economist*, February 23, 2013.

29. Home Affairs Committee — Ninth Report, *Drugs: Breaking the Cycle.*

30. Glenn Greenwald, *Drug Decriminalization in Portugal: Lessons for Creating Fair and Successful Drug Policies* (Washington, DC: The Cato Institute, 2009).

31. HIV rates remained stable, but the number of new cases of HIV/AIDS among addicts dropped substantially. Hepatitis B and C cases had also dropped in number, and deaths from drug use were down or stable, reversing the trend of the 1990s.

32. It is probable that harsh regimes result in higher drug use rates. In addition to the countries already noted, the United States is a very harsh regime, and a 2008 survey found that it had the highest level of marijuana and cocaine use in the world: 16.2 percent of U.S. citizens have used cocaine, while 42 percent have used marijuana. This is reported by Louisa Degenhardt, et al., "Toward a Global View of Alcohol, Tobacco, Cannabis and Cocaine Use: Findings from the WHO World Mental Health Surveys," *Public Library of Science Medicine* 5, no. 7 (2008): 1057.

33. Maia Szalavitz, "Drugs in Portugal: Did Decriminalization Work?" *Time Science Magazine*, April 26, 2009.

34. Wiebke Hollersen, "'This is Working': Portugal, 12 Years after Decriminalizing Drugs," *Spiegel online*, March 27, 2013, translated from the German by Ella Ornstein.

35. Dina Rickman, "Decriminalisation of Drugs in Portugal Was Not a Success, Says Dr. Manuel Pinto Coelho," *Huffington Post*, December 10, 2012.

36. Hollersen, "'This Is Working.'"

37. C.E. Hughes and A. Stevens, "What Can We Learn from the Portuguese Decriminalisation of Illicit Drug Use," *British Journal of Criminology* 50, no. 6 (2010): 999–1022. Also, C.E. Hughes and A. Stevens, "A Resounding Success or a Disastrous Failure: Re-Examining the Interpretation of Evidence on the Portuguese Decriminalisation of Illicit Drugs," *Drug and Alcohol Review* 31, no. 1 (2012): 101–13.

38. Helena Smith, "Greek Addicts Turn to Deadly Shisha Drug as Economic Crisis Deepens," *The Guardian*, May 16, 2013.

39. "Drug Addiction in Iran: The Other Religion," *The Economist*, August 17, 2013: 43.

40. The "crack" we are familiar with in North America is derived from cocaine.

41. See *www.tdpf.org.uk/case-for-reform#responsible-regulation*.

CHAPTER 9: STEPPING OUT IN FRONT: THE AMERICAS

1. "Burn-Out and Battle Fatigue," *The Economist*, March 17, 2012: 43.

2. These included all seven Central American countries, plus Mexico, Colombia, and the Dominican Republic.

3. Heather Walsh, "Chocolate Losing to Cocaine in Colombia as Cocoa Prices Slump," *Bloomberg*, August 16, 2012.

4. Jess Hunter-Bowman, "South America Takes Lead in Calling for End to War on Drugs," *Straight Goods*, June 3, 2013.

5. *http://stopthedrugwar.org/chronicle/2007/aug/03/feature_colombia_announces_shift*.

6. *http://stopthedrugwar*. Also, Connie Veillette and Carolina Navarrete-Frías, "Drug Crop Eradication Alternative Development in the Andes," CRS Report for Congress. Order Code RL 33163, November 18, 2005.

7. Sibylla Brodzinsky, "Colombian Rebels Offer to Support Peasant Protests," *The Guardian*, July 23, 2013.

8. "Experiments in Legalisation," *The Economist*.

9. Ibid.

10. "Thinking the Unthinkable," *The Economist*, June 30, 2012: 38.

11. NORML, "July 31 Uruguay Votes on Legislation," *July 2013 Newsletter*. Accessed at *www.norml.ca/newsletter2013-07.php#uruguay*.

12. Staff, "Uruguay Won't Be Pot-Smokers Haven, President Vows," *Globe and Mail*, August 1, 2013.

13. Uki Goni, "Excitement, but Anxiety too, as Uruguay Sets Liberal Path with a New Cannabis Law," *The Observer*, August 3, 2013.

14. Simon Romero, "Lawmakers in Uruguay Vote to Legalize Marijuana," *New York Times*, July 31, 2013.
15. Isabel Teotonio, "2014 Poised to Go to Pot," *Toronto Star*, January 10, 2014.
16. "Burn-Out and Battle Fatigue," *The Economist*.
17. In March 2012, U.S. Secretary of Defense Leon Panetta cited unpublished figures from Mexican officials and said that 150,000 people had been killed in Mexico's War on Drugs. "Examining the Drug War Death-Toll Debate," *The Guadalajara Reporter*, January 12–18, 2013: 9.
18. "A Glimmer of Hope," *The Economist*, November 24, 2012, Special Report, 9–10.
19. "Kingpin Bowling," *The Economist*, October 20, 2012: 34.
20. Allyn Hunt, "Mixed Signals Keep Many Mexicans on Edge about Drug War Strategy …," *Guadalajara Reporter*, March 22–28, 2014.
21. "The Unmentionables," *The Economist*, May 3, 2013.
22. "Experiments in Legalisation," *The Economist*.
23. Associated Press, "These Countries Mull Over Marijuana Legalization."
24. Jo Tuckman, "Mexico City Legislators Move to Relax Cannabis Laws," *The Guardian*, February 20, 2014.
25. *CBC News*, June 7, 2013.
26. Jason McLure, *Reuters*, June 6, 2013.
27. The Associated Press, "Alaska: Push to Legalize Marijuana Begins," *New York Times*, June 14, 2013.
28. NORML, "DEA Busts in Washington State Despite State Laws to the Contrary," *NORML Canada Newsletter*, July 2013, *http://norml.ca/newsletter2013-07.php#dea-busts*.
29. International Centre for Science in Drug Policy website, *www.icsdp.org/aboutus/science_drugpolicy.aspx*.
30. Associated Press, "Obama Won't Go after Marijuana Use in Colorado, Washington States," December 15, 2012.
31. Accessed at *http://globalgrind.com/endthewarondrugs*.
32. T.W. Farnum, "Colorado Marijuana Growers Hoping for a Rocky Mountain High," *Guardian Weekly*, April 26, 2013.
33. Jenny Kleeman, "Cannabis: Colorado's Budding Industry," *The Guardian*, May 17, 2013.
34. Another person in the business says that his licence to sell medical marijuana is about an inch thick: "They took photos of all my tattoos and scars," he says.
35. Financial institutions, security providers, and landlords serving marijuana businesses can be prosecuted for racketeering, money laundering, and trafficking under federal laws, which also hinder states in regulating banking and taxation of growers and dispensaries. Ashley Southell, "Answers Sought for When Marijuana Laws Collide," *New York Times*, September 10, 2013.
36. A number of banks offered credit card services in the past but these dwindled

to one bank in 2011 due to pressure from law enforcement. *www.thetransactiongroup.net/medical-marijuana-merchant-accounts.*

37. Ariel Shearer, "IRS Targets Medical Marijuana Businesses in Government's Ongoing War on Pot," *Huffington Post*, May 29, 2013.

38. AOL.on News, video "Obama: Legalizing Drugs 'Not the Answer,'" *http://on.aol.ca/video/obama--legalizing-drugs-not-the-answer-517334740?icid=bottom_related_thumb_3.* Accessed March 18, 2014.

39. This appears to be an echo of the advice President Obama received from his former senior drug policy adviser, Kevin A. Sabet. Sabet's new project, Smart Approaches to Marijuana, or SAM, talks about taking a health-first approach, but opposes legalization. SAM's main fears are that our children will suffer, and that Big Tobacco will take over Big Marijuana: "Very likely results of legalization would be Big Marijuana marketing to children and Big Tobacco taking over Big Marijuana." Accessed at *www.learnaboutsam.com.*

40. E.C. Gogolak, "Trying to Sell Wall Street on the Value of Marijuana," *New York Times*, June 14, 2013.

41. "Marijuana Stocks Soar as Speculators See Green," *Huffington Post*, from *Bloomberg News*, January 9, 2014.

42. Dan Levine and David Ingram, "U.S. Moves to Curb Long, Mandatory Drug Sentences," *Reuters*, August 12, 2013.

43. Many police are in agreement with these changes. Chuck Wexler, executive director of the Police Executive Research Forum, a Washington-based research group, says many police chiefs want to see a rethink of mandatory sentencing for low-level drug offences. Charlie Savage and Erica Goode, "Two Powerful Signals of a Major Shift on Crime," *New York Times*, August 12, 2013.

44. Charlie Savage, "Justice Dept. Seeks to Curtail Stiff Drug Sentences," *New York Times,* August 12, 2013.

45. Vanita Gupta, "How to Really End Mass Incarceration," *New York Times*, August 14, 2013.

46. Serge F. Kovaleski, "U.S. Issues Marijuana Guidelines for Banks," *New York Times*, February 15, 2014.

47. Gogolak, "Trying to Sell Wall Street on the Value of Marijuana."

48. Stephen Rolles, *After the War on Drugs: Blueprint for Regulation. Executive Summary*, Transform Drug Policy Foundation, 2009: 19. Accessed at *www.tdpf.org.uk/downloads/blueprint/Blueprint_exec_summary.pdf.*

49. OAS Scenario Team, *Scenarios for the Drug Problem in the Americas 2013–2015*, (Washington, DC: OAS, 2013), *www.oas.org/documents/eng/press/Scenarios_Report.pdf.*

50. Hunter-Bowman, "South America Takes Lead in Calling for End to War on Drugs."

51. Jamie Doward, "Western Leaders Study 'Gamechanging' Report on Global Drugs Trade," *The Guardian*, May 18, 2013.

52. "Breaking the Taboo about Drugs," *The Guardian*, May 18, 2013. The letter was signed by Fernando Henrique Cardoso, former president of Brazil and Chair of the Global Commission on Drug Policy; César Gaviria, former president of Colombia; Ricardo Lagos, former president of Chile; George P. Shultz, former secretary of state, United States, and Honorary Chair of the Global Commission on Drug Policy; Paul Volcker, former chairman of the United States Federal Reserve and of the Economic Recovery Board; Louise Arbour, former U.N. High Commissioner for Human Rights, president of the International Crisis Group; Ernesto Zedillo, former president of Mexico.

53. Global Commission on Drug Policy, *The War on Drugs and HIV/AIDS*.

CHAPTER 10: PROHIBITION, PROHIBITION "LITE," OR LEGALIZATION?

1. As has been mentioned, under most decriminalization regimes, simple possession of drugs remains a criminal offence (for which a ticket might be issued). Efforts to divert users away from criminal sentences, though, generally still allow for prison sentences as the default position.

2. Jonathan P. Caulkins, Angela Hawken, Beau Kilmer, Mark A.R. Kleiman, *Marijuana Legalization: What Everyone Needs to Know* (Oxford: Oxford University Press, 2012).

3. After years of allowing marijuana use in California, evidence is that the drug has become a substitute for alcohol among youth. Since driving while high on pot is less dangerous than driving while impaired by alcohol, and since marijuana causes much less harm to individuals and communities than alcohol, this substitution of one drug for another is regarded to be a positive step. Adam Nagourney and Rich Lyman, "Few Problems with Cannabis for California," *New York Times*, October 26, 2013.

4. ICSDP, "Effect of Drug Law Enforcement on Drug-Related Violence."

5. David Brooks, "Been There Done That," *New York Times*, January 2, 2014.

6. Daniel Schwartz, "Legal Marijuana: How Could It Work?" *Huffington Post* from *CBC.ca/news*, September 4, 2013.

7. *R. v. Malmo-Levine* [2003] 3 S.C.R. 571.

8. UNODC, Vienna.

9. Dawn Moore, *Criminal Artefacts: Governing Drugs and Users* (Vancouver: UBC Press, 2007).

10. Fernando Henrique Cardoso and Ruth Dreifuss, "An Ugly Truth in the War on Drugs," *New York Times*, March 10, 2013.

11. Carter and MacPherson, *Getting to Tomorrow*, 96.

12. Alan Travis, "Decriminalise Drug Use, Say Experts after Six-Year Study," *The Guardian*, October 15, 2012.

13. Home Affairs Committee — Ninth Report, *Drugs: Breaking the Cycle*.

14. See *www.parliament.uk/documents/commons-committees/home-affairs/27248*

%20Cm%208567.pdf. This response was tabled in March 2013.

15. Mariano Rolando, "War on Drugs Has Failed, International Panel Says," *The National Post*, June 2, 2011. Mo Mowlam, another former drugs minister, also called for legalization in 2002. Mark Easton, "Can We Imagine a Britain Where All Drugs Are Legal?" *BBC News*, December 16, 2010.

16. Héctor Aguilar Camín, Eduardo Guerrero, Alejandro Madrazo, Andrés Lajous, Jorge Hernández Tinajero, Joel Chávez, and Dante Haro, *Informe Jalisco: Más Allá de la Guerra de las Drogas* (México D.F.: Nexos Sociedad Ciencia y Literatura, 2012). All translations are by the author.

17. Dale Hoyt Palfrey, "Jalisco's Attorney General Talks Turkey on Fighting Crime," *Guadalajara Reporter*, March 22–28, 2014.

18. Hélène Mulholland and agencies, "Ed Miliband Rebukes Bob Ainsworth Over 'Legalise Drugs' Call," *The Guardian*, December 16, 2010.

19. The TDPF recently reported the export value of opium in Afghanistan at \$2.5 billion or 10 percent of GDP. Accessed at *www.tdpf.org.uk/case-for-reform#responsible-regulation*.

20. Debra Black, "Decriminalize Heroin and Cocaine, Says Top U.K. Doctor," *Toronto Star*, August 18, 2010.

21. BBC News, "Top Doctor Sir Ian Gilmour Calls for Drugs Law Review," August 17, 2010. Accessed at *www.bbc.co.uk/news/health-10990921*.

22. Nutt, *Drugs Without the Hot Air*, 213.

23. Mike Barton, "Why Ending the War on Drugs Will Cut Crime," *The Guardian*, September 28, 2013.

24. Police Foundation of the United Kingdom, "Drugs and the Law: Report of the Independent Inquiry into the Misuse of Drugs Act of 1971," April 4, 2000. The Police Foundation, based in London, England, is a non-profit organization which promotes research, debate, and publication to improve the efficiency and effectiveness of policing in the U.K.

25. See *www.countthecosts.org/blog/news-release-prison-governors-association-criticises-war-drugs-and-calls-government-explore-alt*.

26. Nutt, *Drugs Without the Hot Air*, 282–83.

27. Rolles, *After the War on Drugs*.

28. This summary follows closely the text of the Rolles document, for which I thank the author.

29. In Canada, there is strict control of these in relation to alcohol and tobacco. Some jurisdictions (like the United States) might have difficulty in establishing such bans.

30. Rolles, *After the War on Drugs*, 21.

31. See *www.tdpf.org.uk/case-for-reform#responsible-regulation*.

32. What follows is a summary of the arguments presented by the TDPF in *Tools for Debate*, for which I am grateful.

33. Nutt, *Drugs Without the Hot Air*, 185.

34. ICSDP, *Tools for Debate*.

35. Bill Keller, "How to Legalize Pot," *New York Times*, May 19, 2013.

36. Matt Ferner, "Marijuana Legalization: Colo. Gov. Hickenlooper Signs First Bills in History to Establish a Legal, Regulated Pot Market for Adults," *Huffington Post*, May 28, 2013. Associated Press, "Highlights of Colorado's New Marijuana Laws," *The Denver Post*, May 28, 2013. What follows is derived from these two sources, and I am grateful to the authors for their summaries of the new legislation.

37. Dr. David Nutt, "The Government's Plan to Curb Drug-Driving Is a Car Crash," *The Guardian*, September 27, 2013.

38. Maggie Koerth-Baker, "Marijuana and the Sobriety Test," *New York Times*, February 18, 2014.

39. Phillip Smith, "Moving Toward Legal Marijuana Commerce in Washington State," *Cannabis Culture Magazine*, June 13, 2013. Most of what follows is derived from Mr. Smith's summary of the draft rules, for which I am grateful.

40. Jonathan Kaminsky, "Washington State Pot Proposal Sets Licenses at $1,000 Per Year Cost," *Huffington Post*, May 16, 2013.

41. Jonathan Kaminsky, "Marijuana Leaf Logo Dropped from Washington State's Pot Rules," *Reuters*, July 4, 2013.

42. Simon Romero, "Uruguay Acts to Legalize Marijuana," *New York Times*, December 10, 2013.

43. Associated Press, "Uruguay: Marijuana Becomes Legal," *New York Times*, December 24, 2013.

44. "A New Prescription," *The Economist*, August 10, 2013: 12.

CHAPTER 11: THE OUTLIER: CANADA

1. Adrian Humphreys, "Montreal Mafia Family Sent Weekly Chartered Flights Stuffed with Millions in Cash to Los Angeles to Buy Cocaine," *The National Post*, May 23, 2013; "Quebec Playboy Accepts Plea Bargain That Avoids Life Imprisonment for the International Drug Kingpin," *The National Post*, May 31, 2013.

2. Peter Edwards, "Mexican Drug Cartel Violence Hits Canadian Mobsters," *Toronto Star*, April 19, 2013.

3. Tom Blackwell, "How Rob Kamermans Made $500K as Canada's Top Medical Marijuana Doc — Until Police Came," *The National Post*, July 26, 2013.

4. Eric Grenier, "Majority of Canadians Want to Loosen Marijuana Laws: Poll," *Globe and Mail*, August 29, 2013.

5. MacQueen, "Why It's Time to Legalize Marijuana." Also Ian Mulgrew, "Opinion — Hallelujah! Canadians Agree It's Time to Legalize Marijuana," *Vancouver Sun*, January 19, 2012.

6. Michael Harris, "Out of Our Minds on Drugs," *iPolitics*, May 26, 2013.

7. Mulgrew, "Opinion — Hallelujah!"

8. Samuel Perreault, "Police-Reported Crime Statistics in Canada, 2012," *Juristat* (Ottawa: Canadian Council for Justice Statistics) July 25, 2013. ISSN 1209-6393. Cat. no. 85-002-X.

9. MacQueen, "Why It's Time to Legalize Marijuana."

10. Ibid.

11. Gerald Le Dain, *The Report of the Canadian Government Commission of Inquiry into the Non-Medical Use of Drugs — 1972* (Ottawa: Information Canada, 1972).

12. See *www.cbc.ca/archives/categories/lifestyle/pastimes/pot-and-politics-canada-and-the-marijuana-debate/explosive-report-on-drugs-divides-cabinet.html*.

13. Mike Bryan, "Canada's Bill C-17 (Cannabis Law Revision): Still Prohibition After All These Years," July 13, 2005, *www.cannabisculture.com/articles/4451.html*.

14. Wade Raaflaub, Law and Government Division, Legislative Summary, "Bill C-17: An Act to Amend the Contraventions Act and the Controlled Drugs and Substances Act," LS-488E, *www.parl.gc.ca/About/Parliament/LegislativeSummaries/bills_ls.asp?ls=C17&Parl=38&Ses=1*.

15. Auditor General of Canada, *Illicit Drugs.* The Auditor General also reported that there was a growing acknowledgement by Canadians and parliamentarians that there are limits on the ability of law enforcement to reduce supply. He then recommended that Canada provide better information on the drug problem, better reporting, and more leadership if it were to combat illegal drugs more effectively.

16. *Policy for the New Millennium: Working Together to Redefine Canada's Drug Strategy* (Ottawa: House of Commons, 2002).

17. This is a sly reference to the criminal offence of "living off the avails of prostitution," an offence recently struck down by the Supreme Court of Canada as contrary to the *Charter of Rights and Freedoms*.

18. *Policy for the New Millennium.* The content that follows can be found on pages 465–610.

19. Stephen Harper talks about marijuana on YouTube, *www.youtube.com/watch?v=RFp210pZSKk*. Accessed March 5, 2014.

20. "Welcome to the Middle Ages," *The Economist*, January 18, 2014: 37.

21. Raaflaub, "Bill C-17."

22. Selley, "Marijuana Prohibition Isn't a Conservative Position."

23. "Pot Decriminalization Fears 'Overblown': Expert," *Cannabis News*, from CTV.ca news staff, May 18, 2003.

24. Carter and MacPherson, *Getting to Tomorrow.*

25. Harris MacLeod, "Justice Minister Nicholson Pushes Crime Bill He Used To Be Against," *Hill Times*, February 1, 2010.

26. *R. v. Smith* [1987], 1 S.C.R. 1045.

27. Dan Roberts, "Eric Holder Calls for Criminal Justice Reforms Aimed at Easing Drug Sentences," *The Guardian*, August 12, 2013. Laura W. Murphy, "How to Process Eric Holder's Major Criminal Law Reform Speech," ACLU

Blog of Rights, August 12, 2013.

28. "Eric Holder: 'Broken' Justice System Needs 'Sweeping' Changes, Reforms to Mandatory Minimum," *Huffington Post*, August 12, 2013.

29. Tonda MacCharles, "Small-Time Addicts Don't Belong in Jail: U.S. Drug Czar," *Toronto Star*, November 23, 2010. Judge James P. Gray adds that raising penalties for drug traffickers will encourage them to recruit children, who are immune from prosecution. *Why Our Drug Laws Have Failed*, 53.

30. Gloria Galloway, "Canada Warned Not to Follow U.S. Tough-on-Crime 'Mistakes,'" *Globe and Mail*, March 3, 2011.

31. Sophie Pilgrim, "Almost a century after Denver became the first U. S. city to jail someone for selling marijuana, the same city is today making millions selling the drug through licensed stores in a move that could precipitate the end of prohibition across the country," *France 24*, January 26, 2014.

32. Jon Swaine, "Marijuana No More Dangerous than Alcohol? Obama Risks Undermining Drugs Laws in Foray into Pot Debate," *The National Post* from *The Telegraph*, January 20, 2014.

33. The Ouimet Report. *Report of the Canadian Committee on Corrections: Toward Unity: Criminal Justice and Corrections* (Ottawa, 1969). Referred to by Eugene Oscapella, *Changing the Frame: A New Approach to Drug Policy in Canada* (Canadian Drug Policy Coalition, 2012), 9.

34. *The Criminal Law in Canadian Society*, Government of Canada, 1982. The current Conservative government cut the budget of the Law Commission of Canada (which was established in 1997 as a successor to the Law Reform Commission of Canada, abolished by the Mulroney government in 1993) immediately after being elected in 2006. Treasury Board president John Baird said the government was not interested in funding an organization that had opposed government legislation. "Law Commission of Canada: What Happened," *Voices-Voix*. Accessed at *http://voices-voix.ca/en/facts/profile/law-commission-canada*.

CHAPTER 12: A POPULAR GROUNDSWELL FOR CHANGE

1. See *www.norml.ca/norml_statement.php*.

2. See *http://sensiblebc.ca*.

3. Dana Larsen, "How To Decriminalize Marijuana," *Huffington Post*, June 10, 2013. Also, Dana Larsen, "Marijuana: To Decriminalize or Legalize?" *Huffington Post*, June 14, 2013.

4. See *http://stoptheviolencebc.org/wp-content/uploads/2011/12/STVBC-Breaking-the-Silence.pdf*.

5. See *http:///stoptheviolencebc.org/2012/11/14/domestic-cannabis-market-estimate-over-five-years*. The Canadian Press, "Canada Gang Violence," 3.

6. Stop the Violence BC, *Breaking the Silence*. The information that follows can be found on pages 4–22.

7. The Canadian Press, "Canadian Gang Violence."

8. *CBC News*, "Legalize Pot, Say Former B.C. Attorneys General," February 14, 2012.

9. The Canadian Press, "B.C. Marijuana Legalization, Research Wanted By Majority: Survey," *Huffington Post*, April 18, 2013.

10. "Call to Action — Marijuana Prohibition and Its Effects on Violent Crime, Community Safety, and the Health and Well-Being of Our Citizens," November 23, 2011, *http://stoptheviolencebc.org/2011/11/22/letter-from-former-mayors*.

11. Canadian Press, "Police Chiefs Suggest Tickets for Pot Possession Instead of Criminal Charges," *Globe and Mail*, August 20, 2013.

12. Josh Visser, "Harper Says Trudeau Is 'Promoting Marijuana Use for Children,' but Leaves Door Open to Tickets for Possession," *The National Post*, August 29, 2013.

13. See *www.unodc.org/wdr/en/maps-and-graphs.html*. A recent assessment of INCB data, though, shows that Canada has the highest per capita use of opioids among the countries assessed — 150 percent more than third-place Denmark. Dr. Hakique Verani and Dr. Ian Forster, "Opioids: Addiction Is Not a Disease of Society's Margins," *Huffington Post*, April 10, 2013. They are referring to an analysis done by the Wisconsin Drug Control and Access Consortium.

14. "The World at Six," CBC Radio One, February 5, 2014.

15. LEAP Press Release, "Cops and Judges Applaud Canadian Liberal Party's Marijuana Legalization Resolution," January 16, 2012.

16. See *www.leap.cc/about/who-we-are*.

17. Carter and MacPherson, *Getting to Tomorrow*. What follows can be found at 6, 46ff, and 88–90.

18. Robert S. Hoffman, "How to Stop Heroin Deaths," *New York Times*, February 6, 2014.

19. "Decriminalize Drugs Report Gets No Love From Conservatives, Police," *Huffington Post*, May 24, 2013.

20. Robert Matas, "Ottawa Urged to Legalize, Regulate Illicit Drugs," February 18, 2009, *www.dreamindemon.com/forums/showthread.php?13965-Canada-to-Legalize-Heroin-Cocaine-Pot*.

21. Carter and MacPherson, *Getting to Tomorrow*, 75.

22. Gloria Galloway, "Harper Government to Throw Up Roadblocks for Supervised Injection Sites," *Globe and Mail*, June 6, 2013.

23. Devon Black, "Playing Drug Politics with Human Lives," *iPolitics*, June 11, 2013.

24. Dr. Evan Wood, "Harper Should Embrace Safe-Injection Sites: They're the Law-and-Order Option," *Globe and Mail*, June 19, 2013.

25. Sunny Dhillon, "Report Pushes for Supervised Injection Sites in Toronto," *Globe and Mail*, July 2, 2013.

26. Ben Makuch, "New Marijuana Regulations from Health Canada Change Growing Rules," *The National Post*, February 21, 2013. The Canadian Bar Association estimates there will be more than forty thousand licensed Canadians by 2014 and three hundred thousand by 2024. Craig Elder, "They Grow Pot

Because They Have To. Don't Punish Them," *Globe and Mail*, January 24, 2013. Editorial by Leona Aglukkaq, Minister of Health, *Globe and Mail*, July 3, 2013.

27. The National Cancer Institute has suggested that cannabinoids protect against tumours, may kill cancer cells, and inhibit growth and metastasis, *www.cancer. gov/cancertopics/pdq/cam/cannabis/healthprofessional/page4*.

28. Stephanie Levitz, "Price of Medical Pot in Canada Will Hit New High," The Canadian Press, December 14, 2012. Another source says the price will rise from $1.80 per gram to $7.60 per gram: Elder, "They Grow Pot Because They Have To."

29. Jim Bronskill, "Medical Marijuana: Crime Networks Exploiting Canada's Program," *Toronto Star*, July 3, 2013; and Jim Bronskill, "Feds' Medical Marijuana Program Abused by Opportunistic Criminals, RCMP Says," The Canadian Press, February 18, 2014.

30. Elder, "They Grow Pot Because They Have To."

31. Michael Harris, "Out of Our Minds on Drugs," *iPolitics*, May 26, 2013.

32. Andre Mayer, "Drug Legalization Debate Divides the Americas," *CBC News*, April 13, 2012.

33. Bronskill, "Medical Marijuana." A letter sent to the states by the Corrections Corporation of America set out the requirements for the CCA to consider purchasing a facility. One of these was "an assurance by the agency partner that the agency has sufficient inmate population to maintain a minimum 90% occupancy rate over the term of the contract," *http://big.assets.huffingtonpost.com/ccaletter.pdf*.

34. Sunny Dhillon, "Cash Back: Return of Rare Coins Puts B.C. Asset Seizure Law in Spotlight," *Globe and Mail*, January 29, 2014.

35. Jared Lindzon, "These Canadian Cops Are Fighting to Legalize Drugs," Spring 2013, *www.vice.com/en-ca/read/meet-the-Canadian-cops-who-fight-for-legalizing-drugs*.

36. Brian Hutchinson, "Critics Warn Civil Forfeiture Gives Government a 'Licence to Steal' as Hells Angels Gear Up to Fight Legislation," *The National Post*, October 11, 2013.

37. Andre Mayer, "Drug Legalization Debate Divides the Americas."

38. The Vienna Declaration was signed in 2010 at the XVIII International AIDS Conference. It proposed the redirection of drug enforcement budgets to evidence-based prevention, regulation, treatment and harm reduction programs. Canadian organizations that supported the Vienna Declaration included the Canadian Public Health Association, the Urban Public Health Association, and the medical officers of eighteen of the largest cities in Canada. Carter and MacPherson, *Getting to Tomorrow*, 94–96.

39. Daniel Tencer, "Marijuana Legalization: Liberal Party Lays Out Detailed Economic Plan for Pot," *Huffington Post*, January 28, 2013.

40. Margaret Wente, "What's Justin Trudeau Been Smoking?" *Globe and Mail*, July 27, 2013.

41. Other well-respected Canadian journalists, presumably reflecting received pub-

lic wisdom, accept uncritically that legalizing marijuana will not make it more difficult for children to obtain the drug. Konrad Yakabuski says, "No one (except perhaps Mr. [Justin] Trudeau) believes that legalizing pot sales will make it harder for young people to get their hands on the drug." "Pot needs more than a token discussion," *Globe and Mail*, January 11, 2014. Expert Jon Gould of the Children's Alliance in Washington State, on the other hand, supports legalization largely because regulations will prevent children from easily buying marijuana.

42. Lawrence Martin, "On Pot, Trudeau Puts Himself in the Vanguard," *Globe and Mail*, July 30, 2013.

43. Matt Gurney, "Justin Trudeau on Marijuana — Right Idea, Wrong Reason," *The National Post*, July 25, 2013. Tasha Kheiridden, "Pot in Every Pot? The Argument Against Legalization," *iPolitics*, July 26, 2013.

44. See *http://xfer.ndp.ca/2013/policybook/2013-04-17-Policy_E.pdf*.

45. "Trudeau's Stand on Pot Legalization Gives Harper a Generational Wedge," *Globe and Mail*, July 30, 2013.

46. Martin, "On Pot, Trudeau Puts Himself in the Vanguard."

47. Selley, "Maybe Justin Trudeau Can Convince Stephen Harper of the Insanity of Our Marijuana Laws," *The National Post*, July 25, 2013.

CONCLUSION

1. Konrad Yakabuski, "Republicans Suddenly Get Smart on Crime," *Globe and Mail*, March 20, 2014.

2. Matt Apuzzo, "Holder Endorses Proposal to Reduce Drug Sentences," *New York Times*, March 13, 2014.

3. Associated Press, "Colorado Gets High on Pot Revenue, Marijuana Tourists," *Huffington Post*, March 10, 2014.

4. Redditstumble, "Medical Marijuana Users Threatened with Legal Action by Health Canada," *Huffington Post*, March 15, 2014.

5. Daniel Tencer, "Harper Launches a Witch Hunt on Medical Pot Users," *Huffington Post*, March 17, 2014; Jim Bronskill, "Ottawa to Inform Police if Medical Marijuana Growers Flout New Rules," *Globe and Mail*, March 17, 2014.

6. Canadian Press, "Court Injunction Lets Patients Keep Growing Medical Pot," *Toronto Star*, March 21, 2014, with files from Isabel Teotonio.

7. Jen Gerson, "New Provincial Laws Have Had Great Success Shutting Down Drug Dens, but Critics Question Why They Circumvent the Criminal Code," *National Post*, February 28, 2014.

8. "Vancouver Medical Marijuana Grow-Ops Won't Be Busted: Police," *Huffington Post*, March 5, 2014. Resistance to the new proposals has become a moot point since the federal court granted its interim injunction, but it is important to recognize that British Columbia plans to stand up to the federal government on this matter if the constitutional challenge should fail.

Index

Available at Your Favourite Bookseller

The Nurses Are Innocent
The Digoxin Poisoning Fallacy
by Gavin Hamilton

In 1980–81, forty-three babies died at Toronto's Hospital for Sick Children from a supposed digoxin overdose. Serial murder was suspected, leading to the arrest of nurse Susan Nelles. In order to clear Nelles's name, an investigation was launched to find an alternate explanation.

No one on the Grange Royal Commission of Inquiry had expertise in diagnosis. The post-mortem diagnosis of digoxin poisoning was based on a single biochemical test without knowledge of the normal values. Gavin Hamilton's extensive research shows that a toxin found in natural rubber, a digoxin-like substance, might well have been the culprit in the babies' deaths. He clearly demonstrates that explanations other than serial murder account for the cluster of infant deaths at HSC.

What can be learned from this black stain on Canada's judicial system? One lesson certainly stands out: we can't ever again allow a group of unqualified amateur diagnosticians make life-and-death decisions about such important matters as potential serial murders.

The Couch of Willingness

An Alcoholic Therapist Battles the Bottle and a Broken Recovery System

by Michael Pond

After two decades of helping clients battle addictions, Michael Pond, a successful therapist, succumbs to one himself. He loses his practice, his home and his family to alcoholism, ending up destitute in a rundown recovery home populated by a cast of characters straight out of Dickens.

The Couch of Willingness is a real couch in that home, a couch where Pond is forced to sleep until he surrenders and admits he's powerless over alcohol. But just when Pond gains any measure of sobriety, in sashays his other powerful addiction, Dana, a can of Red Bull in hand and a 26er of vodka in her purse.

Pond's harrowing two-year journey to sobriety takes stops in abandoned sheds, dumpsters, ditches, emergency wards, intensive care, and finally, prison. His riveting account crackles with raw energy and black humour as he plunges readers into a world few will ever have the misfortune to experience.

Along the way, Michael the drunk finds himself shamed and stigmatized by the very system in which Michael the therapist thrived. The dissonance rankles for Pond and, by the end of the story, for the reader too.

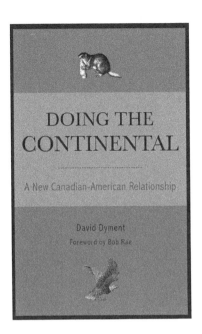

Doing the Continental
A New Canadian-American Relationship
by David Dyment

When President Barack Obama sat at his desk for the first time in the Oval Office in January 2009, one of the farthest things from his mind was Canada. On Capitol Hill the whirling pursuit of interests was intense. In Ottawa, Canada's senior officials were too preoccupied to appreciate that the nations neighbours to the south weren't paying attention to the affairs and concerns of the Great White North. Canada's relations with the United States are broad and deep, and with Obama in his second term in office, the two countries have entered what could be considered a new era of hope and renewal. From water and energy policy to defence, environmental strategy, and Arctic sovereignty, David Dyment provides an astute, pithy analysis of the past, present, and future continental dance between two countries that have much in common, yet often step on each others feet.

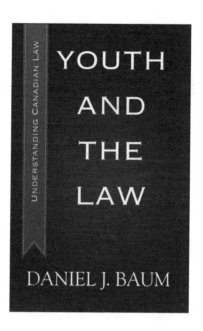

Youth and the Law
Understanding Canadian Law
by Daniel J. Baum

Laws, as they relate to youth and youth issues, can be difficult to understand for those they are intended to serve. In the first book of the *Understanding Canadian Law* series, author Daniel J. Baum breaks down the Supreme Court of Canada's decisions relating to youth in plain language intended for readers of all ages.

Drawing on examples from recent Supreme Court rulings, *Youth and the Law* walks the reader through such controversial subjects as spanking, bullying, youth violence, and police in the schools. Each chapter contains prompts to encourage critical thinking.

Youth and the Law is an objective introduction for all readers to better understand how law impacts the young.

VISIT US AT
Dundurn.com
@dundurnpress
Facebook.com/dundurnpress
Pinterest.com/dundurnpress